GETTING BY

STORIES OF WORKING LIVES

Edited by

David Shevin & Larry Smith

Working Lives Series
Bottom Dog Press
Huron, Ohio

For a complete catalog
of our pubications write to:

Bottom Dog Press
c/o Firelands College
Huron, Ohio   44839

Assistant Editor: Suzanne Smith

Cover Photo by Rebecca Colon
Block print on back cover by Andy Nelson
All rights reserved.

Acknowledgements

Some of the work in this volume first appeared
in the following publications:

Randy J. Abel, "Tsunami" first appeared as a chapbook from Pig Iron Press, Youngstown, Oh.

Sue Doro, "The Cultural Worker" in *Blue Collar Goodbyes*. Watsonville, Ca: Papier-Mache Press.

Diane Goodman, "Jewel on Her Way to Work" and "Love Stew" in *African American Review.*

Philip Levine, "Easter, 1944" in *Image: A Journal of the Arts*, 1996; "The Last Shift" in *Michigan Quarterly Review,* 1988; "You Can Cry" in One for the Rose. NY: Atheneum Press, 1981.

Annabel Thomas. "Laying Ulajean's Ghost" in *Knucklebones*. Kansas City, Mo. Helicon Nine Editions. 1995.

David Watts. "MRI Scan" in *Journal of Amreican Medical Association*, 1994.

The Ohio Arts Council helped fund this organization with state tax dollars to encourage economic growth, educational excellence and cultural enrichment for all Ohioans.

CONTENTS

Introductions: Larry Smith and David Shevin: 5
Preface: The Cultural Worker by Sue Doro : 17

ONE — CARPENTER AUNTS —
FAMILY & NEIGHBORHOOD

Selling Manure—Bonnie Jo Campbell : 24
Carpenter Aunts—Kevin Clark : 26
Champion & Martyrs —Robert Flanagan : 34
William Miller & Letters to My Father—David Kherdian : 45
Emma and Shorty—Jim Sanderson : 50
As If Corn Could Invent Itself & Fair Haven, Connecticut
—Vivian Shipley : 57
Alleghany 95910—James Mason Vaughan : 60

TWO —WORKING CLASS EDUCATION—
THAT WORKING STATE OF MIND

Tsunami-Void: The English Behind the Eightball—Randy J. Abel : 67
Paquito de Todo & Called Susan & Work—G. Timothy Gordon : 77
Easter 1944 & The Last Shift & You Can Cry—Philip Levine : 81
Working Class Education—Susan Luzzaro : 85
Beast of Burden & Minimum Wage & Job Description—Mark Vinz : 90
The Turn of the Tide & Billy's Pecadillos—Tom Wayman : 93
Antonio & MRI Scan & Telling the News—David Watts : 97
A Strong Face—Suki Wessling : 103
Sunday School—Frederick Wm. Zackel : 112

THREE —THE SWEEPER
INGENUITY & PERSISTENCE

Gypsum, Ohio 1937& Lobby Teller Ballad—Debra Benko : 119
Our Fathers & Coal Miner & Breeding—Jeanne Bryner : 123
Between the Sheets—Paola Corso : 126
The Sweeper & Tiny Griefs—Sean Thomas Dougherty : 134
Welcome to the Pit—Thomas Fairbairn : 138
Searching for My Father: A Working Man's Life—Robert Fox : 144
Jewel On Her Way to Work & Love Stew & Late Lunch in the Museum
Garden—Diane Goodman : 155

FOUR —WHERE YOU GO WHEN YOU DON'T WORK— STRUGGLES & GETTING BY

In the Spirit of Free Enterprise & The Gift—David Axelrod : 161
The Factory & Selling Shoes & Killing My Father—Denise Duhamel : 165
Footprints & The Mechanic—Glory Foster : 169
All Packed —Jim Daniels : 175
Cooked & In a San Diego Sweat—Maggie Jaffe : 183
Killin' Snakes & I Was Hitler's Secretary —Lisa Martinovic : 186
Sissies —Peter Markus : 189
Where You Go When You Don't Work —Geoff Penrose : 203

FIVE —CLEANING STALLS IN WINTER— WORK ETHIC & DIGNITY

Past the Corner, Opening Gate & The Way She Could Disappear & Pears—Geraldine Connolly : 211
They Shoot at Houses, Too —Jo Giese : 215
Maw—Julia van Gordon : 224
Breaking—Richard Hague : 231
NoAfterWords —Joe Napora : 235
Cleaning Stalls in Winter & Truck Driver & How I See the Rapture — Edwina Pendarvis : 238
Down Time & Texas 1974 & Field—Daniel Smith : 241
Laying Ulajean's Ghost—Annabel Thomas : 245
Driving the Senior Citizens...—Grant Vecera : 252

Biographical Sketches of Authors & Photographers & Editors: 254

INTRODUCTIONS

[ONE] Losing Class:
Or Why Working Class Writing Really Matters

I arrive at the shopping mall in Steubenville, Ohio, to set up my book table at the front of the WaldenBooks Store. It is 11 am, and I am greeted by a folding chair, a thin card-table with a beige cloth, two book holders, and a stack of my latest (and first) book of fiction, *Beyond Rust*. The book includes a novella set in working class Lorain, Ohio—people surviving mill strikes and closings—and a collection of stories set in the industrial Ohio Valley of my youth. All treat the struggles and endurance of working class people in America. My own "work" (writing) has been done over the last ten years while teaching at a two-year college along the smalltown shores of Lake Erie. Having thus moved from working class to middle class America, I know that such classes do exist. Only those who can afford it risk ignoring that class cultures exist. I cannot. Seated at my display now, I catch my reflection in the window display—my blue denim shirt and my black tie—a true cross-class mix.

Not surprisingly, as I am learning, no one is here at the bookstore to greet me. Though my book cover with author photo is temporarily featured on the back of a Colin Powell book display, there is no line—just me and my laminated newspaper clippings and reviews, a bowl of candy corn which my wife suggested I bring, and a set of books splayed out across the plastic tablecloth, waiting—for my readers.

Eventually people come into the store, some browsing near my display, some daring to pick up a copy of my book, so that I risk casting out my line: "Hi. I'm from Mingo Junction, and this is my new book. It's about the Ohio Valley." When there is no response, I ask, "Where are you from?" Intimacy creates value, I know that, and so I share mine knowing that this whole thing means much more to me than to anyone. As a kid life taught repeatedly not to care so much, but I never learned. If I had, I would never have written such a book. Most people smile and put down my book, reach for a novel by Michael Crichton or a collection of the best of Calvin and Hobbes comics. And that's okay, I say to myself. I like those too.

Gradually as the morning turns to afternoon, I begin to study the crowd: white haired men in caps being guided by their wives. In some of their faces I see my own folks, now gone—my railroader father who probably would have helped me build a book display, my gentle mother who would have told people, "That's our son, the writer." Suddenly a group of junior high girls, unleashed upon the mall, rush up to my table for a look at the book. "Have some candy," I offer. And one picks up the book exclaiming, "You wrote this *whole book*?" I nod and she releases a "Co-ol! Hey, he *wrote* this book. He's an *author*."

Realizing that I may be experiencing the high point of the day, I suggest, "You know, you might write a book yourself, some day."

"Not me," one says, "I write too sloppy."

"You're young," I say and notice that while they are talking, they have restacked my books into neat piles. They do this by instinct, without thought, for which I thank them and sit back down as they head toward the music store. I get out a pad and pen and start writing things down--it seems the right thing to be doing with myself. I'm an author, right?

At one o'clock I go and get a cup of coffee, return, check my watch a dozen times, read the back cover of my book, and watch the parade of faces. The mall's security guard comes along and picks up my book. He looks it over, checks the cover photo, then me, then sets it back down. "Co-ol!" I write him and the girls into some haiku poems.

I have tried to read a few magazines, pretended to be thinking deeply, but mostly I notice the faces—these are the people I try to put into my books. It seems so right and natural, writing of and for a place, and yet something is wrong here? If they haven't read my book, why don't they at least check it out? How do I reach them? What is wrong with this picture? For the first time I notice that the mall's merry-go-round is turning in silence—not to disturb the customers, I guess—but somehow echoing the whole blank mood of the place. Sitting quietly beside my book, I feel the rise of larger questions: What can we really expect from working class writing? How can it reach this working class audience? What is the source of their resistance? Does such writing really matter? And if it doesn't—then, why not? I sip my coffee and search the afternoon for answers.

Opening my bookbag, I pull out the book I have been reading, a study of working class academics like myself. Its title, *This Fine Place So Far from Home,* connotes the dual worlds and deep personal ambivalence of most working class youth sent off to a college life. Immediately the editor, Carolyn Leste Law explains the book's purpose—to tell our stories—"to *stop* being embarrassed after a very long time of consciously hiding our pasts from the view of our colleagues and students, to reveal our working-class roots not in terms of the academy that would seek to degrade them, but to reclaim our past lives, as well as the present lives of our families, through autobiography and to make those lives relevant in critically important ways to the work we do..."(Temple Univ. Press, 1995, 4). These are fierce and welcome words to one who has endured such class bias and denial.

Half a lifetime of puzzling over all this has made me realize how de-valued is working class life in America. The subject of media stereotype, suspicion and scorn by others—*Who are those people and why do they dress and talk that way?*—the working class is the one class seeking to deny itself—to disappear. The goal of the working class, as it is so often portrayed for them, is to escape itself by becoming middle class. At public readings of my writing, I have found working class people uneasy with the elements of poverty allowed in my book; admitting that it exists, they would still deny any basic connection. *"Don't soil yourself with that,"* I hear from those who would deny their own family and neighborhood and the humanity of us all. *"You were brought up better than that,"* echoes in my own head. And in fact we all have been brought up like this, taught this in America where the term "poverty" and "the poor" and "working class" are held synonymous and so deny deeper realities. Like all stereotyping, it ignores the true character and complexity of people to justify their ill treatment. What we don't see is that this poverty of vision in America robs us all. From the working class it steals human dignity and erases a literature.

What I recall encountering at college was a world of ideas and culture, of experience and comfort that challenged and stretched me right out of myself. I liked the study of art and writing, the rich sense of history, the quiet rolling hills, the quantity and regularity of dormitory meals. It was "a fine place," truly "another world," yet tragically one that denied my own past. I did not hear mention of my own working class culture until one day an instructor in an introductory sociology class explained and wrote out across the blackboard the range of socio-economic classes. I was among the "lower" socio-economic class. I never spoke of it there or at home where the college education that I was getting was equally misunderstood. When I would go home I was allowed to talk "that college stuff" for about an hour, much as we tolerated my father's "mill talk" when growing up. Though I didn't grasp all this then, I was in fact being sent away to school— a world that denied my source, my background, my family and working class values. It's a bit like *being* a divided country, and such splits are never healthy. Attracted to a world of ideas across a great river, you are forced to deny your native experience to reach the new land.

For Renny Christopher, a college professor from a family of carpenters, the class conflict has proven interminable. You live with conflicting voices: "I hear my mother's voice saying to me, 'Get your nose out of that book and go do something!'—I take on too much, I over commit myself. Do half again or even twice as much as my colleagues, work seven days a week, long hours. My old self doesn't respect my new self. My old self says I'm living a lazy, over-privileged life. My new self says, what more could I do? My old self says, you're not doing anything productive. My new self says, you don't know how to think....Nothing will ever be enough to stitch together the before and after of this life" (*Fine Place*, 140). Strangers in a strange land and without a guide, we could not understand what was going on; we couldn't grasp that cultural denial, ignoreance, and exclusion of the working class life brought on all of this ambivalence. The two worlds had been kept apart. I believe what many of our parents were expressing in sending their children off to college was their own defiance at being oppressed as well as their love and hope for their children. Much as their great-grandparents had watched their young journey off to American and its promise, they sent their children into a life they really could not comprehend. A college education was paid for twice, by the family's sacrifice and by the emotional pains of its recipients.

When I returned to my alma mater, Muskingum College, to do a reading of some of my writing, I found the choice of material easy. I read the working class poems and stories that had been denied by the old place, and I found students welcoming me in and sharing their own struggles with academic denial. To its credit, the college is now making itself more affordable and giving students from its Appalachian area, a big tuition break. I could only hope that they were also giving them a place inside the culture of the college.

Back at my book table, a woman who was a neighbor of my mother, has asked for a copy of my book. "You're Larry aren't you? I knew your mom and dad. We went to school together." I nod, "Oh, yeah, you lived up on Murdock Street. I used to be your paperboy." She stares at me again, and we laugh. "That's right. I forgot." It is so easy being with her, so that I joke, "You always were good tippers, even though you had that big dog." I hand her a book, wait and ask, "Would you like me to sign it?" She is a bit embarrassed and confused, "Oh, yes, do you do that? I've never bought a book from an author before. This is nice." And it *is* for both of us, but why is it so foreign to her? When she leaves, I take off my tie, and wonder some more.

Though the powers and patterns of exclusion have always been a violation of basic human rights, their workings persist because they are so ingrained in our vision of ourselves. What television show deals realistically with working class life? "Roseanne" has managed to show some of the real issues and has created living characters, yet I fear it survives the ratings battles chiefly by its sense of sarcasm. Almost all of the other shows, including those of minorities, are set in cozy middle class settings. Film treats the working class life chiefly as a disgusting battleground one should struggle to escape. I watched Michael Cimino's celebrated *The Deer Hunter* at a theater near Mingo Junction, where it was primarily filmed, and heard local people object, "Why are the workers always dirty and the families so violent?" We are left with this slummy portrayal of working class peoples' lives. And yet, film and television and books are the most popular art forms, the most accessible and inexpensive. So, why don't they speak to and for the masses? Could it be their corporate control by management executives who keep themselves distant from working people?

Which brings me back to writing and books—an expression that can still speak for and about and to working class people. But what's the problem here? Where are the readers? We face another form of cultural denial. Most working class people don't think they are *supposed* to read serious novels, and certainly not 'poe-try.' Let's face it, whether through school texts or teachers or corporate publishing, the working class is not portrayed as alive and well—as worthy of study, much less of art. Alice Walker writes a beautiful book of poor Black working people making life meaningful in *The Color Purple*, and Steven Spielberg turns it into a family of Black middle class landowners serving themselves. Yes, it's still a fine film, but why did he feel he had to deny the real character of the working life to reach a large audience? In the film, all of Celie's hard work and ingenuity are converted into a convenient stroke of luck that boosts her into middle class.

Our schools often do no better in teaching us to value the particular skills of one's working class background. Speaking of the college where she teaches, Renny Christopher points out, "While my colleagues appreciate my ability to learn new discourses, they do not value my father's ability to learn new trades. They wouldn't even be able to see it. Blue-collar work is simply invisible to them"("A Carpenter's Daughter" in *This Fine Place* 133). We are always extolling young people from working families to "pull themselves up by their bootstraps," and walk away from their dirty working class roots. Why is it people are so amazed when someone from a working class family does well on tests and wins scholarships? They are given patronizing applause in a kind of tokenism that implies that intelligence rests primarily in the middle and upper class. Such equating of class with intelligence is one of the worst qualities of education and academia. Tragically this system becomes ingested and perpetuated by its participants, by its young who learn to deny themselves in order to achieve status. What is not recognized in the whole myth of gaining power through academics and finances is the great loss it creates in the denial of a whole segment of society.

What virtues come out of the working class life? Mary Cappello in her essay "Useful Knowledge" takes on this whole "myth of lack" now perpetuated in America. She reveals how portraying the working class as limiting *marginalizes* people and *de-legitimizes* whole fields of knowledge—something women and minorities and children have long experienced. To grasp this "marginalizing" effect, image that you are listed in this article, but out in the margins of the page, where things don't really matter. In subsequent editions, you will be no doubt be dropped off, edited out. Capello exclaims, "We need to tell the things we see as what we know." Praising working class story telling, verbal directness, persistence, cooperative bonding, and practical ingenuity, she suggests that "A working-class person's daily thoughts, a shoemaker's poetry, may be just the resources higher education needs to divine itself, to plumb the depths of its mechanisms of exclusion, its refusals to know or to find marginal knowledge(s), in the best sense of the word, useful" (*This Fine Place*, 136).Our whole culture needs this. Is the goal of education to prepare us all for middle class life, or is it about recognizing and challenging our talents--all of them?

A man has brought his daughter up to my table. She is high school age with soft eyes and a pretty smile. "Excuse us," says the father. "We read about your book, and I wanted Denise to meet you." I rise, smiling at the blushing child. "She's a writer, herself, see. She won the Power of the Pen Contest last year." I exclaim, "That's great, Denise, let me shake your hand." She tells me her school, and I am thinking of asking her for her autograph, but ask instead, "What authors do you read?" She speaks right out, "I love Whitman and Dickinson as poets, but also Austen and Bronte. What I write are stories and some poems." We are all pleased to be connecting like this, and I sign my name inside her book... "To Denise, an Ohio Valley writer." I tell them the old story of my being a senior at Mingo Central High School and hearing my English teacher announce that a man from Martins Ferry, down river, had won a great poetry award—James Wright. "I remember my own shock when I learned that he had written poems about the Ohio Valley and its people." Suddenly she looked both happy and perplexed, "I wonder why I've never heard of him?"

Conspiracy and denial grow in a climate of ignorance. In the world of writing and literature, where our questions began, there has been a patterned denial of working class writing. At a recent conference of university writing programs held in Pittsburgh, a panel was conducted on "Blue Collar Writing." I believe it was a first for the Associated Writing Programs, so I expected a small turn-out. I entered late into a room packed full of eager faces telling their stories of struggling to find and include working class writing in their courses. One young man from the back of the room suggested that he had only come to the conference because of this panel, adding, "Why do we take this denial? Look around you. There are more working people than any others in this country. Hell, we're the majority." A roar of applause went up, but as the panel proceeded and biased views of working class writing were exposed, another question arose, "Where do we find the books about this?" There was a silence and then I dared to suggest a key book by Carey Nelson, *Repression and Recovery: Modern American Poetry and the Politics of Cultural Memory* (Univ. of Wisconsin Press, 1989).

Nelson is explicit in his accusation of how conservative and traditional "politics" entered the world of literature and education following the "Leftist" writing of the 1930's: "The institution of literary studies cooperated and eliminated the names of political poets from the ongoing conversation of the discipline. Like the leveling movement of the sea, the weight of our cultural memory closed over this part of our heritage, turning it into a shadowed place where nothing could be seen...literary studies as a whole instead devoted itself to establishing the limited canon of modernism." (10) Yes, what he is saying is that works were excluded on the basis of their outlook and their popularity. Eventually the deeply human writing of John Steinbeck, Carl Sandburg, Edgar Lee Masters, Erskine Caldwell, Tillie Olsen were recognized, but always with a disclaimer because of their "populist" and "sentimental" styles. Equally serious, vast numbers of writers were and are excluded from texts, anthologies, and courses because they are thought as part of a Leftist movement. In the world of poetry this means Kenneth Patchen, Michael Gold, Kenneth Fearing, Horace Gregory, Isador Schneider, Edwin Rolfe...become footnotes, and eventually their work goes out of print. For fiction, writers such as Grace Lumpkin, Robert Cantwell, Rebecca Harding Davis, Jack Conroy, William Rollins, Waldo Frank...are denied to us. It took Alice Walker's popularity to resurrect and reclaim the lost writings of Zora Neale Hurston. What this also means is that most readers will never find these books, never know that such writing ever existed or has value. Because whole segments of humanity must be maligned to justify this denial, it is a loss to us all. As writers and a culture we are forced to relearn the human and artistic lessons these writers have earned for us.

The common excuses for this cultural bias are that such populist and leftist writing is full of political rhetoric, is single minded in theme, and limited in form. Uncomfortable with its passion and its commitment to treating social issues, such writing is regularly dismissed as "sentimental" and "propaganda." Yet a look at the writing through old and rare anthologies reveals just the opposite; the writing is free and original, engaged in life's personal and social problems, diverse in its forms, and most important, deeply human. Labeled as "proletarian" writing, it was at first segregated and marginalized, then after time ignored—pushed right off the page. The result has again been a disempowering of a people. Nelson would have us restore writing to its former place where it "had the power to help people not only come to understand the material conditions of their existence but also to envision ways of changing them." He envisions a return to a period in which writing can be seen as "one of the most dependable sources of knowledge about society and one's place and choices within it," wherein the writing "is itself a terrain of political action, that what poetry does to and for people, what people do for themselves with poetry's assistance reshaped the political arena itself" (*Repression* 124, 127, 128). Seeing writing as a necessary alternative to the status quo and as a means of changing it, as a power that should be shared rather than contained, turns writing into a vital and exciting action. I understand the emotion and insistence of that voice. We need blue collar writing, pink collar, white collar, striped, no collar—all kinds of writing that deal intimately and with vision about people's lives.

Eventually, as my afternoon grows, I do sell a dozen copies of my book to people who have heard about it from neighbors or read the announcement in the papers. Information and knowledge are still power tools. Many buyers are from my home town and remember my family. They wanted to stop by and see what I was up to. Some take a pride in knowing me—a real gift—and I in knowing them. Inside their confidence we begin to talk about the mills, the railroad, what's happened to the jobs, the kids moving out West, the puzzle of this economic depression, the memories that still live in them. And I realize that all the answers I have to offer are human, like them. Inside their eyes, I find a good place from which to begin.

-Larry Smith/ July, 1996 (Huron, Ohio)

[TWO] I knew T. S. Eliot. I worked with T. S. Eliot. T. S. Eliot was a friend of mine. You're no T. S. Eliot.

There isn't a college writing workshop anywhere in this country that would let me write honestly about Randy Reynolds.

The material just doesn't conform to stylized ideas of what makes literary art. Randy's story would only invite ridicule from what the academies teach. "The *name*!" one would-be editor would say. "Has to go. It's a cliché, like the rest of him. You're trying to rewrite Studs Lonigan here. Give me something I can believe!" Then a poet would chime in. "Absolutely. No reflection, no *negative capability* in a nature like this. He's class warfare and nothing more organic, complicated or reflective than that. And his drinking. I don't know if he's supposed to be a hero or just pathetic..."

The workshop leader, aware of group pressure and (maybe) partly interested in the material, would nod, encourage developing Randy some more, with cautious words to please make him believable.

Randy was my friend and was all class warfare and he loved this life. Everything there was to rejoice in being big and Irish and from Chicago and sensual and crying big and laughing big and raging big at the bosses—that was him, and by profession he organized for the service workers, having come through the ranks to his board position. For a while he stopped regularly by my own union office, in red-faced proletarian indignation after coming off a long-standing nursing home picket line. He'd talk everyone he could into beers at this little grill off Cincinnati's MacMillan Street, and there he'd demand to be center of attention by telling animated jokes and organizing tales from the battlefront. He'd grab my sleeve.

"Get this. One capitalist gets real emotional, goddamn weepy with another capitalist. He gets buddy-buddy, uncommonly philosophical. He says, 'Do you know what the most beautiful gift, the biggest gesture is that one human can give away to another?' And the second guy doesn't know, so he says, all imploring, 'Tell me!' And the first capitalist's eyes get big and he says, 'Well, HOW THE CHRIST WOULD I KNOW?!'" He'd slam the table with his laughter. He'd be demonstrative enough to knock beer glasses over with almost every story.

I'd would laugh or act in shock, too, for every Reynolds story. The joke about the USX executives who torment Satan in hell by shutting down furnaces and laying off all the imps. The one about the surgeon's conference where Europeans boasted miracles about industrial workers who miraculously recovered major transplant surgeries. They'd be up to look for work again in unbelievable time. Then the American surgeon boasts, "We have that all beat. We transplanted just one asshole from Sacramento to Washington, and the next day, *three million* workers were up and looking to work again!"

Just as passionately, I'd sympathize and strategize over the no-shows at scheduled negotiations, the contracts unrecognized and the human stories of workers stiffed of necessary overtime. Randy never saw an issue as an isolate issue of morality. Every argument was someone's specific car payment or medical expense. Every clause had a name.

These stories he'd tell with Irish flair and emotion. Every future dangled on a contract condition. What an education in application he was! This was singularly useful in the turf where I was, managing contract applications in a "professional" union of broadcasters in three Ohio cities. Our union was militant on First Amendment issues, but not as passionate as the service workers that wages and hours meant survival. Randy was the guy who made the nuts-and-bolts work so much more real. He was drunk when he died on the road, on his way back from a campaign organizing strategy meeting in his home town.

I'm not making a martyr out of the fellow. I've been through my "bosses don't die overworked on the road" rages and my images of trying to make Randy some storytelling Joe Hill type. He just wasn't mythic in ways like that. He was a guy like the Irish Catholics in the neighborhood where I grew up. He was anxious when he was on the make, and that was most of the time. I miss him, and he was my friend: real and predictable and full of enthusiasms too circumscribed by class to lend themselves to rarefied literary invention.

When I try to characterize him after these years in the grave, I think how much he's like the guys in Farrell's stories. Farrell, turn, was just the sort of writer that none of my professors ever encouraged me to read. He was not politically correct for an academy oh-so-anxious to reinforce that men were men and white and dead and Protestant and English, though they were liberal enough to forgive both Eliot's embraces of the Vatican and his Missouri roots. Hail, fair, fair liberals!

Yes, I am grateful to the exceptions, who taught well outside required curricula. In my graduate program, the great resister and voice of conscience William Stafford came to speak. Bill Stafford had been a hero of my undergraduate days. He spoke of his literary voice hearing, above all, his mother in Kansas. The graduate instructor hooted contempt at that very idea, but Stafford was our university's guest. Then I had the blessed opportunity of a workshop with Philip Levine, who taught me that poetry was everything you could not live without. Still, the mainstream of graduate school was such a reinforcement of white man's burden, I'd find myself at dances benefiting the Coalition of Black Trades Unionists explaining to my friends that my dissertation six years overdue at the University was in the "Honky Studies Program." Those requisites were the very reason that, after trying to advance myself through advanced degrees, it seemed like a good idea to chuck the process for something real.

Stylized ideas of literary art—there's a phrase. I was mightily alienated from that world, and came back to it. Today, I never enter the classroom without hoping that I came back on honest terms. When I returned to the dissertation and then to teaching, that act held the sense of getting a union card for the world where writing and books were important. I wanted the importance to be on real conditions, in the world of real lives. I wanted those years of working the chemical plant and being graduate stipend hungry, of slopping tar and working the office to mean something.

As I read the real lives in this collection, the whole education process feels a bit more human than it did while jumping through hoops of Restoration dramatists and morality plays. Back when our graduate school teachers encouraged us to discard proletarian literatures as unfit for study, the impulse was to resist and wonder about their priorities. Who did it to them? Why were the voices of social and cultural dissent so "inartistic"? Was the sympathy of our beats and LeSuers and Dreisers such a broadside to the class pretense running the schools where we studied?

Well, yes. It was.

In the bars after classes, we'd celebrate those vices that good student life precluded. Literature that mattered was one of those vices, a concern as serious as chasing sex and downing booze. The subjects for the literary passions had this in common: they were everything that the classroom would not consider. Class was no place for class. We were in struggle, and the way we bound our culture was so removed from the worlds of Dryden drama and Henry James novels, it found all expression in the barely underground.

Class is after all where you find your struggle, and in this sense, most of us are more working class than of the eminent "middle," where public opinion mavens tell us most Americans place themselves. The retail worker promoted to shift manager and the lineworker handed a clipboard to enact a foreman's role have not leapt from the pressures of job instability or downsizing. The middle management officer at the bank tells me with a sadness, "Well, don't you consider finance if you want to pay the rent!" Nurses aren't placed during our ongoing nursing shortage and doctors struggle with the squeeze of their Hippocratic oath at odds with the greedheads handling the accounts.

Others in the public and private sectors doing advocacy and non-profit work watch prior resources vanish, and a top-down assault on the future of any public funding. All of these realities make one wonder why the corporate-owned media loves to pay talking heads to celebrate a "middle-class" self-defined culture. Where is this middle class? Mostly, people I talk to identify much more readily with the education in the first-in-the-family-to-go-to-college story I recently read.

The story goes that the smart young scholar, awed by the structure presented in the Sociology Intro class, comes home at holiday to tell the parents, "I am learning so much! There is such a clear structure to our economy and I can see it now. There is this upper, and middle, and a lower class. The upper class works to keep the structure in place..." The father roars displeasure. He hasn't had the education, being of the generation that graduated high school into the assembly line. "What kind of trash are they teaching you there?"

"It's the class system, the three classes in the economy..."

"Wrong! Wrong! There are only two classes: workers and capitalists."

The reason so many find *deep* truth in this story is that to "liberate memory" (using Janet Zandy's wonderful phrase) in a class-denying culture is also to claim a real, vibrant heritage. It's the very heritage that class pretense has begged us to deny. To be honest, real and human was and remains the most revolutionary task we have.

So we'd most of us grapple with the ways education refuted our lives. We all have lots of stories and examples, but let the country's great moral struggle suffice. William Faulkner, genius of the Southern soul, preached a reprehensible "go slow" attitude toward desegregation, and activist geniuses like Lillian Smith and James Baldwin would attack him. Faulkner's ideas would gain repetition in our anthologies and from the mouths of our teachers, would run as opinion pieces in *Life*. Smith was being banned and pulled from bookstore shelves. Baldwin's responses languished in *Partisan Review*. Who went to the classroom armed with *Partisan Review*? There the professors taught the received wisdom: "Well, here's what a writer thinks." Who did it to our graduate school teachers? We used to call it "the system," and we were right.

We were right, too, to wonder what Eliot's Dry Salvages had to do with finding our civilized place in this world. The world of literature is a very big tent. The Missourian's theological struggle does illuminate powerful fears. His alienation speaks worlds of denials. Why not learn what it is he denies?

So say all the wonderful writers who responded to the call for manuscripts for this collection. When Bottom Dog Press issued a call for manuscripts, the idea was to make room for stories like Randy Reynolds's. We realize now that the concept deserves a many-volume collection rather than the single book that you hold. We expected a strong response, but not in the degree that was offered.

"I don't have room to put all the manuscripts any more," Larry would tell me as deluges of submissions came our way. These pages are the ones that engaged us most in the work of about 10% of the writers coming forward. Still, it was not quantity so much as quality of submissions that daunted us. So very much honest, forceful and prophetic and varied writing was before us, all from a request on "stories of the working life." And so many different kinds of tales were *true*. It makes sense, now that the book is coming together as a book, that we saw such impressive variety.

What are we, if not various? Here are tales of a culture that loved Archie Bunker, and here are tales of a culture that loved Meathead. In San Francisco, families would laugh at Archie Bunker. Around towns you'd find here in rural Northwest Ohio, families would laugh at Meathead. These are the pure products of America: the Archies and Glorias and Ediths and Meatheads and the families watching in cities and towns, and tired Randy coming home on the Illinois to Ohio turnpikes.

The way we gave an order to the variety was to look at the accepted work, and group testimonies by recurrent themes. The tales showed too much variety to group by profession, and too much timelessness to present chronologically. We begin where it all starts, in family and neighborhood. Then there is "Working Class Education": the glory and despair of the working state of mind. Section three examines the compassion and ingenuity of negotiating the workday. "Where You Go When You Don't Work" looks at the wild everyday grind of getting by. The final section embraces the dignity of struggle as labor creates its soulful treasure.

The result is what we had hoped, the stories they would not teach in school. It is offered in the large spirit of Whitman's "Song of Occupations":

When a university course convinces like a slumbering woman and child convince,
When the minted gold in the vault smiles like the night-watchman's daughter,
When warrantee deeds loafe in chairs opposite and are my friendly companions,
I intend to reach them my hand, and make as much of them as I do of men and
    women like you.

                  -David Shevin/ July, 1996 (Tiffin, Ohio)

PREFACE

SUE DORO

The Cultural Worker

The poem waited for her outside the wheel shop door in the Menomonee Valley train yard. Waited, as if it were one of the countless raw cast-iron train wheels propped upright against the factory wall in the moonlight. Train wheels in long, neat rows leaning like round rusty-brown, 500-pound dominoes. Train wheels waiting to be machined.

So too, the poem waited. It had been waiting for her to finish work since 3:30 that afternoon. Now it was midnight. Soon she would step out of second shift into the dark of the going home night.

Hours ago in the early evening, the summer sun hung low and rosy over sidetracked freight cars in the yard. The poem had gone to look in the window nearest the machine the woman was operating that night. The poem thought that the sunset would surely get her attention. But then it saw her leaning across the table of a boring-mill machine, measuring inside the hub of a freight car wheel with her micrometer. She was straining on tiptoe to reach across the machine's table to the wheel's freshly cut center, and the poem could see she was too busy to be thinking poem words, so it did what it knew how to do.

It waited.

Measuring minutes against the sun's shadows on the dirty cream-colored brick wall, it waited. When five o'clock break time arrived, it waited and watched through a different window as the woman ate half her sandwich sitting at the lunch table by the men's locker room. She was sharing a newspaper and conversation with some of her co-workers. She kept on talking as she reached under the table to feed a bit of cheese to a dusty yellow, scrawny factory cat that grabbed the scrap of food in its mouth and bolted away.

The woman was the only female in the shop, and there were nights when she was lonely for the company of other women. But tonight the poem saw she was having a good time, laughing and joking with her work "buddies."

It was an hour and a half later when the poem checked in again. The woman was standing at the same machine working on a different wheel, listening intently to a short leathery-faced man with a chin full of gray quarter-inch whiskers. He wore a work-scratched green hard hat low over his dark eyes. His hands hung at this sides, glistening with soiled brown train bearing grease. In one hand he held a red-handled putty knife used to scrape lard-like gobs of grease off old train bearings. In his other hand, by their cuffs, he grasped a pair of oily black rubber gloves. The ring finger was missing on that hand. A cigarette bobbed up and down in his lips as he spoke, its ashes dusting the man's brown shirt every so often. The poem moved in closer to hear the conversation above the roar and clatter of the machine. It could catch only a few of the man's mumbling phrases: "love her...the kids don't talk...need more time." The woman was concentrating on the man's hesitant sentences with one eye on the boring-mill's cutting tool, ready to slap the stop button and flip the lever that pulled the cutting bar out of the wheel's center.

The poem went back to wait at the door until dinner break.

In summer, it was still light at eight o'clock in the evening when the break whistle blew, and the poem knew that the woman would go outside to relax on the long bench against the building. Most of the other second shifters would travel up the hill to the tavern, so she was generally alone. Some evenings after eating the rest of her saved sandwich, she'd take a stroll along the railroad tracks heading under the nearby freeway.

The walk was quiet and calming except for the faint rumble of cars far overhead. And if she walked a little further, the traffic noise faded completely. There was a small stream at that end of the valley, and a hill where she'd sit and gaze at the water, listening to it ripple over rocks and chunks of cement. Wildflowers grew along the riverbanks. In springtime there were baby asparagus plants and tiny green onions hidden in the tall, waving grass. Once when she brought a spray of yellow daisies back to the shop, one of the guys found and washed a mayonnaise jar to use as a vase. The flowers lit up the tool bench by the window, and everyone that passed by that night stopped to smell the daisies or to comment on the display. She was pleasantly surprised and happy that not one man teased her about it.

Other evenings found the woman writing in her journal. But tonight there was neither a walk nor journal writing happening at dinner break, and she wasn't alone. When the poem came around the corner of the building, it saw her leaning forward on the bench, holding a small open book and flipping through its pages. She referred to certain passages by tapping the index finger of her right hand on the page while she and a group of seven or eight men seemed to be talking at the same time: "contract...bargaining...Chicago...layoffs in July...four guys fired ...bankruptcy ...they can't...it's illegal...they'll try." The poem decided it was fruitless to try to get into her head. Then the sound of a factory whistle pierced the air, and moments later a foreman appeared in the doorway motioning everyone back to work.

The sun was beginning to slide down behind the freeway overpass. The poem stayed outside.

At ten o'clock the poem looked in the window by the woman again. She was staring out into the deep blackness of the night without even noticing the poem. Her eyes were taking in moonlight silhouettes of axles, train wheels, and oil drums. She watched three crows gliding like slow motion velvet shadows in front of a glowing pink yard light—one of the many fifty-foot-tall globes illuminating the train yard. A shop cat scampered over a discarded train bearing lying in the grass at the base of the pole. A warm west wind brushed the woman's cheek. She sniffed the air, smiling a little, and the poem thought for a moment that she was thinking poem thoughts. She wasn't. She was simply relieved that the night smelled of sweet Memononee Valley wilderness thanks to the west wind, instead of the stockyards to the east of the wheel shop.

"A few more wheels," she commented aloud to no one in particular, and then turned away from the window. Thoughts of home and her sleeping family filled her with a flash of emotion—God, how she missed them on night shift. She shrugged her shoulders, shivering at the same time, like a cat shaking off water. Then she attacked the unfinished wheel in the machine with the frenzy of someone who wished to believe her own speed could control the clock.

And finally it was minutes away from midnight. A full moon waited high over the factory roof like a white ball with a golden ring, outshining any stars. Pink lights cast shadows on the path next to the tracks. The entire train yard was a watercolored wash of pink and black. The poem waited with the moon, holding its breath.

The woman was usually the first ready to leave because her locker was in the bathroom of the foreman's office near the door. On other nights she waited to walk to the parking lot with the guys; however, tonight felt different to her as she stepped out ahead of the whistle.

She was short, but her shadow was ten feel tall. She carried a paper sack of dirty work clothes. The poem was with her like another shadow, walking quickly. The farther away she got from the building, the taller her shadow grew, from the yard lights and the moon on her shoulders. Little rocks and pebbles at her feet crunched under her shoes. Each pebble had its own rosy shadow, like pink moon rocks under her feet. She smiled to herself, relishing the moment.

A cat meowed from the path ahead, scurrying away from the woman's flying feet. Stopping abruptly, the cat turned its head to stare back at her, its yellow eyes frozen in black midair. Then it disappeared under a parked freight car.

Night birds called in the distance.

Now her shadow split in two, growing taller, taller, taller. Racing past more pink lights. Stepping nimbly across one, two, three sets of train tracks. Passing flatbed cars stacked with unmachined axles and rows of wheels. Past lines of mounted wheel and axle sets waiting to be shipped out.

A lone crow cawed at her from a telephone wire. Something stirred in her brain. Some disjointed words seemed to come together. She laughed aloud, and the crow cawed again, leaving its perch to soar over her head into the blackness beyond the realm of pink lights. For a fleeting second she saw its dark wings gleam with a blush of pink. Then suddenly the woman threw back her head and shouted up into the pink and black sky. "HEY...I'm a midnight rider. A cat's eye glider. I'm a second shift mother goin' home!"

She laughed again. Surprised and delighted, the poem jumped *inside her* like a fetus kicking in the ninth month. She hurried along, faster now, running the last few yards past the guard shanty.

Finally, she was at her car in the parking lot. She plopped her dirty work clothes on the car hood to pull her keys out of her pocket. She unlocked the door, opened it, and flung the sack into the backseat. Jumping in, she started the car, revved its engine, put the car in gear, and aimed the old '68 Ford out of the lot. She saw the other workers, just then crossing the tracks, waving at her, and she beeped her car horn a couple times in response.

Now she would have time for herself. A smile, glorious as a weekend, spread across her face. She felt the uneasy urgency she'd buried deep inside all night leave her in a great, earthmoving sigh as she drove through the open gate and turned up the road to the ramp leading from the valley.

And a poem was born, comfortable as a well-fitting work shoe, satisfying as the end of the work day. The poem. The woman. The mother. The machinist. All became one. And she sang to the hum of her car:

> *I'm a midnight rider*
> *A cat's eye glider*
> *A second shift mother goin' home.*
>
> *I'm a moon rock walker*
> *A pink bird stalker*
> *A short tall shadow headin' home.*
>
> *I'm a cool old river*
> *A seasoned survivor*
> *I'm a factory workin' poet goin' home.*

Truck farmer, Ohio © Rebecca Colon

Bonnie Jo Campbell shovelling manure on family farm

CARPENTER AUNTS

FAMILY & NEIGHBORHOOD

BONNIE JO CAMPBELL

Selling Manure

Last year, after school was out, I found myself staring six weeks of unemployment in the face. My mother quickly got wind of this and lined up myriad farm chores to occupy me. Similarly, my darling Christopher assigned me all sorts of house cleaning tasks. Unemployment, I discovered, did not mean free time. The biggest job at my mother's was mucking out her big horse barn. The manure was so deep in some parts that the horses were scraping their heads on the ceilings.

"How are we going to get rid of this stuff?" I asked.

"We're going to sell it," she said confidently.

True to her word, she put ads in the *Kalamazoo Gazette* and *The Kalamazoo Shopper*, offering manure for 35 dollars a truckload. My portion for doing the physical work was 20 bucks; Mom got 15 for providing the truck and the product. Right away we got calls. A surprising number of people wanted the stuff we were anxious to get rid of.

I spent a lot of time inside that barn with my pitchfork, moving layer after layer of manure and urine-soaked straw. The sweat poured out of me like I was a marathon runner. My mother brought me glasses of ice tea to keep my spirits and electrolytes up. I gratefully accepted, but oddly enough, wasn't feeling wretched. As my thoughts wandered, I found myself filled with good cheer. After months of sitting in class, listening to the death drone of professors, and pouring over textbooks, I felt once again like I was member of the world of the living. Moving my muscles this way was reviving me.

Making the delivery was a little embarrassing at first. My mother's pick-up truck was a vehicle of some notoriety. The body was rusting away; the two sides of the bed were held together with shock cords. Some days the weather was in the nineties, and with a half a ton of manure in the back of our truck, stuck in a traffic jam on West Main, we made quite a sensation. I put my hand over my face and hoped desperately that I wouldn't see anyone I knew.

Within about a week, however, I began to see the absurdity of our situation as liberating. As we rattled along in a 4-wheel drive, half-ton pick-up truck full of stinking, steaming manure, I got a different take on the journey through well-kept neighborhoods. I didn't feel like wearing my safety belt, but instead, hung a leg out the window. And strangely enough, I felt like master of all I surveyed. Perhaps this was how a prostitute felt toward a wealthy and respectable client; I might be dirty, but I have something you need.

Finally, I began to take pride in what we did. Mom and I provided an excellent quality product at a fair price to decent folds. And I was preventing my mother's horses from scraping their heads on the ceiling.

The people to whom we delivered manure were nice—after all, only very earthy people would order manure from the farm rather than buying it sterilized in bags from the store. When I unloaded my product onto somebody's garden, I was usually in good company. Customers often tried to help me shovel, but after I rebuffed their advances, they stood back and smiled at the cascading dung, hands on hips, eyes sparkling. They might have been fantasizing about mid-summer gardens brimming with vegetables.

One man was planting a full acre of garden. After I unloaded the truck, he made Mom and I walk with him to a mound on the other side. "Do you know what that is?" he asked. We didn't. "That's llama manure. And this pile over here, that's pig manure. And that's chicken." The pig pile was so fragrant that I figured he'd soon have trouble with his neighbors. But his enthusiasm was touching. I felt proud that our manure was out in the world, mingling with other manures, making things grow.

There is no vocation more honest than selling manure. Consider what most people do for a living. They go to work where they build crap, or sell crap, or move crap, or spin a line of bull over the telephone, all the while trying to convince the customer that their product is something other than crap. When I delivered a load of manure to someone's garden, the customer and I were both upfront about what we were dealing with. All I had to ask was, "Where do you want this shit?"

This experience made me reflect on the idea of work in general. Any job is and important job, whether it is selling manure or selling insurance. People should take pride in what they do, and not assume that a low-paying job or a dirty job makes them a second class citizen. And even the smelliest job, when well-done, has its rewards.

My husband works second shift at a paper converting plant in town. "What are you doing this afternoon?" he asked me one day as I walked him out to his truck. I told him I was going to the farm to pitch manure.

"Aren't we all," he said, nodding. "Aren't we all."

KEVIN CLARK

Carpenter Aunts

Cass had a C-clamp tucked under her arm, a plane in her right hand and was obviously pissed to see me standing there. She knew time was running out. The honeymoon couple was due back from St. Thomas tomorrow and she was rushing to finish the job. "What are you doing here?" she said and let the plane fall to the floor.

"I don't know. Just checking things out, you know."

"Julie, Dad won't like it that you're here. You've got school tomorrow. Jesus. What were you thinking?"

"Cass...."

"That's another thing, you hang out with carpenters you're going to pick up a few bad habits."

"Cass...."

"I'm not done."

"Cass, Dad had another seizure."

"What! Is he...?"

"He's fine. It was mild. Over in a few minutes. Mom's with him. I had to get out of the house."

Cass stooped to retrieve the plane. "I gotta get these doors on the house. Mr. Morton's probably practiced that threshold carry over and over in his mind. There really ought to be a threshold to carry the bride over."

"He'll need a lot of practice to hoist Nellie Creighton over anything. Did you see her coming down the aisle last week? There wasn't room for her father."

"I know. Look, I put down double two-by-eight studs under this floor. Case she wants to resume her tango lessons."

"Where's Deana? Why isn't she helping you?"

"She is. She's upstairs, trying to get the commode to sit right on the wax seal."

"No doors. No toilet. What a love nest."

"Hey, little sister, you can get on the other end of that door over there or you can get your little butt back home."

We moved the door to a couple of sawhorses and Cass turned a knob, adjusting the blade on the plane. She took the metal rule from her tool belt and pulled seven feet out. Marking the spot with the pencil from behind her ear, she cracked her Bazooka gum and yo-yoed the measure back into its silver box. Shaved to a perfect fit, the door was lifted into place. Cass lined up the hinges and I tapped in the pins. It swung free. From upstairs, we heard the toilet flush.

"The sound of success," Cass said. "Deana! Dee? Everything okay up there?" We heard a muddled response and took it to mean that things were under control.

"She's been fucking with that thing for over an hour and a half."

"Hey, you're carpenters, not plumbers."

"Tell me about it. I go up there and she's like trying to use a crescent wrench on the supply line to the shitter. She had it all chewed up and she's skinning the hell out of her knuckles."

"So what'd you do?"

"I sent her down to True Value to get a pipe wrench. Five-ninety-eight! Can you believe that? This dinky little wrench, made in China. I'm telling you we ain't gonna make shit on this job."

"What else do you need to do?"

"Got to put that quarter round trim down along the baseboard. Hey, want a beer? Morton's got a case of Lowenbrau out in the fridge. We've been helping ourselves to the little skinflint's stash all week."

"You know, Aunt Deana will have a fit if she sees me drinking."

"Let her." Cass waved me along toward the kitchen, white with fluorescent light and hard with newly installed Formica countertops. I could smell the glue they used to anchor things. Cass reached in the refrigerator. "Think fast." I caught the foil topped bottle about belt high. "They twist off," she announced and gave her own a turn. "So tell me about Dad."

"There's not much to tell. He was walking into his study with a paper and his evening cigar and bamm! He like stumbles to one side and I see him go down. Then, he starts...well, you know."

"Yeah. It's never easy to watch."

"And, anyway... I called Mom right away. She was on the phone with Aunt Fran."

"Who *should've* been here tonight." Cass takes a glug of beer and wipes her lips with the back of a dirty hand. "Go on."

"That's about it. He's okay. Really, Cass. I think he kind of looks better afterward. Don't you?"

"Yeah it's some kinda release, I suppose. I just wish they'd get his medication right. Jesus, he scares me with those convulsions."

There was the sound of the kitchen doorknob being turned. A disheveled Aunt Deana appeared. Her mouse brown hair clung with perspiration and she was arching her back, still trying to untwist from the cramped behind-the-commode position.

"I thought I heard two voices down here." She saw me move my arm behind my back. It was a pretty obvious cover-up.

"Oh my God, Cass, what are you doing? If your mother finds out about Julie drinking—"

"Dad had another seizure." Cass laid the words out with a tone that said this is serious, your worry is bullshit. Deana caught her breath and then exhaled.

"He's okay?"

"We think so. Still, y'know, it's always scary, and Julie saw the whole thing."

"Julie." Deana put her hand to her mouth.

Cass went on, "Anyway, Julie needed to see her big sister and her Aunt Deana. Y'know. Get out of the house and all."

"I understand." Deana came over and gave me a hug. "Got any more of those cold?" Cass turned and opened the refrigerator door.

"Help yourself."

We all moved to the back porch and watched a nearly full moon climb over North Mountain. My thoughts were with Cass. How she knew how to handle every situation. How she could talk herself out of trouble, nearly every time. We smoked up her Camel Filters and then went inside to put down the quarter round.

It was going on midnight when we got the last strip down. I wasn't very good with finishing nails, so Cass decided that she should drive them and I should follow behind her and sink the heads with a wood punch. Deana was cleaning up the mess she'd made in the bathroom. Later, I got the home improvement tour.

"We spackled in here after we hung the sheet rock." Deana was flipping on light switches as we went through each upstairs bedroom. "Let me show you the insulation job we did in the attic."

"Oh, for Christ sakes, Deana. Let's get out of here." Cass was downstairs tipping another Lowenbrau.

"I'm just going to show her the attic."

I followed Deana up the narrow stairwell to the attic. It was like other third-floor spaces in these old houses. Tall, almost another story with steeply pitched gables.

"It was hotter'n hell up here, Julie. We had to have both these exhaust fans going." She flipped one on to demonstrate. "Had to use both just to get the air moving." She flicked the toggle on the second fan and it sparked. Then, total blackness.

"Uh-oh. I think we blew a fuse."

"Deana?"

"Yeah, Julie."

"Keep talking, okay?" I was shuffling my feet, afraid to step left or right and wind up falling between the joists and through the ceiling of the floor below me.

"It'll be okay."

Then there was the sound of Cass, running up the steps. Flashlight in hand. Big sister to the rescue.

"Nice going, Edison. Now we've got to replace a fuse."

"Carpenters, plumbers, and electricians, too. Good thing this isn't a union job," I said.

Deana and Fran were solid, just like their work. We called them the Carpenter Aunts. Mom's little sisters. They started the contracting business just after Vietnam. As army corps nurses they'd seen some pretty ugly things over there. Somehow they also picked up an interest in working with wood. Aunt Fran had dated a Seabee and later she went to trade school. Deana was the business manager and project estimator.

They bought and restored a big Victorian house over in Eagle's Mere. It had a wide sweeping porch with a great view of the lake. I guess they got along. They were quiet for sisters, but seemed to always know what the other one was doing, where she'd be, what she might need. They stuck to the house. Didn't go out much. Old houses have a way of holding you prisoner with the upkeep.

A V.A. loan got their business started. It only took a pick-up truck and some power tools to begin. People liked their work and their prices. They promised to bring Cass in with them after she graduated and when the business picked up.

I loved Cass. She was the older sister every sixteen year old girl should have. When my friends talked about their older sisters and their boyfriends and fiancees, I found it all so boring. Cass rarely dated. Never had a steady guy. She couldn't be bothered with make-up or dresses and she was the first girl to take shop class at Sullivan County High School, back in '72. Maybe it's something in our genes. She loved working with wood.

I remember how she'd sit on the back porch hand-sanding things. Working the grain smooth, then polishing it until it shone. She used to say, "Jesus was a carpenter's son, sure...but he didn't really pick up on the trade, did he? First thing you should learn is to keep your hands from between the nails and the wood, right?" Mom would go into a tizzy over such blasphemous talk. Cass would get grounded, but sneak out anyway. She showed me how to get onto the porch roof and use the downspout route to freedom. Dad figured it out and threatened to put in a new gutter, but he knew that wasn't going to stop her.

She moved out when she was seventeen. She already had a job as a finisher at the cabinet factory in Dushore. It was part-time after school and the only other woman worked in the front office, but the foreman was the cousin of an old family friend and gave Cass a chance. Cass learned the job quickly. She was paid minimum wage plus a piece rate of seventy-five cents a unit. Cass sure showed those guys. Even Dad was bragging, saying, "She's whipping those cabinets out like a three-armed shoe-shiner at a Shriner's convention." Pooey. Spit-polished and ready to ship.

*   *   *

        I helped her when she moved out of the house to her first apartment. It was a two-bedroom dump over the donut shop on Laporte's Main Street. Jack Furman, the baker, owned the building. It had a sweet aroma that could make you hungry for donuts at any hour, except Cass said after a week of living there she couldn't look at anything glazed or sugar coated. When she got around to painting the walls, it temporarily drove out the deep fryer confection smell, but it wasn't a real pleasant trade-off.

        We painted her place together. Cass showed me how to mask the trim so you don't get the base color all over it. We put down drop cloths and had pizza delivered from Rusty's Bait, Tackle, and Frosty Cup out on 220 North. We used to joke about the toppings. You know, like if you asked for anchovies, you could end up with minnows. We just got extra cheese that night.

        I remember glancing out the window at the empty street below. It was past dinner time and the county offices were closed. The streets were quiet, except for a lone jogger. I think it was Jeremy Shoates, some creep who used to be a track star in high school.

        "Hey, Cass?

        "What, Sis?"

        "Do you ever think about meeting somebody and getting married?" It was a subject I hadn't raised with her for a while.

        "No."

        "Never?"

        "I don't know? I guess I used to. Do you need a paper towel?"

        I wiped my greasy hand on the front of my jeans. "No, I'm okay."

        "Why do you ask? She teased, "Are you planning on getting hitched?"

        "No, I just think you'd make some guy a really good wife."

        Cass wanted to laugh, but had her mouth full of cheese that stretched from her teeth back to the slice in her hand. She tore off a towel from the roll and wiped her lips. "I'll never marry, Julie. It just won't happen."

        "But you're so pretty. Talented and all."

        "Well..." Cass picked up her beer and just looked up at the ceiling. It was getting near dusk and we were losing the natural light.

        "I'm just saying that I know of at least two guys who'd love to go out with you."

        "Julie! What are *you*, the Laporte *Love Connection*?"

        "Cass, Frank Stowacre and Bobby Diehl. Either one would give his left testicle to go out with you."

        "No way! They're losers. They wouldn't even know what to do

on a date."

"All right." I knew she'd say no. I just worried about her. The only life she had was her job and this apartment. I didn't want her to end up like Mom's sisters, Fran and Deana in their forties and living together like a couple of nuns. No romance.

"We should put the lids back on the cans now," Cass said. I got up and started pouring paint thinner over the brushes.

"Hey, Cass? Can we go to the Genetti sometime?"

"The Genetti? In Williamsport? What's at the Genetti?"

"Sunday nights, they have a band and an all-ages dance."

"Sure, Julie. If you want. Who's there this week?"

"Oh, not this week. They have that all-girl band this week, The Vixens."

"So?"

"So, I don't want to see an all-girl band."

"Why? You hang out with all-girl carpenters," she laughed.

"It's different."

"How's it different?"

"You know. They say these Vixens are like, you know, lesbians."

"And lesbians can't play music?"

"No. No! It's just that people will think things."

"Like we must be lesbians too, if we go see this band?" Cass had stopped wiping the rim of the paint can. I felt like I'd said something wrong.

"Look," I said, "it's no big deal, we could go Sunday. I don't care."

Cass looked distracted now. "Yeah, well, I'm pretty busy this Sunday. We have to go out to Forksville and do an estimate."

We never did get to the Genetti, even when those boring, slow summer Sunday evenings rolled by. Instead, we'd go to her place and drink, listen to the stereo, or if she could score any weed, we'd get high. I never asked her again about Frank or Bobby or any guys for that matter. When I think back on that conversation and those sickening paint fumes, I think I knew then, but she never said anything. She wouldn't.

The next time we really talked about anything like that was at the honeymooner's house the night that Dad had his seizure. Deana eventually fixed the fuse and we left the Morton place unlocked because we weren't sure if the honeymooners thought to take along their keys. It was late and the temperature had dropped to the point where you almost needed a jacket. Cass had her arm around me.

"How was school today?"

I was going to lie, but she caught me off guard.

"Julie, you're blowing off too many classes."

"It's okay. Really."

She wasn't buying it, but went along with it. Resignation in her voice. "So what did you do today?"

"I copped the old man's wheels and went for a cruise. You should've seen this guy I picked up today."

"Picked up?" Cass stopped walking.

"Yeah, I sort of gave him a lift."

"Somebody you know?"

"No, he was hitching out on the highway. Going to Laporte."

"Julie, you can't just pick up strangers." We started walking again.

"I know. I know, okay? But he looked really cool. He wasn't big or nasty looking."

"Oh, that's reassuring."

"He was wearing this flannel shirt wrapped around his waist and he had really cool-looking hair. You could tell he wasn't from around here. He said he came all the way from Ohio. Can you imagine? He was on the road for like four days. I dropped him at the courthouse. Anyway...nothing happened."

"Julie, listen. Don't tell Mom any of this. You can't be doing this shit. Believe me, I know what I'm talking about."

"They already know. Big deal. So I skipped school and took the old man's car. It's not a federal crime. You used to do the same things."

"And?"

"So I'm grounded. Two weeks, no phone, no television. I don't give a shit."

"Julie, I don't care if you play hooky or go on joy rides with the Pontiac. Just promise me you won't be picking up any more hitchhikers, okay?"

"No problem. This guy wasn't much fun anyway. I think I shocked him when I asked him to come along to the Falls with me."

Cass paused and then started walking again. Walking faster and with more of a stiff stride. I had trouble keeping up.

"What's bugging you!" I shouted at her back, but she just kept walking. Mad at me, I thought. When we got to her apartment she said she was tired and needed to go to bed. I wanted her to tell me what was wrong, but she waved me off.

"Get home. You don't need to be in any more trouble and I'm just tired, that's all."

Late that summer, I began to feel like all my flirting with guys was leading up to something. One night at Rusty's Frosty Cup, Tommy Homan put his hand on my thigh and started rubbing me there. I told him to quit, but didn't really insist. He laughed and kept on stroking me, real soft and gentle. I felt like we were in on a secret, his hand on me right there under the table, while several of our other friends sat oblivious on the other side.

We didn't have sex that night, but I thought about having sex a lot after that. Just thinking about it screwed me up, but I didn't feel right asking Cass and there was no way I'd approach Mom on the subject. I was counting on Cass for answers, big sister advice. But now, we weren't talking the way we'd been. It was awkward. I felt colder towards her, like someone who'd been betrayed. She was still this crazy girl, a real lunatic, but somehow I knew she couldn't help me with this. My head was filled with guys, while Cass couldn't care less about them.

A week later, I went to the Weis Market in Hughesville for some things. I knew that Frank Stowacre worked there as a stock boy. I was looking for some pasta when I heard his voice from just around the corner of the aisle. He was talking fast and friendly with some other guy. They were stooped down low, stocking shelves.

"Yeah, honest to God! Jeremy Shoates gave it to her good once." You could tell from the snickering that they were talking about sex. Guy talk. Then the other guy said something that grabbed me.

"You talking about that dyke from Laporte?"

"Yeah, you know, the babe in the bib overalls. One time, Shoates was hitching a ride home after practice and she pulls up in that truck of hers. Jeremy says he made up some story about losing his keys on a run somewhere back by the landfill. She drove him back there and he did her right there in the middle of the road."

"He liked her?"

"Hell no. Shoates said he just wanted to teach her a lesson. That Cass, so fucking uppity. Acting like she don't need it from any guy."

Something turned deep and vile in my belly and I wanted to rip their snickering tongues from their mouths. Pound my fists until bloodied. Leave them whimpering. Wondering what hell had just unleashed. Instead, I went out to the Pontiac and put my head on the steering column. None of this was right. I wanted to go see Cass. Tell her I knew. Make up some story about beaning them both with a can of Contadina. But I couldn't do anything. I couldn't stop the tears.

When my breathing slowed again, I could smell the nearby dumpster rank and pungent. The afternoon sun created a sundog off the windshield. Sensations only, no thoughts.

Then I jolted upright at the sudden sound of a power saw screaming through wood.

ROBERT FLANAGAN

Champion

[Two chapters from *CHAMPION*, a novel-in-progress set in
Toledo, Ohio in 1954. Pat McCandless is thirteen.]

Headed uphill, Pat stood on the pedals, rocking from side to side,
pressing down with all his weight. He'd gotten a good lead on the downhill run but was scared shitless they'd catch him now. What if they had
switchblades? All he had with him was his book bag. The heavy bike
topped the rise. He looked back. The closest one, the one with the stick,
was more than a block behind him now, and all three had slowed to a jog.

Legs trembling, he kept peddling. If he coasted they'd know he
was tired and make another rush at him. Three more blocks and he turned
off Dorr street onto Upton, then he stuck out his legs and coasted, free.
His heart pounded hard. He was smart to take off the second he spotted
them, instead of trying to act friendly, hoping not to tick them off. Sweat
ran into his eyes. *Smart?* What a moron to ride through the Bardos' turf,
short cut of not. If they'd gotten that stick into his spokes, that would've
been all she wrote. That'd be great, race across town to surprise Mom with
his big news and show up with his school clothes ripped and bloody, the
Schwinn Roadmaster stolen, and his teeth kicked in. The Bardo gang didn't
just push you around, they were out to kick ass. Like the time Pat gave up
his Mud Hens cap but got whipped with that bike chain anyway.

Upton Avenue dead-ended at a gate made of iron spikes with a sign
above it: *Welcome! You're in the Company of Champions!* Guards in gray
uniform blocked the walk between the gate and the guard house, and high
chain link fencing topped by barbed wire ran all around the plant. There
was no way you could get in without a pass. He leaned his bike against a
tree for a quick getaway, though he didn't think they'd chase him that far,
of try anything with guards there. He hung on the fence to watch for her,
his heart beating against the chain link. He hated feeling scared, hated
worse knowing how he felt. You tried telling yourself you were just excited from the chase, worked up from riding fast, but you knew. You were
scared, you ran. The bastards.

A woman walked up to the front gate, two men behind her, and the
guard passed them through. Not Mom though, not even close.

She'd be surprised to see him. Mad too at first, since he wasn't to
ride so far from home, but once she heard his news she'd understand, he
thought, and probably be happy he'd been picked for something special.

He untied the windbreaker from around his waist and put it over
his sweat-soaked shirt. At his bike he got the new glasses from his book

bag and slid them on, then went back to the fence. Coke bottles, four eyes. But she was tired of catching him without them. If he didn't need glasses like the school nurse said, then why had she spent good money on them?

The grinding and stamping noises made it sound like a war was going on inside the plant. They'd had to wear ear plugs the time Mom had taken him through Champion, and he'd been amazed at how loud it was, and dirty. The rows of plug tamping machines, all pipework and tubes and steel plates, looked like things you'd tie martyrs to until they gave up the faith. How did she stand it night after night? Yet on their tour she'd acted happy, yelling *Hi* to people and showing off Pat as her bigboy. The women made over him, shrieking that he was cute, and someone shouted to ask was he going to work there, because his mom could get him in when the time came, no problem, not if he was half the worker she was. He'd smiled at people and said oh sure, oh he didn't know, oh maybe, stupid stuff, but not loud enough for anyone to hear him anyway. Watching the set-up men wrestle heavy trays of cores and insulators and gaskets to the machines, he knew he'd never be able to do the work, not like her.

He walked along the fence, plucking at the wire, The factory was one giant building after another, their windows as big as billboards, and made up of row on row of small gray panes. Fat gray pipes ran up the red brick walls, and metal boxes sat on the black roofs like pillboxes. The whole place was fenced and guarded like an army base. Maybe besides spark plugs Champion made secret weapons but Mom wasn't to tell. Dad might let it slip sometime when he was home from the veteran's hospital, when he didn't really know what he was saying.

The shift whistle blew and everything went quiet, like a cease fire. Pat stepped behind a tree to dig into his shorts and adjust his truss. He heard a rush of noise then, not machines but voices, and looked to see people stream from the buildings, first trick rushing out. He moved back to the fence. Second trick workers were coming in in twos or threes, some through the front gate but others by side entrances from parking lots flanking the factory. He looked to one side, then the other. He'd thought everyone used the front, he had no idea where her ride parked or which gate she used. People swarmed past him, groups mixing and separating. "Shoot." He'd miss her for sure. After all the rush and nearly getting killed, now he —found he was looking right at her but hadn't known who it was. Behind the wire she headed his way along with Gil Ford, her ride to work, and Elsie Glick, one of Gil's riders, coming from a lot off to the right. In an orange sweater and black slacks, and smoking a cigarette, Mom walked with bouncy steps. Nights when she got home from work she would be all worn out. 'Oh Laws,' she'd say, sighing, 'I'm so tired I could just die?' When Dad was still at home he'd be sure to get out of bed and have a cold beer waiting for her then, and she liked that. But when she sat at the table to relax he'd pace around the kitchen in his robe, taking up a dish rag to dust the counter or radiator as if midnight was a good time to start cleaning house, then stop and look at the rag like he didn't know how it got in his hand and flip it into the sink, all the while going on about how lucky they were Mom had landed the Champion job, not that it wasn't hard on her, oh no, it was a real grind, he knew that for a fact, from first-hand experience at Red Man Tobacco and Armor Meats, and the city street department. One job of another it was all the same, you knew which end of the stick you'd get. The bosses, your big industrialists, your financiers and politicians, they were never ones to give anything away for free, not even your Stranahans, who were a pretty decent lot all in all. Poor Dad didn't see how he got on people's nerves, talking all the time or else couldn't help himself. If only he'd sit and be quiet and give them all a breather. But no, he kept asking her if there was anything else she wanted, a baloney sandwich of a bowl of cheerios. Only to be left alone, she'd tell him. If everything would just leave her be, she believed she could sleep for a week.

But now, laughing with Gil, she didn't look worn out and beat down the way she did coming home nights, she looked like someone you'd see in *Life* magazine, not a mom but someone pretty and young. A knockout, like Dad always said. Seeing her now, you wondered why she had to do such hard, dirty work. Why didn't she try to go on stage or get into the movies? But if you told her that's what she should do she'd laugh it off, like you were trying to put one over on her but even she wasn't dunce enough to fall for that malarkey. The same when you said how pretty she was—just save your guff, she'd tell you. Yet she really was good looking, even if she didn't know it. Other people knew it. You could see by the way Gil looked at her that he knew it.

Just as Pat began waving she turned to walk away from him, along with Gil and Elsie headed back toward one of the rear buildings. "Mom!" But she couldn't hear him over the people crowding through the main gate, calling names, cursing, telling dirty jokes, like kids getting out of school. "Madge McCandless!" But she stepped through an open, dark doorway and he lost her. "Damn." She'd have heard him if it weren't for that pack of loud clowns crowding through the gate. He kicked the fence, saw a guard give him the fisheye, and backed off. *"Damn!"* She never was at home. Gil picked her up about the time school got out, and even when Pat ran straight home he was too late, they were gone, and she wouldn't be back until nearly midnight. He went to his bike and gave it a kick, kicked it again and sent it clattering onto its side, it was his bike, it was none of the guard's beeswax what he did with it. He never wanted it anyway. All he'd wanted was a used one, some banged-up thing nobody'd bother to steal. But on his birthday there was the Schwinn Roadmaster in the living room, his big surprise. Shiny black and white enamel, horn, headlight, fenders and chain guard—everything about it way too flashy. 'Mom!' he'd said. On his card she'd written 'Happy Thirteen!' What was she thinking?

Did she want to get him killed? Maybe she was trying to make it up to him for Dad being gone, he didn't know. Or showing off maybe, now that she had a good job, by giving him something they really couldn't afford. That *he* couldn't afford anyway. But she'd looked so proud standing beside the bike that he had put on a grin to match hers 'Wow!'

He stood the Roadmaster upright. If the Bardo gang didn't steal it, the coloreds would. Or smash it just for something to do. Wop punks with their steel-toed motorcycle boots and sharpened belt buckles, like the shines always looking for trouble.

At least now she wouldn't be mad at him for riding over to Champion, out of the neighborhood. She didn't see him so he wasn't there. It'd be better anyway to tell her at home, without Gil hanging around. Hey Mom, guess what happened at school? No, something *good*. I got a part in the school play. I got picked. I play the father.

He saddled up and rode the long way home, Upton to Bancroft instead of Dorr to Detroit. In the cinder lot behind DeWald's Bar and Grill, he got off his bike. He took a good look around, saying a prayer to Saint Gertrude of Nivelles who guarded you from the fear of rats and mice, then bumped the bike down the cement stairs and into the low basement to chain and lock it to a water pipe. He thought he heard something, but shook it off. He went behind the big furnace to knock on an unpainted plank door. "Cap? Wanna hear some good news?" Some people complained about a colored janitor living in the building, but Pat was glad to have someone there to watch over things. Cap had worked at Republic Steel before he got hurt. Now he hauled ashes from the furnace, swept the apartment stairs, and kept a ball bat beside his cot for any thief fool enough to sneak in where decent people stored their belongings. "Cap? You home?" And he'd gone after the rats with poisoned bait. Every so often now you'd find one curled up in the lot with a pool of bright blood by its yellow teeth, though usually they hid away to die, leaving an awful stink.

Climbing the open flight of stairs, Pat heard the neighbors—Mrs. Pike telling Mr., laid off again and hitting the bottle, that he'd just better not get started, not tonight, not if he knew what was good for him.

He unlocked the apartment's back door with a key he wore on his scapular cord, then rushed to the toilet, sudsing the bowl with his strong stream. Mom's things cluttered the shelf below the medicine cabinet— Lux facial soap, Lustre Creme shampoo, eyebrow pencils, cold cream, rouge —and he began straightening them. He could see Gil Ford laying his hand on her shoulder as they walked to the Champion plant from the parking lot, Mom smiling like it was okay, like she liked it. He set a tube of Viv lipstick on end, then left off trying to put her things in order. In the kitchen, he turned on Dad's old radio. Fats Domino sang "Please Don't Leave Me." There was a note taped to the stove but Pat acted like he didn't see it. He made a sandwich, singing with the radio, swaying back and forth. He liked to dance if no one was watching. "Pleez doan leave me." His mouth full of peanut butter, he sounded a lot like Fats. He took a quart of milk from the Crosley refrigerator Mom was buying on time and sat at the table, eating the sandwich and drinking from the bottle. Often she'd wonder aloud why their milk always tasted like peanut butter, and he'd shake his head, sorry, but he couldn't help her there.

Under the salt shaker lay a long white envelope. At first after Dad left he hadn't written home at all. Now they got a letter each week. He pulled it to him. The envelope was torn open, its flap ragged. Mom never thought to use a knife or fingernail file. On the back she'd printed 'Needs slippers,' which meant they'd be going down to see him again. Whenever Pat's sister Ann drove them to Chillicothe, Dad always was just getting out of bed. His eyes looked raw and red and there were white, flaking patches beside his nose and mouth. He had plucked out his eyebrows again, and this time all the hair on his head too. It was growing back, but coming in white instead of red. He wore a little soft blue hat that looked like a base-ball cap with the bill cut off. A skullcap, he called it. When Mom got them coffee from the cafeteria, he'd use a dish towel to drink his. He draped the towel around his neck, held one end of it in his right hand, grabbed the other end and cup handle in his left, then pulled the cup up to his mouth without spilling a drop, even with his hands trembling so. Neat trick, Pat told him. He always acted cheerful at the hospital. He didn't want anyone to know how creepy it made him feel to see the disabled veterans walking around like zombies, and Dad looking like his own grand-father. But the visits had made Dad tired, so now they just wrote back and forth.

> Greetings and Salutations! I trust my loved ones are in good health and fine spirits. The good Lord willing I will soon be back in the bosom of my dear family. Each day brings new hope. The doctors do all they can for us here. We should give thanks to the Almighty for such kind and patient souls. Fervently hoping to se you soon, I remain...

It was dated Monday, October 11, only three days ago, but might as well have been written months past for being the same old stuff—God bless, thank the Lord, no news, no jokes. It didn't sound anything like Dad. Though the handwriting was better, steadier. When he'd first written home they could barely make out what he was trying to tell them. Pat tucked the letter into the envelope addressed to The Robert F. McCandless Family in big loops and swirls, the Palmer Method Dad learned as a boy back at Saint Patrick's school.

He tilted back on the chair to pluck the note from the stove, a bank slip with Mom's block printing on the back.

> I made veg soup - heat up for supper - don't just
> eat peanut butter - I want you in bed when I get
> home.
>> love Mom —turn off the stove

In the refrigerator the soup was still warm. She'd check to see if any was gone so he served up some, dumped it down the toilet, rinsed the spoon and bowl, careful to leave traces of soup, and set them in the sink.

Then he sat back down at the table. Good News!' he wrote on a Toledo Trust deposit slip, then balled it up. He wanted to see her face when he told her. He had made the play, he was almost the lead. She'd get mad if he waited up for her, but he was good at faking being asleep and waking up, and she never caught on. *If* he could stay awake that long. Though maybe he really would wake up when she tucked him in. Every night she came into the living room where he slept on the pull-down Murphy bed to wish him 'Good night, Good morning, God bless you,' doing it all at once since he was gone mornings to serve the six-thirty mass long before she got up. If he wasn't too dopey maybe he'd remember to tell her his news then. Or just wait another day and tell her on Saturday when they both were awake. Weekends were the only time they had together now. Even then, cleaning the apartment, running to the A&P, and to church, they didn't get much time to talk.

If the play was on a week night, Mom probably would have to miss it. She couldn't take off work, he wouldn't want her to, that was her job. And even if Dad was back by then, he couldn't go, not to a place with a crowd and noise.

Still, he was happy for them that she'd gotten the second trick job she bid on. She made better money now and they got along fine without having to ask anyone for help.

MARTYRS

He climbed the back stairs to their apartment over the Ideal Furniture store. All the way up he could hear "Your Cheating' Heart," Hank Williams sounding lonely as a lost dog. Since Williams died last year, Mom played him all the time. It was so *unfair*, she'd say, for him to be taken like that, a heart attack in the back seat of a car on the way to Canton. As young as he was? And just when he'd made it big? After growing up dirt poor, his father a war veteran in a hospital like Pat's Dad, and his poor mother having to run a rooming house. It was awful to think of him dying, just when he finally got a chance to enjoy life.

Pat slipped his key into the lock and eased open the door.

Mom sat with her back to him at the kitchen table. Dressed for work, she sang along with the record. "But sleep won't come, the whole night through." If she thought anyone else was home she'd clam up. She hated her voice. 'Oh laws, it's so *na*sal, like I've always got a cold. I sound just like a cat!' She was right too, she sang through her nose and off key, but Pat would tell her no, she did fine, that hillbilly music all sounded that way. He liked hearing her sound happy for a change.

In the living room the record ended and the needle scratched like radio static in the grooves

"I'll get it," he said.

"Oh laws!" Mom started, twisting about. "Pat? What on earth!"

But she loved scares, anything exciting. He went up the narrow hall past the bathroom and bedroom to the living room to change the record. Then she called to him, no, just stop it, she was done, so he shut down the old victrola. And what was he doing home so early, she wanted to know.

He came back down the hall to the kitchen.

"Don't you look nice," he said.

The green jumper left her long arms bare, and her neck looked long and smooth with her hair braided and coiled at the back of her head. Her lipstick was the same color as the sweater draped on the back of her chair, a licorice-whip red. She had to be the prettiest woman in the factory.

"Oh, well." From a roll of the gray half-inch wide adhesive tape that Champion Spark Plug gave out free to plug tampers she cut a finger-length strip and stuck it to the edge of the table where a dozen or so strips hung. She lay the scissors beside her coffee cup and fixed him with a look "I asked you something, didn't you hear?"

He moved around the table to stand beside her. Taking the scissors, he cut a strip of tape and stuck it in place. "How many more you need?"

"Six or so. *Pat.*"

"We got out early, that's all."

"Why?"

"Saint's feast day."

"What?"

"Saint Ignatius, martyr, patron of sore throats."

She lookied to see if he was kidding.

"When the lions were eating him in the Colosseum, in Rome, he called out Jesus's name. He didn't stop till they'd ripped out his throat."

"Laws! Even so, I think they ought to keep you the whole time."

"They do, just not today."

"They must know what they're doing, but still."

She always spoke of priests and nuns as though they were strangers from another country, or planet. A non-Catholic, she seemed to have no idea of what they were doing or why, yet was willing to trust that it was for his good. His sister Ann, the smart one in the family, had said a Catholic education was a good thing, so it must be. Mom herself showed no interest in it. She never went to see his teachers or talked to Ann about it, so had no way of knowing that school wasn't let out on saints' days, that today actually was the feast of Teresa of Avila, virgin, and that Saint Ignatius, Bishop of Antioch's feast day was that Sunday. But Pat knew virgins bored her. It was martyrs she liked.

She slid a cigarette from the Philip Morris pack on the table and lit it. As he cut eight more strips of tape he glanced at her, enjoying how graceful her hand was in lifting the cigarette to her lips, the way she seemed to sip at it, just like kissing the tip, her hand sweeping the cigarette away then in a little dip and rise, as wisps of smoke slipped from her nostrils like incense, Her face took on a dreamy look and he wondered what it was she dreamed about. A brick house for one thing. Good jobs for him and Ann. And Dad back home from the veterans' hospital, not crazy anymore.

He put an arm around her shoulders and gave her a quick little hug. "I'm glad we're out early," he said, "so I can see you."

"I know, Doodlebug. Me too. But they shouldn't cut corners."

"We got extra homework to make up for it."

"Then I suppose."

"And guess what?"

She sipped from her cup and made a face. *"Cold.* Toss this out?"

He dumped the coffee into the sink, rinsing the cup under the tap. "Remember the drama thing I told you about? I made it!"

She looked at him, half-smiling.

"The school play." He came to the table. "I got a part, a big one, the father. Maybe you can come see me, you and Ann."

"Oh, good. That's nice." She brought the cigarette to her lips, then took it away. "And this, it's a part of school?"

"Sure."

"Because I want you getting all your schoolwork done."

"It's like a school club. Like altar boys." He lifted the sweater to her shoulders but she shrugged it off and he dropped it back on the chair.

"A play?" she said.

"Yes, Mom! On a stage? Come onnnn."

"Come on, what? I never claimed to be brainy like some people."

"A *play.* Like on TV? Goodyear Playhouse—"

"—I just didn't know you were interested in—"

"G.E. Theatre, Kraft Theatre, Fireside Theatre, —"

—that kind of thing. And I don't want you watching—

"—Studio 57?"

"—so much TV."

"I don't." At the refrigerator he took out the milk, lifted it out his mouth, then stopped and filled a glass. "A lot of kids tried out. I didn't think I had a chance, but I got it."

"Good for you then, I'm glad you beat them."

"Thanks."

"Be sure to tell your sister Ann, she'll be happy."

He sat across from her. Dumping his bookbag out on the table, he started on homework, sentence diagrams.

"Now don't look like that, dunky-doo," she said. "*Potsy.*"

"Like what?" With a milk mustache and crossed eyes, he got a laugh.

"I just want you to do good in school so you can get a good job and be able to do for yourself. That's why you're at St. Ann's that costs more than Monroe school, to learn the right things." Stubbing out her cigarette, she began taping her hands to protect them from the tooled metal cores she ran through her machine. "School's a lot like work."

"You're telling me?" Groucho's voice and hand waggle, the pencil as cigar.

"Now I'm serious. You have a job, you have to do it."

"I know. But I wish you could stay home, just for tonight."

"You know I can't."

"I *said* I know. I was just saying—"

"So why say it?"

"If you were sick you could."

"Don't even say that. I'm *not* sick and not going to be either. Your poor father's sick enough for all of us."

"Mom, okay. I'm sorry."

"We're you on time this morning?"

"Sure. I always am." Though he'd tried to wait up for her the night before, making it to a little after eleven, and that morning had dozed off twice during the school service. Then after lunch he could not stay awake, no matter what, and finally told Sister Petronilla he had such a bad headache it hurt to keep his eyes open. Some trouble with his glasses, he said the doctor said. He had medicine at home though, if he could just—

"Well, I'm glad. You've been really good about that, and that's good. I hate it when my supply boy's late. It puts me behind the entire night." Finished with the right hand she started on the left, wrapping strips around the first two joints of fingers and thumb, then laying another across the tip, like a boxer getting ready for a fight. "I have to turn out five thousand plugs a night if I want to make top rate, no matter how I feel. That's what I get paid for."

"But when I get a job..."

"No no, what I mean is, I *do* it."

"Right. But why can't I get a paper route?"

"You know what your father says, he's worried you'll get hurt."

"Yeah, but he's not here."

"When he comes home, we'll see."

"What if he doesn't come home?"

"Why wouldn't he?"

"I don't know."

"You want him back home, don't you?"

"When he's okay, sure. If the doctors are sure he's okay."

"We all want him home, I wrote and told him. He needs to know."

"Mom, I never said I didn't want him home."

"Nobody said you did. Now listen, I'm trying to tell you something. About work. What I'm saying is, even if I wanted to stay home, I wouldn't. I do the job no matter what." She lit another Philip Morris, blew smoke, waved it away. And, she said, she made her quota without down time too. Some of the girls bragging about making quota, a lot of it came from down time. They just knew how to play up to their foreman and repairman. That one hunkie, Bettina! Laws, the sweaters she wore. Not that down time wasn't a good thing.Mom was darned glad the union had fought for it. Because now, say a broken core jammed your machine, you got credited with the number of plugs they figure you could have done in the time it took a repair man to get you back on line. But she always tried to make her quota without down time. It was harder to make tops now that she was running aviation, the plugs were a lot bigger and trays heavier, but to her, a machine operator didn't deserve top rate unless she had five thousand plugs stacked up each night where you could see them and touch them. If it was only on paper, really it didn't count. Not the way she saw things.

He took two left-over tape strips, laying them across his knuckles.

Once she'd gone six weeks straight without down time, the record on her floor. Of course a lot of that she owed to Polish Teddy, her set-up man. He always supplied her machine first, and never let her run out of cores or silament powder. He was kind of sweet on her, she guessed, and she felt sorry for him because he was fat and homely and oh honestly had such godawful breath that none of the girls there would look at him twice. So whenever she baked anything she took some in for him, hermits or banana cake, whatever, And she took her foreman Ronald Fenn some too because when she broke down if he had a machine free he'd switch her to it rather than give her down time. They all knew she'd a lot sooner work than sit around gossiping. It there was anything she couldn't stand, it was not having something to do.

She glanced at the clock. "Laws! Look at the time!" Stubbing out the cigarette, she got up. "Potsy, clear up here for me, would you?"

"Sure." He backed away in front of her, bobbing and weaving, flicking jabs and crosses just short of her.

"Look *out* now." She grabbed the red sweater and her baggy black work purse big enough to hold her lunch and make-up and other things. "Salmon patties in the frig."

A horn beeped out back—shave and a haircut, bay rum.

"There's Gil."

"Why's he always hanging around?"

"He's my ride, you know that." She stopped at the door. "And don't wait up tonight. Now I really mean it. You need more sleep, your sister tells me that all the time."

"Bye." At the door he called after her, "See you tonight!"

At the lip of the back stairs, she threw him an exasperated look, then hurried on down, her head sinking from, sight past the Ideal roof line.

Gathering eggs © Roger Pfingston

DAVID KHERDIAN

William Miller

Bill Miller fixed radios, traveling from home to home from his apartment on the corner of La Salle and Hamilton Streets. I can still see him, walking by himself, groomed in a well-worn suit and tie, and with an inner, imperturbable quiet.

For some reason he did little repairing in his own home. We would phone him (or somehow get a message to him in the days before we had a phone) and he would come in the evening and fix our radio. Why he came in the evening I do not know, unless of course he had another, regular full-time job, like all the other men I knew. In one or another of the factories, that is. Nor did I know that he was "colored," as we called the blacks then. I only knew that he seemed different from the other men, and for this reason I was attracted to him.

I was not any more or less attracted to him once I learned that he was colored (mulatto actually, another term from that time), because this was merely a fact to be attached *onto* him, whereas what compelled me to notice him and to go on noticing him, with that first edge of wonder and admiration that comes when we encounter a mystery, was something else, his quality of quiet dignity and pride, that I was unable not to notice.

My wonderment, if I can put it that way, was of course my own groping nature itself, for wherever I looked my eye always stopped and became attached to the non-commonplace, the thing that misfitted the design. I did not put any great importance on the fact that I too was different, even though I knew I would never fit in myself. My subject of study, in the beginning at least, was not myself but others. I didn't realize then that I was looking for confirmation for myself, as well as models from whom I could learn. I was simply watching and learning—indirectly and unconsciously. The impressions I was taking were leaving a deposit that was beyond the concerns or comprehensions of the mind.

Mr. Miller—for that was his name—smoked cigars. He smoked them in a way that I had never seen before. And all cigar smoking that I have witnessed since, and for some years I was a cigar smoker myself, has been a poor approximation of the way he smoked. In that time and place, each man was known for something, and this "thing" often carried such importance that it became, for others at least, the man himself. It was therefore not surprising that he seemed legendary to me for the reason alone that he smoked his cigars with a particular expertise.

But there was more to the matter of his personality and his influence on me than that, because in addition to smoking a cigar professionally, Mr. Miller fixed radios.

And he was colored.

And he was a bachelor and lived alone.

All of these things, in my child's mind, made him different and special.

One day I asked him about his cigar smoking. I wanted to know why I never once saw him re-light one of his cigars. He told me, in the soft-spoken way he had, that he was able to keep his cigar lit for over an hour at a time by knowing just when to puff on it, and just how *hard* to puff on it, depending on the moisture of the tobacco, the climate and temperature, and of course depending on how far down the cigar had been smoked. I was amazed and couldn't take my eyes off him. Or his cigar. I don't know what enthralled me more, the feat, or the style with which it was accomplished.

But in the end the thing that seems to lie at the basis of my remembrance of Mr. Miller was his dignity and self-respect. I had all along assumed that these qualities were his inherently, but it may have been that he acquired them through suffering, and out of a deep, personal need to make something in himself that could deter prejudice and discrimination. I do not know. If this was the case then it may have been—again unconsciously—why he served as a model for me, and why in fact I admired him as much as I did.

From Letters to My Father

ONE

Every time I passed that unpainted
storefront building on State Street
I remembered that you and Mother once
lived in an upstairs apartment there
beside your relatives, who still owned
the building, but no longer ran the
businesses downstairs.

For some reason we were relatives
but not friends. It had to do with
their stinginess and their fears,
and with their old country ways
that became more pronounced in time,
unlike my mother who was becoming
more liberated by the day.

Once during a strike, when you were
unemployed—or was it a lay-off
or another recession—we had
stopped at their restaurant,
and I remember seeing a sweet roll
under glass that I had wanted
but couldn't have. I blamed the
Hardys, as they were now named,
because it seemed such a simple
need to fill.

And that is all that comes to mind
of that incident, although what made
it unforgettable was probably my
embarrassment, and your own
loss of pride that I would have been
witness to.

The building is now gone, but is
there in the mind, where remembrances

are lived. And I won't let it go
because you did time there
and so did I. And not just there
but up and down that block. Our place
of home that was always more my
home than yours; your home having
disappeared completely,
as mine would one day begin to do,
bit by bit.

TWO

I think of him trudging off
in winter snow by
morning dark
to wait
at the corner
bus stop
end of our block

And the lonely, tubular
light of the bus
traveling the deserted
streets of our town
taking those early morning
men to their jobs

And also walking home
in summer, four miles
of city streets, from
the factory gate to where
I stood on the sidewalk

Or sometimes on the porch
waiting to be greeted
as he had waited to greet
me, pressing a nickel or
dime into my palm,

still warm from his hand,
money he had saved from
the fare, that I was to use
for ice cream,
or whatever else I might
want

THREE

I would hear the furnace clank
and know you were shoveling
coal into its orange hungry mouth

and I would roll over in my
half-sleep, curling my body
for additional warmth

while Mother rose and readied
breakfast, calling me to dress
before the parlor vent

that brought a draft of warming air
from where you had been
before you went off

trudging down the cold
dark street of icy wind-swept snow
in your heavy gray coat

waiting at the corner for the bus
that would take you
to the factory gate alone.

JIM SANDERSON

Emma and Shorty

In 1943 somewhere around Pecos, Texas; Shorty and Henry sat in a cold bunk house with nothing but bed rolls, a poorly working heater, and a bottle of bourbon to keep them warm and talked about Henry's agricultural deferment from World War II and his future. Shorty was too crippled, too old, and too short to get into the service. And at the time, Shorty had just glimpsed over the edge of fifty to see his future. Alcoholic, displaced, with no hope of ever being more than what he was, Shorty had only death as the next great event in his life. Shorty, like Henry's father, knew the sad truth that over-worked, under-paid cowboys, if they weren't lucky enough to find a wife and get into some other business or get real lucky and manage a ranch, became crippled-up old men in their fifties who lived in cold bunkhouses off a rancher's sense of social responsibility. Henry had left his home because of the woman his father picked to marry. Henry couldn't cock his head or hold his tongue right while praying to receive the Lord's transmissions like his mother could.

So small he often had to buy a boy's saddle, Shorty was too abnormal or ugly to ever find a woman, but he could make a horse do anything. Years later, Henry would tell everybody about the way Shorty rocked in the saddle and moved with the rhythm of the horse and how "pretty" the horse looked with his muscles working "fluid-like" beneath its skin. Once, with his reins in his teeth, a pistol in each hand, guiding the horse with his knees, Shorty had ridden through the West Texas prairie and blasted at jack rabbits to show the cowboys how the old Texas Rangers had scared the hell out of Mexicans, Indians, and Yankees. When Henry and a wetback buddy first tried to become cowboys, they had seen Shorty do this, and doing this trick was how Henry tried to remember Shorty. When the "wetback" Henry had gone to cowboy with got cut up in a bar fight and then got deported, Shorty had become Henry's best friend.

That night, Shorty lay on his bunk, took a long swig at the bottle of Old Crow bourbon, then passed the bottle to Henry. Henry sat in his bunk with his sleeping bag wrapped around him, listened to the whir of the kerosene lantern, and watched the shifting shadows as the wind, not just a draft, blew in through the cracks in the cabin's lumber to shake the lantern. He took the bourbon that he was just learning to drink and appreciate and took a long swig from the bottle.

"For a young man like yourself," Shorty said, "This war might be a good thing."

"What sense is quitting a job and a deferment to go get killed?" Henry asked. Shorty reached for the bottle and shook his fingers for it.

"What you think you gonna become here?"

"It's a job. A cowboy is better than what I once was."

"Yeah, but you join the service and make it through a war, you are a hero."

"So, what good is a hero?"

"So what good is a cowboy? Ain't been a real cowboy, let alone a useful one, in fifty years. We ain't nothing more than heirlooms." Shorty took a drink from the bottle, lay his head down, and looked up at the ceiling. "The worst that could happen is you get killed. But war has to end, and if you ain't dead, you're a hero. You stay in the army, you become a sergeant or something, and you got a roof and three squares assured to you. Can some fat ass rancher offer you that?"

"I could be a sergeant," Henry said to confirm Shorty. Shorty raised his head up just a bit, stuck the bottle between his lips, and sucked out the last of the bourbon just as Henry reached for the bottle. "Jesus, Shorty," Henry said. "I got hardly none of that to keep me warm." Henry looked at Shorty to see him silently staring at the ceiling on the verge of screaming or shaking. "You okay?" Henry asked.

"This war is a big thing and is gonna give a lot a people a lot of chance. It is going to shake things all up."

Henry stared at his friend whom he had thought too mean and too by God proud to be on the verge of crying, and then, looking closely at his friend for maybe the first time, Henry saw his future. "You want to enlist with me?"

"They already refused me," Shorty said and an alcoholic tremor went through his body. "Goddamn it is cold," he said. "It bites into your bones." Henry knew what Shorty meant. The bourbon didn't really help against the cold; the warm tingle it left in your throat, chest, and stomach just took your mind off the cold.

Maybe, since Henry couldn't pray right, the Lord had given Shorty a message for Henry. Henry looked at this angel of the Lord, "I got this blanket stuffed into my bag. You want it?"

"It's yours," Shorty said, and Henry watched him shake from the alcohol or the cold chills that ran through him. He reached above his head to turn off the kerosene lantern, so he wouldn't have to listen to its whir, or watch its shadows, or see Shorty.

* * *

Henry got trained just in time for the Normandy invasion. He got mad when Travis Lilly, a fellow Texan from Houston, only twenty-two years old, was made corporal over him and put in charge of Henry's squad. Henry thought his five years of varied experience gave him more common sense ability. He began to fear that rungs on his career ladder were slipping out of his fingers and from under his feet.

Travis Lilly, for his part, must have doubted his own ability to lead men. He had been in the army no longer than Henry and now had a minor part in waging the most important battle in history. But, he must have gained confidence in his own ability when he and Henry hit the beach side by side. They dove head first into the sand and came up coughing and spitting it out. He turned to Henry and was the first one to see the former cowboy staring dumbly at the shattered wood of his rifle's stock, then at his own finger tip lying in the sand.

As Henry had raised his rifle to fire, a lucky German bullet or a stray American bullet had hit his trigger finger then shattered the stock of the rifle, sending splinters of wood into Henry's chin and cheek. Travis Lilly must have at least thought himself less shocked and disoriented than the poor cowboy. "I didn't even fire," Henry said. He held up his broken rifle. "What do I do now?"

"Jesus fucking Christ," Travis said. Since Travis Lilly was the corporal, Henry figured Travis should give him some advice, should order him to do something, but Travis said, "I guess you should pick up your finger." Then they heard a lieutenant or someone who sounded important shouting to advance. Travis Lilly got to his knees and elbows, then to his feet, and ran forward. Henry followed him.

When they dove into the sand again, just next to a coil of barbed wire, Henry borrowed a handkerchief from Travis Lilly and wrapped it around the shredded knuckle of his trigger finger. Henry also tried to cock his head and hold his tongue just right to pray like his mother prayed so he could pick up the Lord's transmissions, but everything was going too fast, like in the movies of World War I, so Henry again failed to contact the Lord.

Henry followed Travis Lilly on into France. He followed him and the rest of his squad for three days, right off the beach and into the hedgerow country of northern France. His rifle was useless. He was afraid it might go off and shoot somebody, so he pulled out the clip as best he could with his one hand and drug it behind him by the barrel, the splintered stock scraping against the ground. He figured since it was the only weapon he had other than his bayonet that he should keep it; maybe he could use it as a club.

On his third night in France, Henry tried to follow Travis over a brick wall. As he grabbed the edge of the wall with his right hand, he screamed from the pain that shot through his trigger finger all the way into his shoulder. He fell backward and tried to twist in mid-air to regain his feet. When he hit the ground, he broke an ankle. Travis and a Georgian minister named Wesley Zirkel felt along Henry's ankle and listened to him scream. They decided the ankle was broken. "Guess now you just can't go with us no more," Travis said to Henry, shook Henry's left hand, then led his squad over the wall.

Henry was unconscious when another squad with a medic found him and sent him to the rear. He was carried back to the beach in an ambulance and put on a ship, just like a hero. And when he was recovering in a hospital in London, a colonel came by and gave him a purple heart and a citation for bravery for stumbling after his squad for three days with a shot off finger.

The finger had gotten infected and the doctors had to trim it down below the knuckle of the forefinger, nearly to the knuckle on his hand. The compound fracture of his ankle was worse. The doctors cut into it once, put it in a cast, then took the cast off and cut again. He got a letter from Travis congratulating him on his million dollar wound, the kind all the draftees prayed for. Henry, the desperate cowboy, immediately volunteered to go back to the front. His doctors and the colonel who gave him his purple heart mistook him for a hero because he wanted to stay a soldier, but they said his missing trigger finger would keep him out of combat.

Nearly one year after he enlisted in the army, two days before he was to be released from the London hospital, the colonel who gave him his medal told him Travis Lilly had been killed in what was beginning to be called the Battle of the Bulge. And then, on his last day in the hospital, the colonel shook Henry's hand (the one without the trigger finger), told him the army needed more like him, and gave him an honorable discharge. "I'll re-enlist," Henry said. The colonel cocked his head at Henry's remark and said, "No, son. You've done your time. Your country owes you. You are disabled now. Go home. You have a pension coming."

* * *

A cedar chopper, according to old hill country folks was the lowest form of human life in the Hill Country. Too ignorant or stupid to find work, they settled on chopping down the cedar and clearing the brush off land that ranchers or farmers were trying to develop. Shipped to Fort Sam Houston in San Antonio, Texas, Henry drifted toward the Hill Country and became a cedar chopper. He worked with a large woman who had a red face with her gray hair always pasted to her forehead by sweat, Emma, and her semi-retarded son, Bud. Emma had supported herself for years as a cedar chopper and was known to all the Hill Country ranchers and farmers as a cheap hand. "Used to have some good men work for me," she had said when she hired Henry, "Now they are all off at war."

Almost a year after Emma had hired him, during a warm spring day, Henry was working with her and Bud clearing brush away from a creek and cutting cedars for the owner of the property who wanted to turn his useless land into pasture. Like most cedar choppers, Henry had welts across his face, hands, and arms from the slaps of tree limbs and brush. Though his right hand with its missing finger didn't always hold an ax or a scythe very well in those pre-chainsaw days, Henry developed his own way to chop and saw; he got used to his sweat dripping into the cuts on his face and arms and making them sting like hell, the gnats and horseflies buzzing around his head, and the taste of saw dust and grit sticking to his teeth and lips. Cedar chopping, he learned, was no easier than cowboying.

After working until they damn near gave out, they quit at four o'clock and drove to get a beer at Fischer, what was to become Henry's home town. When he walked into Marie's, Henry got his first view of Sam Penschorn and Pete Proctor bellied up to the bar and talking about their peach crops. He saw black-haired Evelyn without a trace of a gray hair. And Emma introduced him to the owner of the land they were clearing, a doctor in Fisher named Jack Hillier. Other people from around town were in the bar, and by five o'clock, more begin pushing in to hear a politician who was going speak. The area representative to the U.S. congress, a Lyndon Johnson, was going to come by and talk up some votes. A lot of people knew him. Most just used him as an excuse to take off of work early.

A native of the Hill Country, Johnson gave Henry hope. He promised to make life as easy as possible for the returning G.I.'s, to make sure they had money for college and loans to start businesses and buy property. Nothing was too much for the men who had whipped ass in Europe and the Pacific. And Johnson promised to improve life for the common man in the Hill Country. The army corps of engineers would be building dams to bring electricity and irrigation to the entire Hill Country, he promised. After he was through speaking, Johnson walked through the small crowd to shake hands. As Henry stuck out his hand for Johnson to shake, the congressman looked down at he missing trigger finger. Henry smiled, and Johnson seemed to know Henry lost it in the war. To Henry, that handshake was his personal guarantee from the congressman and future senator and president that, though he was out of the army, his service had been rewarded. As Henry saw it, Lyndon Johnson was in Marie's tavern in Fischer, Texas to make good on Shorty Martin's speculation.

The next morning as they started a new day of clearing Dr. Jack Hillier's land, Henry paced off a barb wire boundary at the back of the property. It was a spring day and cool; the overcast sky would keep the heat down until about noon when the sun would come through. Henry heard the cicadas in the trees, noticing their rhythm for the first time. Though he had never heard them in West Texas, their sound was a natural part of summer and spring days in the hill country. He looked around him at the cedars, some tall enough to provide decent shade (no shade in west Texas, he thought). The live oaks gave even more shade. He stared at the shadows of the trees on the ground and thought of what a pretty and cool thing shade was. At night, he noticed, the gulf breeze would blow through the trees and cool down the heat of the day.

He started to climb up the highest hill on Doc Hillier's property, slipping over the limestone rocks, his ankles rolling inside his boots. He bent over to look at the yellow, orange, and green moss that clung to some of the rocks where the water from springs dripped almost year round. He felt the moss and the cool spring water and stuck his fingers in his mouth to taste the water-sweet, clear, cold. He continued to climb, and as he came over the top and stopped on the ground that begin to level out, he looked south and saw Emma and her retarded son taking axes to cedars; and beyond them, he saw the gravel road they came on, Ranch Road 12; and still farther on, he saw two peaks higher than his own stretch into the low haze of a sky. And between the peaks, he saw fields of bluebonnets, Indian pinks, and sun flowers looking like waves of color.

He tuned west and walked across the gently sloping part of the property that formed a nearly level green pasture. Green, he thought; in West Texas, pastures were brown. He continued until he came to tall grass. He pushed through the grass toward the sound of water falling on rocks, spitting against the gnats that flew into his teeth and lips, then saw the head waters of Fischer creek form a mossy pool, spill over the limestone rocks that acted as filters to purify the water; then he saw the water slow down to again make a green pool. As he got closer to the pool and stuck first his arm then his face into the water, he saw that the green came not from the clear spring water but from the mossy green rocks on the bottom.

As he walked back to Emma and looked at their work, he tried to remember what had been the most beautiful thing he had seen in West Texas. Horses! Shorty on a running horse, its muscles working smoothly under its skin and Shorty rocking with the gait of the horse. When he got back to Emma, she yelled at him, "Where the hell you been?"

"Looking," he said.

"Stop looking and start working," she said.

As he pulled on gloves and picked up an ax, he yelled over the noise of axes biting into trees to Emma: "You think that Doctor would want to sell this land?"

Emma cracked a smile. "He ain't like these hard-headed square heads, hold on to something just cause it's theirs. This land is worthless and he ain't got enough of it. Price is good, he'd sell in a minute." She laughed and swung her ax into a tree.

And a thought, as straight and as quick as a Kraut bullet, hit Henry between the eyes. He and Emma and her retarded son would clear off the land; Lyndon Johnson would give him a loan; Jack Hillier would sell him the land. And then, in the natural pasture above him and in the land he was now clearing, he would raise horses and watch them run across his property. Here it was. One year short of thirty, Henry could stop running. Emma, an angel of the Lord, bearing His message, had shown Henry how.

* * *

Two years later, with his own land, a new stallion and Stetson hat, and money in his pocket, Henry had a banana split at a downtown San

Antonio five and dime with a young girl. He had stopped running from women as well.

When he married Rebecca, adopted a little Mexican boy whom he named Kyle and then had his own child, a daughter, Victoria, Henry saw the perfection of life, the promise of America, and some proof, maybe just some, of a God who wouldn't talk to him but didn't hate him. Henry and time had stopped. Emma and her retarded son, like God's very own angels, or like cedar choppers, just disappeared. When Henry died, lapsing in and out of consciousness, with Rebecca gone, deserting before the kids could even know their mamma, Kyle grown up rich and plowing up his property, Victoria married to a man who despised him, he yelled out Emma's and Shorty's names.

Mining workers, West Virginia © Edwina Pendarvis

VIVIAN SHIPLEY

As If Corn Could Invent Itself

I've come back, father, though to a day I didn't want
        to see. I walk all the way around your
        porch, a tunnel like the stand out
on the road where you laid corn in double rows and

piled up the tomatoes I sold for you. I lean right over
        your face boxed in ivory silk.
        You never once said *love* or
to come back here so I would see what death

will look like if death will wait this long for me.
        Maybe it's true that the dead
        return in dreams with messages but
you won't, tougher than the calluses I still can

feel on the palms of your hands. At grandma
        and grandpa's golden anniversary,
        we played blindman's bluff. *It,*
I groped for my cousins who had already gone

back into the house. Never once telling, you let
        me search, calling to the dark, until
        I stood crying in the back field.
What can I do to get back at you, to pull the word

from your set lips that I still need to hear. A solar
        eclipse, giving no light, needing
        none, I tried to be you. Hearing
and seeing without thinking like or as, you never

looked up or back or even on when you plowed
        Father, you had no need to label,
        certain furrowed ground would shift
from brown to green. Seeds not words planted crops.

Fair Haven, Connecticut

No longer paved with shells, Pearl Street has oysters piled
      around doors not crushed to feed the ducks
      but bleached by one hundred and fifty years

of work in the shallows. Built into hills on sides of the Quinnipiac,
      houses from the river, stilled faces lifting lace
      to peer out as they did when Fair Haven led

the world in exporting oysters. Trees hang on the banks, roots
      exposed like the tentacles on squid or the scrub
      pine at the rim of pits left by miners like my father

in Harlan County. Shovel then empty the bucket and back again
      was not so different than stripping away land
      that surfaced to air not green water. Fill with bits

of coal almost blue in the sun was bulldozed back leaving earth
      not good for anything but holding the surface
      of my family's world together. There's no smell

of sulphur but when I wade into the Quinnipiac waist deep, it's old
      hair I smell. There are no oyster crops for light
      to bounce from but darkness, almost breathing

from the remaining beds as if the muck from United Illuminating
      is trying to take over, pooling like shadows
      in the corner of a dirt floor. I come here to hang

over Grand Avenue Bridge so often, my fingers number green
      chips on the rails; I know which arch the gulls
      prefer. Salt marshes move with the tide, ring

the river's mouth and on sunny days, landfill shines as it washes
      to Long Island Sound, past oil barges, past
      Lighthouse Point, past the breakwater. I still

think I can make rocks walk, time them to fall between every third
      ripple, dropping one by one; I never tire of this
      one-sided catch or spruce pilings with slick creosote

soaked sides or the air like my mother's arms. At night, I can hang
      my head over the pier and as the moon mirrors up,
      stars are dropped like sweat on blackened faces

of fishermen who pushed wheelbarrows overflowing with oysters
      up the Quinnipiac's banks to wives waiting
      in above ground basements to shuck off sharp

spines. Women spent all day every day, forcing briny meat to yield,
      shelling, packing oysters in salt that were shipped
      and sold in Chicago, London, New York and Paris.

Pearls they found were strung, twisted twice around their necks.
      Each wore the life her man dug out, proudly beaded
      in black like my father's lungs or albino drops of blood.

JAMES MASON VAUGHAN

Alleghany 95910

Long before zip codes directed mail to Alleghany the town was known by a different set of numbers.

Sixteen to One meant yellow-bright gold in white quartz matrix, more shiny and bright than any ring or coin,

Mint brick or wedding band or hi-grade hoard in a miner's basement.

Ninety cents an hour labor. One dollar for muckers. One and a quarter for miners, Sundays and holidays off.

Time and a half for Saturdays. Grab your checks at Sbaffi's store, pay your bill and get the change.

Van Dorn the foreman, with a nympho wife. He roamed the labyrinthine tunnels, stopes, eyes like radar following the

Beam of his carbide lamp atop his hard-hat, probing for the hidden yellow veins where golden clumps gave up their ancient

Lairs to his miner's pick, mixed with muck in his specimen sack to hide its gleam to a stashing place above a beam

Near where an iron grate quietly blocked alien access from the bushes along Kanaka Creek.

Those were the days of energy and a war-shattered mind refusing to give up its combat memories years in the making.

With the grand finale a Kamikaze slipping through the screen around McArthur's cruiser on the way to Mindora,

Laying waste the lives and limbs of hundreds dead and dying in the heat and smell of blood and guts and stench of burnt crisp

Ash of human shapes in harness and in prayer, like macabre scarecrows in a field of death.

I worked topside with Shelly Kuhfield. He was married to Rachel. They lived in a neat cottage with a picket fence,

Down the side of a hill below Casey's Place, where the lower road branched off to the Sixteen to One.

Shelly came to the mine as a donkey driver, hauling supplies by pack animals up from Grass Valley and Nevada City.

That was before the Old Tyler Foote's Crossing road would bear the wagon through the switchbacks hanging precariously

To the cliffs on stone support patiently placed by Chinese laborers imported for the dangerous tasks before abandonment.

Shelly was wiry, tough as rawhide, taciturn, no spare words, rolled his own, knew the ways of greed and gold,

Long since cured of the fever that blinded me and many others. His open eyes and ears knew best to keep a closed mouth.

He knew what went on underground, was good a running the hoists at every level of the mile-deep mine.

I was there six months before knowing what "hi-grade" meant. Doing hard labor topside, shoveling snow and concentrate.

Being a low-lander and dumb they taught me to run the crusher where the iron jaws chewed up the quartz exposing flashing

Filigrees of gold so beautiful and tempting, always moving toward the ball mill's monotonous roll, eating quartz and ore

And iron balls and water to be digested by its magnesium lined stomach before being secreted out its anus end as grey muck

Through its cone of metal mesh into the troughs where water pulsed from hidden traps below trapping the heavy ore from the iron

Pyrites and galena on the way to the vibrating floatation tables where the fine stuff gathered in riffles for Hunley's pouch.

Old Hunley had the keys to glean the traps. The mercury smoke from his retort shack meant he was refining the amalgam into molten

Gold poured into iron molds for bricks to be shipped out by U.S.Mail to the San Francisco Mint, at twenty-nine a troy ounce.

After the Ridge Road was paved as far as Forest City, in the forties, trucks replaced the mule-drawn wagons and snow plows.

Worked at keeping the road open in the winter except when the snow got too deep and hardy men on skies and snow shoes

Met the stage at the Oregon Creek covered bridge on Highway Forty Nine to pack in the mail and whiskey on their backs.

Babies got born in Alleghany without the help of doctors. People passed their lives in seasons tied to the rhythms of the

Sixteen to One and the mountains' idiosyncracies. Every year, in summer, a new teacher or two came up from the valley below to

Replace those who experienced the peculiar culture of Gold powered ecology and ethos of isolated Alleghany life.

There was a little church with fading paint among the firs on a knoll at the end of a little used path. It was more like a

Chapel with a gingerbread steeple too small for a bell and with a steep roof to shed the snow.

On occasional Sundays a priest from Nevada City trekked up the long grade to hold mass and collect the gold-dust quilt offerings

For his own dispensations to piety. The gravestones in the weed grown cemetery bore dates of previous generations.

Nowadays, people preferred to die in town and have proper funerals, and not be carried out of town in a truck or sled.

Because in those days I had seen too much of death, too many burials at sea, heard taps too often, like a refrain;

Seen too many mangled corpses with blood running in the scuppers and body parts shoveled overboard to the frenzied

Sharks feasting on the holocaust of war. Taps and gravestone priests and parsons seemed then to represent a God

I no longer believed existed, but now I know there is a God but I have no truck with priests or evangelists.

Such is the nature of cynical experience.

The Sixteen to One is surrounded with chain link fences and signs of NO TRESPASS. New technology locates the treasure veins.

The miner's drill now probes virgin shafts for golden orgasms.

Rachel still lives alone in her cottage down the hill below Casey's Place, and Casey and Etta are long ago buried in glory.

Casey's Place hasn't changed much, inside or out. The ghosts of hard rock miners, muckers, vagrant higraders, haunt the stools.

The sound and thud of mortar and pestle wafts up from the basement below, gritty white sand saturating the floor.

That was a year to remember.

Alleghany Town, Summer 1950 © James Mason Vaughan

Field workers in Ohio © Rebecca Colon

WORKING CLASS EDUCATION

THAT WORKING STATE OF MIND

RANDY J. ABEL

Tsunami Void: The English Behind the Eightball

"We can guess—no, we can be quite certain that it was not a mark
on his forehead like a postmark—life is hardly ever as clear and
straightforward as that."
- Hermann Hesse, *Damian*

"Almost before he knew it, his mind, which till now had been with
him in this place, was being taken over by the water, carried away
on its rushing, cast far away...."
-Yukio Mishima, "Fountains in the Rain"

When the Old Man comes to visit, we have lunch at *the beat*—soup,
foccacia, coffee. Dad loves the "beat blend" and serves it to his buddies
back home at their poker gatherings. He takes pride in explaining that its
the special concoction from a coffeehouse where his son works in Youngstown, Ohio. I figure they couldn't care less where it comes from, only that
it keeps their old asses awake long enough to ante the next hand. But Dad
goes on and on about his son, who wants to be a professor of English or
Literature or Someshit... "here's a picture, here's something he wrote about
the family, here's an old letter he sent me from the Middle East, terrified:
'watching death fade into the horizon...' that's a helluva line, there." Dad's
pride seems to know no boundaries. Mine runs in different currents.

Back at *the beat* I introduce Dad to the gang and imagine each of
my friends and acquaintances to be instantly overcome with some powerful new understanding of who I am and from what sort of stock I spring.
And it's almost as if I'd coached him beforehand, when upon meeting two
professors, Dad refers to himself as a "displaced steelworker." I'm grateful for his choice of phrasing.

*See me now (all ye who marvel at the mystery of my inner-strength)
in the light of my glorious birthright—Son of **Displaced Steelworker**! Displaced to the second power. Proletarian Pugilist cast into the post-indus-
trial suck-void. Buffed surfer on the bitchin' curls at the leading edge of
the rolling tide of accumulating nothingness and despair. Know me now,
my compatriots, to be a Steely Sanctified Warrior among you!*

At the counter, Dad makes his usual eighty or ninety corn-ball
wise-cracks, then apologizes to an amused Jen for his "silly banterings."

"Oh my God," Jen laughs, "I thought Randy was the only person
on earth who used that word on a regular basis. Wow, Randy, this *is* your
father!"

And there's certainly no denying that... however, there always seems to lurk some shadow of the old shame—lingering remnants. "To be the very blood of that hated blood," as Charles Bukowski said, "made the windows intolerable/ and the sounds and the flowers/ and the trees ugly." These were times when Wayne's "silly banterings" were made vastly less entertaining by the constant presence of booze on his breath and a barstool on his ass. Sometimes there was venom in his words that pushed me to Mom's side of their constant battle for our favor. *Whatsizname*, she would call him, or the more impersonal *Whatsizface*, which I understood to be the most powerful obliteration of Dad's humanity.

What's his face? I must have wondered, *His face is that round, stubbly, strangely scarred thing that banters, snores like a chainsaw, eats hamhocks and peanuts, sucks down Pabsts like a flabby Popeye without spinach, bristles my cheek as sandpaper when we hug and floats in my dreams like a sing-along ball—always away, away: through the GATX plant to his girlfriend's apartments through the Glass Tower Lounge and off into the darkness, away, away where it pops with a loony-toon "pfwt" like a bubble in the head of a frosty mug of draft. Pfwt.*

But now there's a pride in owning our kinship, and a safety in everyone's having known me first—their having gotten the facts sifted through in my own style, my convenient packaging. My banterings have prepared most of them for this meeting, and Dad provides living proof of my blue-collar genes (*jeans?*), which I choose to exploit at the moment as my gritty reality.

After lunch we take a drive along the Mahoning to look at where all the old bars and mills were. I play Tom Waits tunes, hoping to increase the urban/industrial feel of the afternoon. Dad is put-off by the discordant parts and would probably rather hear a "lite rock" station, though he doesn't say so. I imagine that the Old Man and I will at some point get out and stomp around on ancient slag piles, kicking scraps of metal, maybe finding a battered, rusty lunchbox or clipboard, but I'm the only one dressed for it (me in my steel-toed flightdeck boots, Pops in his keds) and Dad's kidneys are making even car sitting an arduous task. There's still much to be said and felt and I have big expectations for our next-day visit to the labor museum.

My older brother, Greg, is with us at two o'clock the next afternoon, when we head to the museum after coffee at *the beat*. We three are the only people in the place as Dad wanders, giving rapid commentary to almost everything he sees. Pointing to the round fountain-sink in the locker room display he tells us: "I was working once in a part of a foundry that didn't have showers... and I got so dirty that I had to put a brick on that foot-control thing there and climb into this damn thing... my whole body in a fetal position. It worked, though. Goddamn you could get filthy in all that soot!"

But he doesn't linger on the eyes in the photos like I expect him to, like I find myself doing. When we get to the one of the worker with half of his calf sheared off, Dad says: "Look at his face... they must have him drugged so far out of it that he doesn't give a shit about anything." My take on the guy's look was vastly different: I saw a placidness in his eyes, an intense strength, a mark of struggle—but now I'm not sure. A model of his old mill catches Dad's attention and I'm reminded of a familiar pillar of our family's labor connection—the Old Man's passion for expounding the minute details of every one of his toiling endeavors. From hot-rolling to dishwashing, the finite motions of the mundane were a mainstay of Wayne Abel's barstool and lounge-chair litanies. I feel like I could have written the standard operating procedure manuals for all of my father's nine-hundred occupations... like I could have walked in cold and performed tasks with the ease of an old-timer. Maybe that's why I ran screaming from Dad's bars to my school books: there had to be jobs out there that just couldn't be interpreted in a four-hour sitting. (This could also serve to explain why I went into military intelligence—so that I would be *legally bound* to refrain from being as annoying as the Old Man on the job-description front.)

When my time to work draws near, we all leave the museum and Dad and Greg head to Struthers to visit one of Dad's old mill buddies. On the porch at *the beat* I give my father a hug and our faces are sandpaper and sandpaper. He is Dad in sweatpants and keds and kidney problems and no pension. I am his son in Y-town—displaced, dysfunctioned, dicking-around on the floodplain.

Three days later I'm in a local used bookstore, searching a book of Kenneth Patchen poetry for mill-related pieces and discussing the legacy of dead industry with the woman at the counter.

"I'm the next wave, " I explain to her, "The first generation jilted out of a respectable working-class option. It's an odd spot, you know?" Her look is suddenly apprehensive and it occurs to me that I don't know her at all, and that she may be getting the impression that I'm insane. This may require another approach.

"I'm sure you know Bryn..."

"Yes, I do. I've seen a lot of his stuff."

"Well, his art comes from the same perspective—criticism of American industrial dysfunction, the cruel nature of capitalism, and, especially, fear of this terrible void left by the last wave of despair. That's what all his steely-nightmare sculptures are about... Bryn's the next generation, too."

Her smile is pleasant, patronizing. "I think I understand."

She doesn't think I'm insane, she knows that I'm *full of shit!*

But would I lie about this? Would I conjure some proletarian personae to impress a stranger in a bookstore? Was my beat old man not just here, proving with his very flesh and blood that I have the boasting rights of displacement? Can she not see the currents of ignominy etched on my face—the heartbreak, the tradition of maladjustment? Was my face not the tragic face of steely, sooty, collective struggle? Did my scars, **our** *scars not render me visible?*

"I think we might be getting in a whole anthology of Patchen soon, if you're interested." She's ringing me up. We are capitalists.

"Yes, I'd like that." She pities me as one pities would-be cheezers in smoky nightclubs.

"Okay. Why don't you give me your name and phone number and I'll let you know when they come in." An interesting twist on the cheezer analogy, but no consolation.

I give her the info and she stares for a moment at the name that she's just written down before asking, "Are you related to any Abels in New Castle?"

I hesitate, then confess, "All of them."

"What's your father's name?"

"Wayne."

"Oh my god!" Her smile is no longer confused or patronizing, "And you *look* like an Abel! You look so much like your dad!" She is staring at me.

"How do you know him?" I am smiling pleasantly... for some reason I'm also terrified.

"I know the whole family. We grew up together... my sister is your aunt Joyce's best friend. My maiden name is Jacobs. I can't get over this!"

Neither can I. "Did you live on Franklin Avenue?"

"No, but we were neighbors when they lived..." She proceeds to relate tales from her past that mesh strangely with an Abel history that has been fed to me all my life. The mixing of contexts is disturbing— normally New Castle's east side is oceans away from Youngstown's south side—and the distance works for me. Now I'm standing on a completely new shoreline.

"...You have to give them all my best."

"I sure will. You know, my dad was just visiting earlier this week from Harrisburg. He lives down there now with the rest of them."

"Oh really? So Joyce got a teaching job there and everyone else followed?"

"Yeah, they all trickled-down eventually, looking for jobs. Hey, Trickle-down Economics... it works." We both laugh. "Actually, only seven of the nine went down, over about a ten-year period, my old man being the last."

"I remember that he was a big guy, a football player, right?"

Dad rarely speaks of his football days. I know that he was no star, but that his size and strength made him usable in a second-or-third-wave capacity. Somehow her mentioning it makes me uncomfortable. Does she remember or did she ever know that Wayne's mill-working put bread in nine mouths while Grandpa sat on his ass at the Traveller's Inn?

"I guess he played a bit at some point. Yeah." I want to seem pleasant, but hurried, "I think I need to pay you for this." We are capitalists .

"Oh, I almost forgot... that'll be three fifty."

Opening my wallet, I realize that all of my cash has just recently been sucked into my gas tank. "Can I write you a check?"

"Sure," she says.

"Do you need to see some i.d.?" She is silent. I look up from my scrawling and she is looking to see if I'm joking.

"With that face," she asks, grinning, "how could I doubt your being an Abel?"

"With this face, " I respond, a bit dryly, "why the hell would anyone lie?"

She's looking at me like I'm insane again and I wonder if she now has historical justification for believing it to be so. Suddenly I am contextual, exposed. I'm eager for a quick exit, heading for the door.

"Make sure you say 'hello' to everyone for me," she's grinning warmly again, "I still can't believe that you're an Abel."

"Well, I am... and I sure will. Good-bye."

Outside I return to the Ocean, where the Tsunami still roars and rages toward the infinite void. It has finally peaked. I am shooting the curl—terrified, naked.

Heading north on Market Street, my thoughts are full of Dad and football. How is it that she remembers him for something like sports, when *work* was such an dominant reality of his life from such an early age?

...a big guy, a football player...

His cousin Darryl was the celebrated gridiron hero-- five-year all-pro guard with the Giants, galloping terribly for Tarkenton and "The Giff" in the sixties. Shit, he wasn't that much bigger than Wayne, how the hell did Darryl manage to make it out, stutter-stepping to cheat his breeding and avoid the dark, well-worn path from the county high schools to Mesta Machine or Pennsylvania Engineering, or over here to Youngstown's fiery grottos like Dad?

Darryl got to scrap with destiny long before it laid guys like Dad flat on their backs. Now I don't even get the privilege of standing at a millgate, books in hand, yelling: *"Kiss my ass, slave-drivin' bastards! "* That's what's really pissing me off right now. Kenneth Patchen got to do it... James Wright got his chance, too. They even savored, bittersweetly, the exquisite poetic tension of having their own fires fueled by active furnaces that were *in there waiting*.

Where's my infernal tension, my fighting stance against the dense, drooling jaws—the deafening din of industry? What's left of my opportunity to rage against the curse of my breeding, this terrible, swelling Tsunami?

Tsunami, tsunami! Taskete, taskete!

We had followed the rocky, precipitous path down the dark side of Enoshima Island to the clammy caves and the craggy shoreline of Sagami Bay. In the webs covering the lampposts of the ancient fishing village and the trees that lined the trail, there were spiders the size of my fist; and, near the bottom, some smart-ass tickled the back of Ray's neck with a leaf, making him jump and scream like a little girl. It was all like Dante meets some "After School Special" meets David Lynch. The caverns we explored were filled with jagged scraps of metal, probably turrets from WWII, and some contained dark, eerie Buddha shrines surrounded by unlit candles. We were quite drunk and Corbett, the Ragin' Cajun, decided that we should swipe the one and five-hundred yen coins that filled the laps of some of the statues.

"What the fuck Buddha gunnha do with yangs in here?" Corbett was menacingly loony and had the build and demeanor of a pitbull, so we normally took what he said under serious advisement. We scooped up the coins and offered them in faithful supplication, later that night in Whiskey River, to our god, Jim Beam. We were simple, devoted crusaders.

Three-quarters of the way through our circumnavigation of the island, we happened upon a crevasse in the coastline that was backed by an insurmountable, sheer wall. The only way to continue our journey was to wait for a wave to fill the crevasse, swim the gap and amble quickly up the rocks on the other side. We were splintered as to our course of action. Some *Beam Team* members argued for heading back to the village the way we came, rather than throwing ourselves into the early April ocean water. Others, including me, fiercely defended the objectives of our quest to conquer Enoshima and the night and Buddha. The dispute ended when the Pitbull threw his jacket across the 15-foot gap and leapt feet-first into the drink. Seconds later, he was on the opposite rock, barking orders like a crazed combat general.

At Corbett's command, everyone began throwing flashlights and jackets to the other shore and, one by one, Teamsters swam the little wave-swells and were hoisted onto the rock. I was the last troop left. Everyone listened and scanned the churning darkness for signs of a coming wave, while my head was bent in concentration—imagining the sudden, mysterious undertow that would surely carry my drunk ass out to sea. Another tragically funny one-liner in the "Navy Mishaps" bulletin.

Ray heard it first: "Get ready, Randy, here comes your ride!" Somebody yelled "Now!" and I stepped into the abyss just as I heard another voice scream "*TSUNAMI!*" and the world became soundless, boundless motion...

Except for the rush, somewhere in the turbulent silence, of a running tap— and farther off, the sound of a Hank, Jr. tune on an old juke.

It was the summer of 1988. The old man had just kicked my ass all over a pool table for the third time, and we were in the head of the Mechanicsburg VFW pissing-out Yuengling, a cheap Eastern Pa. beer with octagonal honeycomb bubbles composing its head—like an alcoholic mosaic or riprap.

Out in the bar waited an assortment of Dad's buddies that must have been time-warped and transplanted from the Glass Tower back home. Like the Tower drunks, the Mech'burg vets offered shooting tips and regarded me as a protege—an upstart young-buck who wasn't quite yet in on the game but was already thirsting for it, bellying-up to it. And it was apparently Dad's intention that night to make the *primary rule* more clear— to pass it on to me just as it was accorded him. He was to present it like a package: a terrible, treasured heirloom he could place in the palm of my hand.

I have loved some women
Bocephus was emoting and I noticed with a measure of drunken disdain that the old man
wasn't washing his hands.

And I have loved Jim Beam...
"Kid, I want you to know something."
But they both tried to kill me
"Yeah, Pops." I was about to turn off the faucet when he grabbed me by the arm, turning me to face him.
Back in nineteen seventy-three.
"Listen, I don't love you and I never did." His eyes were cold, vacant. He seemed to be angelically white—looming and hovering.
Over and over,
"You needed to know that."
I wonder how I got in this condition...
The tap was running. "Whatever, Dad... the tap is running."

Someone got a grip on my sweatshirt, someone else grabbed a leg of my levis, and I was pulled onto the rock just before the monster wave slapped me against the cliff wall. As soon as I was vertical we all had a good laugh, put on our jackets and headed for Whiskey River with our Buddha-Pilgrim Booty—victorious, sopping-wet circumnavigators and survivors of the Tsunami-Void.

I don't remember stopping here in the parking lot of the Market Street Revco. It's raining hard now and the streets of Youngstown are even emptier than usual. Struck with this deadly emptiness, I try to capture it for use in the poem that I've been working on about "our scars." But right now I can only relate it *very specifically* to Wayne Abel and that emptiness, the cold whiteness that filled him that night at the VFW and that I've seen in more diluted forms, even in the years since he's been sober. I want to call the vacancy a weathered harshness, augmented by years of victimization. I want to know his eyes to be the eyes of a fighter. But all I really see in his hollow moments of clarity is a desperate search, a groping that says: *None of this is doing it... filling it.*

I can see the Void in him because I've come to know it well. And I see the Tsunami raging through him because I've felt it crash over me and I know the sting, the heartbreak that brings Dad's bitter words, because often I cannot see for the acrid haze of my own groping, and I can speak nothing but venom for the brine that fills my mouth as *this unnameable shame*, the unstoppable wave.

I can't blame Wayne Abel any more than I can make him now into the father that I always needed.

I can't portray him as a folk hero any more than I can deny the drunken-grunt reality of most of his old mill-hunkie existence.

I can't write a poem about Y-town any more than I can *beat that fucking Tsunami* into submission...

But I can sure as hell try. With words on paper, at least, I'll have a fighting chance to get my best hold. Maybe I'll start in the morning—this will require much tea and many a cheapy-assed duplex sandwich cookie. I'll stop at the Belmont Giant Eagle on my way home.

Somewhere in the Abyss, the old man and I are shooting stick in an old, beat poolhall—straight out of *The Hustler*. He's wearing Keds and sweats, I'm in my flightdeck boots, jeans and Harley-Davidson t-shirt. We both drink Squirt from funky green bottles. As I rack 'em, Dad reaches back under his shirt to scratch the area of a pimple on his right shoulder. It must be a hurter; he scrunches his face—his eyes squinted intently with the exquisite pain, and I notice that they look just like they do when his attentive listening explodes into laughter, those uncontrollable peals that rock his whole form, but store their focus and intensity in the deep, fatty recesses of that squinting.

When did I learn to mine those depths, seeking to glean transmissions of acceptance and joy? When did I first laugh into a mirror and know that laughter is a billion ripples of joyous surprise with the squinting twinkle of my father's eyes?

I've racked the balls tightly by a method taught to me by the old man long ago in the Glass Tower—alternating solid and striped, with the eight-ball in the center, buffered. Dad takes a swig of Squirt, chalks his worn old cue, leans, squints, takes his aim and thrusts—clean-blasting a dead-on solid sledgehammer—shockwaves of clatter, chaos, conception.

"O-kaay!" he laughs.

"Christ, Pops!" I cry.

The old proprietor has looked up, smiling from selling cigarette papers or fishing tackle to a young kid. His weathered old face looks like St. Anthony of Padua or Grandpa Abel or God... I still can't tell the difference.

Dad has sunk the seven, now he's dropped the two, now the three. I'm afraid that he'll run the table, but as he takes aim on the four, he miscues and the ball skips off and onto the hardwood floor with a thunk and a roll, past two other tables, finally stopping as it meets the bottom of the men's room door. We both laugh as I retrieve it and gauge my first shot— eleven in the far corner pocket, which I miss completely.

I swig Squirt as Dad misses another shot. Then I hit the eleven into the side, but on the next shot bank the fourteen off the rail and right up to the left corner pocket, where it kisses Dad's three and rests there like a kinetic conspiracy. Pops and I both shake our heads, grinning; then he chalks, bends to it again and proceeds to run the table like a two-bit, punk-ass hustler (which he was and is). I'm disgruntled and pride-struck as he saves that damn three for last—taking several angles of approach before executing a shot that kisses my fourteen into his three, and both of them into the pocket.

"That's the way it goes m'boy... the best-laid plans... *c'est la vie, c'est la vie.* All right, Randolphski, show us your stuff." And into the large end of his cue like Keith Jackson, "It's been a rocky start for Abel-the-Younger thus far, folks, but I'm sure we can expect *big* things from the Young Buck from here on out! Woah, Nellie!"

And I hit the twelve, then the nine, then ten, thirteen, fifteen. Dad is brimming as I check my angles on the eight—aiming for the corner by which he stands. Behind him, the proprietor watches, sipping Schlitz; behind *him* I can see typhoon rains outside the pane glass, in the red-blue neon glow of the Void.

"I say, keep your eye on the ball, Son. Eye... ball. Eyeball... that's a joke, Son, cain't *eat* it!" Dad's Foghorn Leghorn is awful, woefully un-southern, but it does its job of breaking my concentration with a laughing moan. I chalk to regain composure and take my aim again.

"Remember, Son..." Dad starts suddenly. I glance—slightly perturbed—at Dad, at the proprietor, at the Void.

"...It's all about English."

Smiling, I thrust and sink the eight *solid*.

My break.

[Youngstown, OH/ Mechanicsburg,PA/
New Castle, PA , 1995-96]

Randy J. Abel in Youngstown poolhall, 1996

G. TIMOTHY GORDON

Paquito de Todo

The men who work *paquito de todo* pour hot tar from a steel drum
    in the hot sun
outside Paul's catering to *touristos*, mostly, for breakfast, and
    sometimes locals,
torn tees, red bandanas gripped round their throats in crisp twicetied
    knots,
doorags turbanning heads in tight skullcaps, one grading the black
    shovel backward,
his "patrón" pointing to the bulky can, "*Mirá! Aquí!*," before oiling
    right down
to the gutteredged street, squeegging, evening, what unworked dust
    and mud
rakers with sharktoothed gears pulled apart, sealing each sidewalk
    crack
with a stooped, twostep slide and wiping excess away with an
    insider's thick thumb,
sometimes siphoning water off the green garden hose to drink, rinse
    rags, then lacquer
the rest behind velcro rollers, back and forth across tarry goo, the
    dozen or so orange cones
corralling their quarter, off the Paseo, men working their small plot
    through the long blue day,
sons of the earth, far from pueblo, *llano*, where no pinion,
    wildplum, grow,
their little of everything outside Paul's *limpio,* clean.

Called Susan

Somewhere in Temple, Texas,
That schoolgirl face is still baling hay
From the flatbed back of a Ford pickup,
Alone, then, peering ahead to the careening
Cab wheeling its half-felt self away
From the gonedown sun in a howl of dust, now,
Fumbling forward to the cab door strung wide
Open for her overall arrival, and wrenching
Those high whining gears back with both hands
Into 2nd as easy as "Good-Morning!" coffee, who
Knew most every steer and star by name (or
Something better) when curfew came late and
Polite upon this land reckoned by bad teeth
And grammar and shit, she, waiting, called
To oddball blue loves owned on the gramophone
By cowpokes in Nashville, Macon, parts hid
South of stars, plenty far from dreams, she,
Blue as the bluing moon herself browsing
The flat outback of Franklin for love too,
Wondering how the ground got by, seedtime
And harvest, inside the truck, crooning
Eddy Arnold and Loretta Lynn—waiting, called Susan,
Just starting her silent and starry nightwork with God.

Work

These hard-at-it, down-at-the-mouth croppers and jobbers,
Depression people, who married, and loved, out of great need, or pain, or
shamed forlornness, who woke early for the most important,
sometimes only, meal of the day—coffee—if lucky, *peones,*
      pobrecitos,
herding their hands and feet and sheep for *patróns* or making a
sticky go
of a vegetable patch or stinking Pie Town chicken farm, or mining at
Mogollon, Mádrid,
way down the blind, gritty shafts, or railroading for AT, & SF at the
      corrugated locomotive
workshop in Gallup or down the line at Thoreau, measuring out flour for
      frybread
and pinto beans and potatoes for mock shepherd's pie or tortillas, for
      supper,
some lucky child's eating day, nailing *Sangré de Cristo, Santa Maria,* to
      the mudplaster
and adobe wall, rosary and scapulars dangling from their eaves, my
      father's long, blue,
flowery face and white baker's apron suddenly out of the beeshaped
      ovens, the resurrection
of bread, kneading out each lump in the dough for the leavens, and my
      mother,
pressed to a printed dress, bric-a-brac belaboring each wall, no matter
      where she lived,
the plaster lion fronting the bannister, like the swallows at Puye erecting
      a living in *vigas*
from straw and clay and sheer stonecliff, and not much else, chafed in a
      city, in boxes
for houses, in closets for rooms, sprinkling the green water bottle over
      the scorched
ironingboard cover, gathering in every tight pleat of my sister's Sunday
      skirt, getting it all right,
like the starched, white-on-white shirts, hankies and blouses, wide,
      verandah ties,
a blitz of clothes, and lost in a sometime reverie (*Long Ago, and Far
      Away?*) of Joni James

or Rosey Clooney from the upright, fullsize Crosley smiling back some
>secret insouciance
to herself, calling her to a moment, or maybe to another man, or, maybe
>even, to those eyes
of the County Kerry poor on the dunes above the shore caught in the
>fireglows of peat and moss,
the scoliotic sea before them, the late afternoon sun stropping the
>farthest waves,
and the heavyshoed horses' tracks against the soft, wet sand, galloping
>past the last milepost,
and out of sight, their faces rehearsed in loss,—then, later, board and
>clothes faded, put away
in each separate childdrawer, as if urged by invisible necessity, remem-
>bering fingers and toes,
hands and feet, darning all the holes in socks and mittens with severe,
>pointed needles,
reminding us of who we were, what we had become, small shapes of
>motion, and light, and touch,
and inevitably, work.

PHILIP LEVINE

Easter, 1944

Mrs. Rousak fixed a big fresh ham
the way Walter liked it, a little
overcooked to be on the safe side,
little dumplings floating in grease,
spiced with fresh green stuff, dill, potatoes
mashed with melting butter. She'd risen
just after dawn to get it all done,

which meant she probably hadn't slept
at all because with still more war work
she was on six days, though she worked nights
just across the way. If you lifted
the shade you could see the factory
sulking on Sunday with no one there
to make certain the machines were fed.

"Did anyone go to church today?"
Bernard asked. Walter and Val hadn't,
Mrs. Rousak hadn't. She was sorry
he asked. "Bernie, now," was all she said.
She turned her head to one side as though
the phone were ringing and lit up
a cigarette and took a deep drag

to brace herself for what was coming,
the familiar sermon on Jesus
Christ that moved Bernard close to tears.
He was her middle son, the frail one
so unlike his father, gone twelve years
into America, gone, thank God,
forever, she hoped, a violent man

her sons and daughter were better off

for not knowing. It was so quiet
everyone could hear when my knife slipped
on the meat and almost cracked the plate.
I raised my head to apologize,
but Mrs. Rousak's little half smile
stopped me before I could get a single

word out, it was so lovely and so sad
at the same time. Sunlight was falling
through the kitchen window, it was warm,
almost comfortable. I closed my eyes
a moment, and prayed Bernie wouldn't
start on Jesus and the Jews. A war
was coming closer, it gave us work,
it gave us food, it gave us our lives.

You Can Cry

I am in an empty house, and the wind
is blowing the eucalyptus so that the branches
sway slowly with a great sea sound,
and although it is dark, I know their movement
having seen it at dusk for years of summer
when the long day's last winds rose suddenly.
The five great branches lifted in soft light
and let their dusty leaves hold the moment
and then settled back with the long sigh
of an old man at that hour setting
down his tools. And I remember that man,
Old Cherry, his black head running with gray,
bowed in his bib overalls, letting the scarred
handle of the sledge hammer slide through
his thick fingers and burying his ashen face
in a red bandana, twenty-eight years ago
beside a road long since dismantled
and hauled off in truck-loads of broken bits.
If he rose now from the earth of Michigan

where he rests in the streaming gowns
of his loss, Old Cherry Dorn, and walked
over the whole dark earth with one hand
stretched out to touch a single thing
he'd made in a lifetime, he would cross
this continent to where the last sea fills
my house with the wailing of all we've lost
until there is nothing left but dust falling
into dust, either in darkness or in the first
long rays of yellow light that are waiting
behind the eastern ranges. Do you hear
the moaning of those great lifting arms? That
is the sea of all our unshed tears, that is all
anyone can finally hear, so you can cry,
Cherry, you can cry forever and no one will know.

The Last Shift

I had been on my way to work as usual
when the traffic stalled a quarter mile
from the railroad crossing on Grand Blvd.
Then I saw the moon rise above
the packing sheds of the old Packard plant.
The moon at 7:30 in the morning.
And the radio went on playing
the same violins and voices I didn't
listen to each morning. Back in the alley
the guys in greasy dark wool jackets
were keeping warm by a little fire
made from fence posts and garage doors
and tossing their empty wine bottles
into the street where they shattered
on the frosted roofs of cars and scattered
like chunks of ice. A police car dozed
across the street, its motor running.
I could see the two of them eating
sugar doughnuts as delicately as two

elderly women and drinking their coffee
from little Styrofoam cups. Soon the kids
would descend from these lightless houses,
gloved and scarved, on their way to school
with tin boxes of sandwiches and cookies.
They would slide on the ice and steal
each others' foolish hats and laugh
while they still could, their breath
pushing out into the morning air
in little trumpets of steam. I wondered
if anyone would step from the faceless
two-storied house beside me, all of its
rooms torn into view, its connections
and tubing gone, the furniture gone,
the floors ripped up for fire wood.
Up ahead I could hear that the train
had stopped, the bells went on ringing
for a minute, the blinking arms of light
went from red to nothing. Around me
the engines began to die, and then
my own went. It was strangely quiet,
another town or maybe another world.
I could feel a deep cold slowly climbing
my legs, which wouldn't move, my eyes
began to itch and blink on a darkness
I had never seen before. I knew
these tiny glazed pictures—a car hood,
my own speedometer, the steering wheel
the windshield fogging over—were the last
I'd ever see. These places where I had lived
all the days of my life were giving up
their hold on me and not a moment too soon.

SUSAN LUZZARO

Working Class Education: Working It Out

No one was saving for my college education. When I would come home from school with my report card, my mother would be diapering one of the four babies who came after me. She would put the baby in a high chair or a playpen and take my report card from my reluctant hands. "Why all these 'C's' in citizenship?" she would ask. "Why can't you raise your hand when you want to talk?" Though I was at the head of the class in every subject but math, citizenship grades were what counted in our house— not scholarship.

Whoever that studious, pigtailed girl was in elementary school, by the time I arrived at the junior high school I was completely someone else. I cut and bleached my blonde hair. I got madras shirts, blue jean wrap around skirts, and I got belligerent, as my parents were wont to say. I only cared if boys looked at me. I only cared if boys wanted to "go" with me. A ring hanging from a chain around my neck was a goal only rivaled by my desire for long fingernails. My voracious demand for new clothes could not possibly be met—even though my father worked in an aircraft factory during the day and at a gas station at night. Though I loved to read and was often in trouble for reading with a flashlight after bedtime—reading seemed to be an entirely separate phenomenon from school or education. School was somewhere you had to be until you didn't have to be there anymore— it was disconnected from any future goals. My future was amorphous; I only imagined it had something to do with love. I was free-floating, like a dolphin at Sea World in the big school tank; I had no particular future, and no particular tasks, other than swimming in a small circle, eating, and oc- casionally performing tricks. It got so bad that at one point the counselor called my mother in and told her that he looked for me to get pregnant and drop out of school soon. That was in the eighth grade.

As a young adult I blamed my parents because they had not given me sufficient direction. It took me a long time to understand that they weren't negligent or thoughtless, and I was not simply a girl waiting to get preg- nant and married; I was raised according to the culture of our class and the expectations of my gender. Deportment was a value, an ethic. What I needed to sustain myself in any conceivable future was the ability to be "good" and to follow directions. I didn't need high scholarship marks, or to excel in any particular subject because it was inconceivable that I would go to college. I needed to know how to behave, to be on time, to do my home-work—not because it would be an avenue of knowledge or insight, but because it had been assigned. My parents had internalized the educations they had received and they were passing them on to me.

Neither of my parents had gone to college. My father, who once told me he used to lay in haystacks whittling the shapes of airplanes pass-ing overhead and imagining a bright and shiny future, left his tiny Mis-souri town shortly after graduating from high school. He went to Wichita and took a course in airplane mechanics. Shortly after graduating from high school in Iowa, my mother followed her brother to Wichita where he attended the same school my father was attending. It wasn't long until all of them came to California with little more than a bag of tools. Though they were all very intelligent, they never conceived of themselves as col-lege material, nor did anyone else. Both of their families were poor and were pleased that they had been able to help their children finish high school.

The single breadcrumb trail that I could follow to college was thrown down by my mother's mother. My grandmother had attended a teach-ers' college, then gone on, briefly to work as an editor for a small newspa-per in the Iowa where she fell in love with the typesetter, my grandfather. My grandmother never lost her desire to write—I inherited that desire. In my parents' house there were also, always, books. My mother worked part-time shelving books at the library—whatever our home may have lacked materially was compensated for by books. And because my mother worked at the library we were exempt from the overdue fines, a decided advantage for people who checked out twenty-five books at a time.

I did finally make it through high school—no thanks to my coun-selor or myself. I never took a single class seriously except French, and in a small town in southern California French is probably the most useless subject I could have invested my energy in. But French was exotic, it linked me to something larger than the little world of family and friends. I sup-pose I believed if I could speak French I could go to France to live. I always got A's in French. The rest of my grades were abysmal until I at last latched on to a steady boyfriend. He graduated a year before me and believed that if I was doing well in school I could not be flirting with other boys; so for love I at least got passing grades.

Then it was on to the great conveyor belt out to the community college. My parents didn't see the point of it, nor did my boyfriend, (nor did I for that matter), but they all agreed that if I took secretarial courses I might improve my employability. I had so far landed only one job the pre-vious Christmas as a gift wrapper and was fired before the actual Christ-mas rush for failing to comprehend the art of making packages pretty. So I took literature classes on the side simply because I loved to read, and typing and shorthand were my mainstay. Though my parents hadn't taught me to drive yet, and certainly we couldn't afford another car; it would all work out because my boyfriend could drive me to and from the slightly enlarged dolphin tank every day.

I finished my first year of college with a 1.5 grade point average in sixteen or so secretarial courses (typing has, however, served me well), and two literature courses and finally fulfilled my junior high counselor's prophecy—I left the community college to marry and become a mother at the age of eighteen. And I have to say I loved having babies. I loved being pregnant, loved nursing babies, reading them stories, taking them for walks. I didn't love the poverty that constantly pressed in on us in those days. Neither did I love the enforced isolation that so often encases young mothers--especially those who don't drive. And who would be surprised by the fact that my husband's and my relationship steadily deteriorated as he went on with his college and career, while I got chubbier and chubbier and surrounded myself with babies. (Well, actually only two.) In spite of the babies that I loved, those years were the dregs in many ways. We received government assistance food—salty canned chickens, hunks of butter, hunks of cheese, packages of mashed potato mix. These could only aggravate the chubbiness. But I think I can focus on a time period that was probably the worst—when I became hooked on the soap opera "Dark Shadows" and sat before the tv every afternoon enthralled by the macabre romance while downing a gallon of Rocky Road. I wanted more from life, but I didn't know what it was or how to get it.

Recently, a number of studies have indicated that at-risk students are often saved or aided by a particularly supportive relationship with an instructor. Likewise, I believe that in general, if you are not born with a silver spoon, your life can still be altered, improved, by simple human intervention. Dan LaBotz—friend to both my husband and myself—was a student of literature at UCSD and earned money on a teaching assistantship. He began to come to the house in the afternoons with one of those unbreakable plastic net bags you can buy in Tijuana filled to the top with books. He would give me reading assignments; he even set up a chalk board in the kitchen and would lecture while helping me clean out the refrigerator or wash the dishes. I awoke from my torpor. I regained my love of reading and I gained new attendant joys—I loved knowledge, I loved connecting ideas, which is a form of study. Dan's visits lasted for only a brief while, but I will always be grateful to him for re-igniting my joy in reading, and for revealing my passion for learning. From then on I became insatiable. I read everything: Simone de Beauvior's *The Mandarins* and *The Second Sex*, Lenin and Cherneshevsky's *What Is To Be Done*, Albert Camus' *The Plague*, Doris Lessing's *The Golden Notebook*, everything written by

Herman Hesse. Even though I was very much alone, and often had no one to discuss these books with, and when I did I mispronounced the author's names, I became a changed person—my mind had entered the big fish tank of the world.

One day I read in the local paper that the community college was going to open a child care center. By now my son was four and my daughter was close to three. The ad said they would only accept children three years of age or more—but I was resolved to go and plead my case. When the head teacher said yes—my problems had just begun. I had to petition for re-entrance because my grade point average was so low. My petition was approved—but I still did not drive and further had no car.

What I did then was part of the times and does not seem possible nor advisable nowadays. Perhaps the country had not had its first mass murder yet, or perhaps the world was really a different place. On the first day of class I made a sign that said *Southwestern College*, took my babies by the hand, and walked to the corner to hitchhike. The whole procedure was very difficult. I worried about our safety. I worried about the kind of ride or the kind of driver we would get. I worried about being on time; sometimes the distance though short would require more than one ride. I worried about my babies feeling abandoned in the day care center; in fact, I often stood outside crying as I watched their initial integration into the world beyond mother. I had very few clothes, and not enough money for books. But more than anything—I had no time to study.

The process, once begun, was by no means smooth or direct. But I was committed. My grade point average steadily rose. Little by little, I acquired study skills and self confidence. Some years I would take off from school and go to work because we needed the money. Most years I attended only part-time so I could be with my children, brush their hair in the morning, pick them up after school. (Oh yes, Janet LaBotz, sister to Dan LaBotz, finally took pity on me and taught me to drive.) It took me twelve years to get my Bachelor's Degree. By the time I received my BA with an emphasis in English, I knew I could write and I had learned self-discipline. I was fortunate to get a part-time teaching position; I had a poem published in *The American Poetry Review*; and human intervention rescued me again. Sandra Alcosser, a recently hired professor at San Diego State University, looked around at her students and said, "These students need a terminal degree." She proceeded to create an MFA program at the only school I could hope to attend and still maintain my place in my nuclear family. It was a three year program and this time I only took three years to complete it. I even graduated with some sort of special recognition written on my degree—because by this time I had begun to conceive of a minus on the side of an A as something akin to a bullet in my heart.

It wasn't until recently when I attended the Breadloaf Writers' Conference in Vermont as a scholar that I was able to conceptualize how education might be otherwise. The difference was tangible, sensual even. The grounds of the campus was Emersonian. Green, isolated, idyllic. There were clay tennis courts and ponds, a fireplace in the library, dining rooms with polished wood floors and linen table cloths. There were isolated Adirondack lawn chairs in the middle of vast green expanses which reminded me of the movie *Man Facing Southeast.* The students who attend there during the regular year for the most part must not anticipate working to supplement their incomes because the towns are distant and small. I began to really think about that other kind of education. The one that was planned for before birth. The one that your parents believed was your birthright and had saved for. The one that was facilitated by parents who had degrees, who could thread their children through educational and administrative hoops. The one that can truly aim at any profession. The one where your job is to study.

This kind of education is so radically different than the ones my students receive in the community college where I now teach, the community college that I first attended, that I hitchhiked to with my babies. My students are often supporting and raising families. This semester, in fact, I had a student working full time, attending college part time, and participating in the difficult process of raising a Downe's Syndrome baby. Two out of three of these students come from families in which no one has an advanced degree.

The faces of my students mirror my own when I first attended. They are uncertain yet optimistic. They are weighed down by work and familial responsibilities. They are not sure if they are wasting their time and should get on with "real life," and "real jobs." They are increasingly burdened by the rising cost of tuition and books. They are keenly aware of the quixotic nature of the job market. They are afloat in a large tank for purposes unknown, or that can only be revealed to them by human intervention, by hard work, or by luck. The route to a degree for working class people is circuitous at best. College was never in our future—the odds are stacked—but we are a determined lot.

MARK VINZ

Beast of Burden

Summers meant the flour mills and
good money as a sampler for the USDA,
an endless circle from packing floor
to boxcars, where I had to check the bags.
The loading crews all knew I was a
college boy, told me every day
I'd better stay in school or I'd end up
like them—some dumb animal doomed
to carry hundred-pounders on his back.
When they asked me what I was studying,
I'd lie and tell them chemistry. They'd
smile at that, knowing the white coats
in the lab had decent jobs, and out of
the heat, too—120 degrees most days
on those sidings. Sometimes I'd help
carry a few bags from the chute, learning
to flip them into neatly forming tiers.
Just when I'd feel good about my muscles,
they'd say again I'd better stay in school or
they'd kick my ass all the way to St. Louis.
There we'd stand in those stifling boxcars,
sharing a forbidden smoke whenever
the conveyor belt broke down, talking
about the icy beers we'd be having soon—
when they'd go their way and I'd go mine,
covered with flour dust and sweat
that dried into paste across your skin
and took a long time to scrub off.

Minimum Wage

Most Saturdays I worked the night shift
at the Kansas City *Star*—what they called
the slave labor crew, assembling the
Sunday editions—winos, drifters, dropouts,
a few high school kids and guys home
from college looking for a little extra cash.
If we got lucky we'd be done by 5 a.m.,
drag our aching muscles home and swear
this would be the last time, though we also
knew we'd probably be back—the place
they'd hire you, no questions asked.

The mail room regulars were big shots
on Saturdays, every one of them a foreman
screaming orders, making sure none of us
was hiding in the john or sleeping behind
a stack of papers. Once I asked the loudest
if he'd ever heard of Hemingway. *Sure,*
he said—*I fired that greaser months ago.*
So watch it, or I'll be firing your ass too.

One time I had to get a paycheck
on a weekday morning and discovered
all those foremen did exactly what
the rest of us did on the weekends.
None of them would acknowledge me—
or maybe they never noticed, heads down,
skin turned gray from years of printer's ink,
hacking from the paper dust that filled the air.
That was the week I never came back.

Job Description

Three nights a week I tended bar
at a college joint where all
we could serve was 3.2 beer,
mastering the lingo as I went along:
two of anything, *a pair*, and three
a crowd; *Rocky in the Armor*,
a can of Coors, and 86, *kill the order*.
Most of it slips, but I do remember
girls who weren't impressed by
bartenders, there were no tips,
and a big part of the job was
pouring drinks for the owner,
a local legend who kept his whiskey
in a paper bag beneath the bar.
When he couldn't stand up I'd have
to drive him home, hurrying back
for a few free rounds, to blast
the jukebox and help the waiters
sweep the place up. The only rule
was *never turn the lights up high*.
We all were learning, even then,
what we couldn't bear to see.

TOM WAYMAN

The Turn of the Tide

light flickers on the sear leaf
as a dry wind
nudges the underside

> when the train brakes to a halt
> the watcher on board perceives
> his car start to roll backwards
>
> and then it does

the green wind
bears the details of moisture
warmth, pollen

> as a mind
> contains and offers
> a party in the landlord's basement
> during the 1950s at Kitimat, the names of grandnieces
> the lineup for mission food
> in the Tucson once
> pouring cement for the south tower
> of the Granville Street Bridge
> a Portuguese curse memorized
> with the help of a co-worker
> whose name was, whose name was

> > the closest edge of the sea-foam
> > dampens, then soaks
> > a grain of sand
> >
> > the next tumble of water
> > slides up the beach
> > just short of that dark grain

a gardener
scoops handful after handful
of rich loam
from the bag he holds

he paces forward
scattering the redolent composted soil

across the ground
the gardener digs into the sack

all forenoon
afternoon

until he bends further
to reach into the container

appears stooped, shuffles
in his rough palm

hard granules show amid the
moist peat moss and earth

each dip into the bag
now draws more

ash-grey
bone meal

until his hands cup
only what has been

burned and crushed
this substance falls

between shaking fingers
into air

      the child's crayon
      does not want to stay within the lines
      printed on a page

she pushes the color strongly
across the paper
and onto the tablecloth

her line sets out

    each wave
    breaks spectacularly on the beach

    while at the center of the lion-headed surf
    an undertow calls back the water

    to ocean's core

Past Dryden Station
the boxcar
cools in the Fall night
When the chill grips him
he opens his bag
and removes the newspaper
He takes one sheet
scrunches it into a ball
places it beside him
Then he lights the wadded paper, the flames
explode
The eyes of the other two men
in the car
turn toward the blaze
He warms his hands
as this fuel stiffens to black
crumbles
A minute later
he draws out another sheet

Hammering and screech of the wheels

The paper dying and flaring

Heat and ice

Billy's Pecadillos

Conrad stops me
coming out of the store:
That your lawn mower
in your trunk?
Good.
The community cemetery
grass nees cutting.
Can you do it with me?
I would, I reply, except
I'm on my way to take the mower
back to Sears: the deck is cracking.
Look here: both places
where the handle joins.
This is the second time
in a year and a half
this has happened.
But, hey,
how about Billy?
I know he and Joan have
two lawn mowers.
He'd likely be glad
to volunteer.

Can't ask Billy.
The woman who lives next door to
the graveyard
used to go with him.
It didn't end well.
I wouldn't want her
to look out a window
and see Billy that
close.

DAVID WATTS

Antonio

He hisses through
his tracheostomy
as his daughter does
his talking.
She tells me
about his smoking,
his emphysema, his
operation that took away
his speech.

His fingertip
covers the red ring
at his neck
as he heaves
a few words.
"I want you...
to be my...
doctor...
I want you...

to treat me...
as a friend..."

By now I have lost
any regrets.
He is family
and I see it will not
be easy.

I examine him.
I study him.
I learn his future.
His daughter tells me

not to tell him
what will come.

Now he sits
and smiles
and thanks me
as I do not tell him
all I know.

But I am troubled.

He wears a small
Italian hat. He
is proud of
his family.
He says, "I
am so glad to
be here with you."
He says to me, "Doctor
you have too much
to think about
to worry so hard
for me."

MRI SCAN

I arrive in a place
of strange light,
the kind
that takes away
intelligence.

I am dreamless.
I am made of the same stuff
the walls are made of.

I am a photograph
by the long door
of the closet, empty
in the center where I sit.

They say the magnet
draws particles from air
through the body,
energy that shakes the cells
and makes them cough up
their whereabouts.

I am a tube in a tube
with no exit sign,
a plastic cone
with sides that clack
and groan, my heart
shudders, my bones ache,
I could swear my skin rises
on a bed of crepitations
like tinfoil over Jiffy-Pop.

I am exaggerating,
but I can no longer tell
what is real. I imagine
the whole Van Allen Belt
sucked through my body,

my flesh shimmering
like atmospheres after space wind.

And I wonder
if now the soul
might leave the body
and drift as vapor
over the ordeal of tissues.
But then
the body would be alone.
So I remain, lie still and witness
the dissection of my form.

And like Indians who feared
the photograph, knowing something
is lost there,
I wonder
if we ever are the same
ever are,
after anything.

Telling the News

> *He is the best physician*
> *who is the best inspirer of hope.*
> > -Coleridge

She would come
and ask
as I knew she would

in that way of asking
that cuts through
deception.

I wanted to leave room
for optimism,
but she fixed

her eye on me,
embraced me and asked
what was it

I found. I said I didn't
know for sure,
clinging to the vanishing

safety.
But she closed in: then what
is your most accurate

opinion? The procedure
was just finished
the small tissues I plucked

still swimming in the formalin
that would bring them
like tea leaves

under the pathologist's eye.
And I thought she still
might be reeling

from the Valium
I'd given her.
Was she ready

for my accuracy?
Her eyes did not waver.
Another cancer, I said,

most likely.
She asked
about the little butterflies

that might be fluttering
through her body
looking for a place

to light. I said
I didn't know.
She wondered if surgery

would cure her.
I said I thought
it was necessary

to save the bowel
from obstruction.
Then I allowed a little reach:

It was possible
the cancer could be
contained.

She let my words drift
unclaimed.
I can't lick this she said.

But it sounds like
I might have a year or two
of peace.

She thanked me
and not knowing why
I let her walk away.

SUKI WESSLING

A Strong Face

The night was sweltering and the car exhaust had piled up a fine mist, creating a spectacular sunset of human folly. There was still a deep, red glow over the filling station across the road, and the blue sky was just dark enough to let a few stars shine through. Or were those satellites? Casey wasn't sure. She'd forgotten how to tell the difference.

Casey shifted in her high heels. She'd thought it was a pretty stupid idea to begin with, but what did she know? She was the odd one out, the woman, the affirmative action employee. She was, in fact, the only one not wearing a tuxedo. She had wanted to wear a tux, but Johnny "Mr. Cadillac" Johnson had thought it lacking in taste.

"What we want here," he told Casey, "is a New Year's Eve sort of atmosphere. Not the Exotic Erotic Ball."

On this hot July evening, Casey was too confused about New Year's Eve to even wonder what her wearing a tux had to do with exotica or erotica. But Johnson was from Concord, a conservative white community across the hills, and he had only moved his dealership into this den of sin because, and Casey remembered his words exactly, "there's no black people over there and dammit, they're the ones that's buying." So there was no accounting for what he might think people wore to such a thing as the Exotic Erotic, and Casey didn't want to be the one to tell him that they wore little if anything at all.

"Nothing" was exactly what she wished she were wearing right now. On Johnny's suggestion of New Year's Eve, Casey had decided to wear that slinky red thing she hadn't been able to wear last year because Bobby had the flu and was throwing up green bile as the new year was counted in. The slinky red thing had stayed in her closet where, she reflected, it belonged. Long-sleeved and floor-length, it seemed to be made of some industrial-quality polyester designed to trap bodily fluids. She was sure that when she took it off she'd be drenched in the stinky sweat she could feel running down her back, and David would quickly forget the amorous overtures he'd started earlier.

"Hey, maybe you should work nights more often, baby," he'd cooed, nosing at the crook of her neck. "You sure this is really for work?"

"No, actually Johnny Johnson and I are going to elope," Casey had answered, and had received a barking laugh into her shoulder as David pulled away.

"You, Johnny Johnson, and what wig?" David said through a giggle. He'd seen Johnson's girlfriends, featured on the fender of the latest model in his ads. 'Big hair and big boobs' had been David's summation of Johnson's taste. But this time he didn't bother, as he had in the past, to assure Casey that hers were not lacking, short and small though they were.

"How you doin', Stillwell?" a voice boomed behind her. Casey turned away from the streaming traffic and saw the be-tuxed form of Harvey, the dealership's top salesman. Harvey, Casey had informed David, was OK. He called everyone by their last name, and made no exception of Casey. His ability to use sports-talk in nearly any situation amazed her. She suspected that he used it to hide a rather sensitive nature that had been brutalized by a lifetime of selling overrated cars for a man who, it was quite apparent, carried his brain between his legs.

"I see old Johnson's got you on the sidelines like a cheerleader, eh?"

Casey grinned. "You're my biggest fan, Harvey."

"If he'd only put you up to bat, he'd see what you can do."

"Well, you look nifty," Casey said. He did, actually, look rather well in his tuxedo with the red carnation in a buttonhole. He had slimmed a bit recently, Casey thought. Put in some decent clothes, he might even be handsome.

"Don't want to turn up in a ratty uniform for the play-offs," Harvey answered.

"Some play-offs," a dour voice said to Casey's right. Bob Muscago—Boob, Casey called him when she talked to David—scraped at the curb with one badly-shined shoe. "More like a last-ditch attempt."

"It's not so bad, Muscago," Harvey said with a wink to Casey. They liked to make fun of Bob's moodiness. "We're not down for the count yet."

"You seen Johnson yet? Looks like a corpse tonight. Said it was something he ate. I think it was something he said."

"Something like, 'We've got inventory to move, for no cash down'?" Casey asked.

"How about 'Biggest New Year's event since the thirty-first of December'? It's gonna be a bust. Nobody's gonna come out to buy a car from a bunch of penguins on a Wednesday night."

"Hey, penguins and a cardinal," Harvey said, in Casey's defense. "Besides, it hasn't started until the fat lady sings. We got a whole night to put the gameplan into action."

Bob snorted and walked back toward the showroom. Casey glanced up to see that the red glow was gone from the sky. A truck rattled by and spewed diesel fumes onto the sidewalk. Coughing, Casey and Harvey retreated.

The lot was lit so brightly Casey could have thought it was day. Rows of new-model Cadillacs obscured the lingering legion of cast-offs: last year's model priced to sell, trade-ins that Johnson had been sure could be moved and bring in a little cash. Cash was, he liked to say, the key.

"Cash is the key," he said, striding onto the blacktop like a stuffed penguin, afraid he would burst. His face was ashen and he was breathing shallowly. Casey was sure he'd be doubled over in pain, if he weren't a man, if he didn't have face to keep. "We'll do credit, but cash is what we're looking for."

"You've made sure of that," Muscago muttered. His voice breathed into Casey's ear from behind. He'd never have the guts to confront the boss to the face.

"I'm just going to be in the office, if you need me," Johnson continued. He attempted to paste a grin on his face, but it formed the sort of animal-like grimace David's cat made through the window when she saw a rival.

"We'll do just fine without you," Muscago muttered, but this time it was into a momentary lull in the constant traffic noise from the street. Johnson glanced over at him, and because she was in front of Muscago, at Casey.

"Good," he said, looking pointedly at Casey's chest. "Pretty good, I'd say."

He turned and lumbered off past the cars, into the well-lit showroom.

"I can't decide if he means you'll be good for the guys, or good for the ladies," Muscago said into Casey's ear again.

"I think he read in a car dealer's magazine somewhere that ladies like to buy from ladies," said Lester, the fourth and last employee. He leaned casually against the long front of one of the latest models. Consistently half-asleep, Lester amazed Casey with his constant grasp of what was going on around him.

"Or maybe he just wanted to keep one around, for his own amusement," Muscago said with a sneer in his voice.

"I'm not his type," Casey snapped, and stepped forward so that she wouldn't be able to feel Muscago's breath on her neck. She didn't like their hovering, their constant talking about her and theorizing about her effect on sales. She put her hands on her hips, wishing for large pockets to hide them in. This is what she hated about women's clothing; it didn't provide escapes the way men's jackets and pants do. Usually she wore a suitcoat that gave her a bit of armor against the world.

"Casey's a key player on our team," Harvey jumped in to her defense. "I don't see you filling any function, Muscago."

"Maybe I'll just go home," Muscago said, and Lester laughed.

"Maybe you weren't listening. We're supposed to be here until we sell."

"Or until we die of boredom," Muscago finished.

"And what would you be doing that's so much more exciting?"

Casey asked. She nodded to Muscago's answering silence, though he was still behind her and she could only assume that she'd properly put him in his place. "That's what I thought, Mr. Excitement."

Casey clasped her hands behind her and walked off to the edge of the lot, not bothering to wait for an answer. She didn't need one. Nothing they had to say interested her. She'd been more at home at the mill, developing a library of sick jokes and forming comraderie through shows of strength. This more genteel job left her constant thinking of David, of stupid little things they did together. She liked to think of doing the dishes, he washing, she drying. She liked to think how he'd take mounds of soap bubbles and smear them on her face to form a beard.

"Who wears the trousers in this family?" David had liked to joke when she still worked at the mill.

But they'd lost that joke when she'd "moved up" into women's suits and shoes with small, nubby heels. "Wheelin' dealin' woman" was what he called her now, imitating Johnny Johnson's ads and mocking her serious study of "sales theory."

"Next thing I know, you'll be wanting to become a lawyer." He was only joking, but in a way that never ceased to surprise Casey. It was not inconceivable to him that she would become a lawyer. It seemed inconceivable to the men on this lot that she could fill a function other than decorative.

"And it's Stillwell, up to bat for the Cardinals," Harvey said, stepping up next to her and grinning.

"Yup," Casey answered, because there was nothing else to say.

At eight-thirty, not a customer yet in sight, Casey went to the bathroom to remove her nylons and emerged to see Johnson turned positively green. He leaned against a wall, gasping for air in more than his usual heavy-smoking manner. He held his belly, which had been let loose from the cumberbun that had been strapping it down.

"You OK, boss?" Casey asked. She had a certain fondness for Johnson, disgusting and sexist though he was. He reminded her why she should be in love with David.

"Sick," Johnson gasped. "Must be something I ate."

Casey put her hand expertly on Johnson's forehead. "You might be right," she said. "No fever."

"What should I do?"

"Go home, drink some Pepto-Bismol, and sleep it off," Casey recommended.

"Good advice," Johnson muttered. He tried to move away from the wall. "You women always give good advice even if you can't sell cars."

He lurched into the hall and caught himself on the next wall that presented itself in front of him.

"You want someone to drive you?" Casey asked.

"Naw. I'll make it." With great effort he straightened up and walked toward the door in a line that might nearly have passed a sobriety test.

Casey watched him go. "Good luck. Good riddance," she recited, but she felt no joy in it. She leaned against the wall where she'd found Johnson. The sick feeling in her stomach had not left with him. Was it the job? Was it David? Was it taking care of little Bobby, whose father had run off into oblivion? Maybe it was the never-ending stream that kept her moving, treading, unsure about whether she should go the easy way or turn and swim against the current. Most people she knew were happy enough just letting themselves be drawn along, but Casey had never been willing.

"Just stop!" she'd yelled once at David. He had looked up, hurt and confused.

"I was just watching TV," he said. "What's wrong, Casey?"

"It's just....it's just...." Casey had mumbled, retreating back into the bedroom.

David didn't understand angst. In school he was studying it, but he had none of his own. He shouldered burdens without questioning why. He suffered differences with a smile and a good attitude.

"Won't it bother you to be so much older than the other students?" Casey had asked the first time they'd gone out. David was telling her that he'd decided to go back to school, to the university he'd dropped out of ten years earlier to care for his family.

"I think I'll provide them with perspective," David answered wisely.

"Didn't you feel angry at your family for making you support them all those years?" she had said in response to the story of his father's death from cancer.

"We all have obligations to bear," David had said. "Do you want more wine?"

He had served her wine and he owned cloth, albeit cheap cloth, napkins. His parents had gone to college and now all of his siblings had graduated, too. He was able to see past Casey's mannish haircut and her gruff manner into what he called her sensitive soul.

"It's too bad you never got a chance to study," he said non-committally. He and his napkins and his wine and his books and good enunciation and his gentle treatment of Bobby moved into Casey's apartment. He went back to school. She went from heavy work at the mill to selling cars along a neon-lit strip. She shelved her coveralls and bought dresses, the sort of things she'd seen David's mother wear. She practiced a new tone to her voice and learned to eat with the fork in her left hand and knife in her right. She tried not to do heavy work, hoping to lose the bulky shoulders that David assured her made her look like a fashion model.

She bought a slinky red dress that made her sweat, and wondered whether a man like David would really love a woman who thought that

Brie was a name and Truffaut was something you ate.

"You're so cute," David would reply to her gaffes. "I love it when you do that."

Casey couldn't decide if he was being patronizing or if he really did love all those things that distinguished her from him. Casey couldn't decide much of anything at all.

She peeled the high heels off her sweaty feet and padded out to the lot.

"Where's Johnson?" Lester called out. Now it was just the four of them: Lester, Bob, Harvey, and Casey.

"Gone home," Casey said, feeling the blacktop gouge warmly into the soles of her feet. "I think it was something he said," she said with a smile to Bob.

He responded with only a further scowl. "No reason for any of us to be here."

"Listen, am I going to have to play coach now?" Harvey asked, clasping Bob on the shoulder. Bob shrugged himself away and took a few steps toward the street. He was a black silhouette in front of passing head-lights.

"I'm outta here," Bob said, turning toward them, nodding decisively, and making for the employee parking end of the lot.

"Good bye. Good riddance," Casey said to his retreating black figure. But she didn't say it loud enough for him to hear. Her voice was drowned in the street traffic. Her dress shone obscenely in the brazen lights of a car-filled parking lot on a Wednesday night.

After Lester had followed Bob's lead and Casey and Harvey were left alone in the spotlit parking lot, Harvey reached up and cut loose a balloon. He handed it to Casey.

"Happy New Year's," he said, and she didn't know whether he was saying it to her, or reading the fancy lettering on the side of the balloon.

"I hear these metallic things kill dolphins....or something like that."

"Yeah, but they're cute," Harvey answered with a jolly air.

"True." Casey took the balloon from him and felt it pull upwards. When she closed her eyes, she could imagine that she was upside down, that it wasn't the helium floating up but rather gravity pulling down.

"So what's up with you?" Harvey asked, turning the world upright again. "How's the boyfriend?"

"Fine," Casey answered.

"Uh-oh," Harvey said with a smile.

"What?"

"Doesn't sound fine."

"No, really," Casey protested. "It's fine. Everything's just....fine."

"Fine," Harvey echoed.

"Fine," Casey said with a smile. She followed Harvey, who had started down the row of cars, wiping a finger tenderly along each hood to check for dirt.

"Damn cars get dirty every day, with all this smog."

"He's in school, you know," Casey said, continuing her thoughts out loud. "And I, I like this job. It's good enough, I suppose. Better than the mill."

She paused and followed Harvey, who was listening but not answering.

"And, I guess, I just wonder if we're right for each other. We're so.... different."

"I doubt we're going to have any customers tonight," Harvey said. He stopped and turned toward Casey. She might have thought he was ignoring her, but he spoke in a consoling way. "Want some coffee?"

"Sure," Casey said with a grimace. Coffee was another thing she'd learned about from David. Coffee was not that watery stuff they sold at McDonald's or that bitter stuff that brewed for hours in the dealership's lounge area. Nevertheless, she followed Harvey into the showroom and paused to tie the balloon he'd given her to the handle of one of the show models.

She watched Harvey as he went to pour the coffee. He was a tall man, big and tall, Casey's mother would have said nicely, though one couldn't deny that he was overweight. His father hadbeen a pipefitter, she had found out in conversation one slow day. Harvey had become a salesman very young. He was going to find a better life, he had told her, and if she didn't know Harvey, she might have heard some bitterness in his voice.

Was this a better life, Casey wondered. She had thought that David would think so, when she got the opportunity to quit the mill and do something less "blue collar." But David had conveyed neither approval nor disapproval. He had said, as he always did, "If it makes you happy," and had only expressed sadness at the disappearance of her coveralls and Forty-niners hat. She had been dressed that way when he'd met her. Coming home after her last day at the mill, he met her at the door with one of those little disposable cameras. He got the picture framed and put it on the TV. "Casey as I first knew her," he would announce to friends, family, Bobby, or even the cat if no one else was listening. He had been working at the mill, too, as a secretary. Casey had never met a male secretary before. They had giggled over their role reversal over hot chocolate and he had lent her books to read during her breaks.

"Maybe I was just fooling myself," she said out loud, looking up at Harvey, who stood over her with two cups of coffee.

"You want some advice?" Harvey said, handing her a cup. He didn't wait for an answer. "Learn to sell cars. You're here. You've done a few deals. You're getting in the swing of it."

"I'm glad you have faith in me, Harvey."

"I do. I have faith in you." He shifted uncomfortably, still standing over her. "Come on. Let's look at some stats."

He walked back to his office and Casey followed. She stood next to his desk as he pulled some files from a cabinet.

"Muscago," he said, pointing at a chart. "Only five percent of total sales were his the first month. Four the next month."

"Yeah, but he sold more cars than me."

"We're in a slump now. Nobody's buying Caddies. But they'll come back. And look at Johnson, the boss man himself. Sometimes he hardly sells at all, and when he does, it's usually to his friends."

"I guess some of us just choose the wrong friends," Casey said.

"Stillwell, I'd buy a car from you if I didn't love my old clunker so much." He turned away abruptly and shoved the file back in the drawer. "I really would," he said with his back still turned.

It was one of those situations, Casey thought, that you could break with a word, like a hammer on glass. Like when she and David were sitting in that cafe, and he'd just said, "Do you want another chocolate?" and he touched her hand, and she could have pulled away, she could have said, "Yes," and broken the feeling so easily, but instead like helium floating upward they'd moved toward each other...

Harvey turned, and it was much more like gravity. He stepped close and pressed his lips to hers. His hands didn't touch her at first, and then they grabbed her waist. He pushed her up against the desk, his hands moving to cup her bottom. He pressed himself up against her with a crackle of rented tux and hot breath that couldn't penetrate the armor of her dress. He planted one very wet kiss on her neck and looked pleadingly into her eyes.

"Gonna bring me in for a homerun tonight, Casey?" he asked huskily. As if embarrassed, he pulled her against his chest so that she couldn't see his face. He thrust himself against her and she could feel the scratchy material of her dress sliding against her wet skin.

Casey pushed against him and let him fall back on the desk as she stood up. He looked so pitiful and pleading, she almost felt that she had to do it, the way she had to give Bobby candy even when she really shouldn't. But she just couldn't imagine....and when all was said and done that was the part she really liked. She couldn't imagine giving him homeruns, being "down for the count," having his "little teammates." True, she also didn't know if she could imagine a continuation of her life with David, his sweettalk and his admiration, his easy acceptance of their differences. But she knew that for now she had only the strength to tread water. Maybe David, standing on shore and watching the world slip by with the detached air of an intellectual, would offer her a hand. Maybe not. But even if she had to depend on her own strength, it was better than grabbing onto Harvey, who was plummeting by her with abandon.

Casey looked at Harvey, who at this moment was in the same predicament as her and maybe could understand her dilemma, who stood uncomfortable and lonely before her in his ill-fitted shoes. She shook her head.

"Sorry, Harvey. I think I'm gonna have to walk," she said, biting her lip, wondering if she'd used the right terminology.

"Yeah, that's what I thought," Harvey said, standing up and smoothing his tux. He had on that strong face, that face that David in his sensitive life had never had to create. A face that Casey often wore herself. "You're a real lady, Stillwell. You're a real good fighter."

"Not much of a team player, though," Casey suggested.

Harvey smiled, nodded. "Sometimes, Stillwell, things just work out. Remember that. Get going. I'll close up shop."

"OK." Casey edged toward the door.

"See you Friday?"

"Looks like it." Casey wondered if she should say something else, if maybe she'd dashed someone's dreams. But Harvey in his strong face turned and shut the file drawer with a slam. Casey slipped out of the office before he'd have a chance to look at her again.

FREDERICK WM. ZACKEL

Sunday School

The taxi rolled down the California Street hill.

"Shame you gotta work on Sunday afternoon," Naomi Lewandowski said, letting the hill do her work for her.

The passenger, a businessman in a three piece suit, stifled a yawn. "No choice. It's the only time the Hong Kong market and the London office are both open." God, do I hate Sundays, he thought.

A cable car was stopped in the intersection ahead, and tourists from both sides of Chinatown were ready to surge and board the cable car. Naomi Lewandowski left the left lane, entered the right lane.

"You'll blow the red light," the passenger warned.

Naomi said no. "The Don't Walk sign starts flashing a full fifteen seconds before the light turns red."

The taxi entered the intersection of California and Grant Streets as the light turned red and the tourists all stepped off the curb.

She squeezed through the tourists. The grip man angrily rang his bell twice at her, but she ignored it. The feud between cabbies and cable cars was as old as the City itself.

The passenger was wide awake now. "That was close!"

"Vaseline on both sides of the cab," Naomi said.

"You really know your lights," the passenger said, impressed.

"You gotta, in my business." Naomi started braking. "Just like there's no way I'm gonna get the green light down at Kearny."

She pulled ahead of the cable car and slipped back into the left lane. She hit her horn and startled the hell out of a tourist with a camcorder in the middle of street. She eased around him, took her foot off the gas and coasted downhill.

There she could forget about parked cars pulling out in front of her and concentrate on the beautiful day in front of her. Sunday afternoon in San Francisco. Sunny blue skies, and a crisp wind off the ocean. A shame she had to work, but a good day to go for a drive.

The light turned red at Kearny. She stopped gently. She looked both ways. She had no pedestrians. She took the opportunity to check her mirrors. No one behind her, no one in her blind spot. The cable car was still a block back up the hill behind her, still loading up, and no one was passing it on the inside, heading her way downhill.

She looked ahead. The Financial District was deserted. A few cars were parked in front of the tall buildings. Except for a lone BMW coming up the street, Naomi could've shot a cannon down California Street and never scared a business suit.

She looked right on Kearny. The traffic coming up Keary was light, a half-dozen cars maybe. She knew the big blob of traffic was stuck down near Post Street, a full five blocks away, held back by synchronized lights.

The Beamer was jet black, had the sunroof open, was sitting in its left lane across the intersection from her. The Beamer was brand new, a forty grand investment, and it had flipped on its left turn signal.

"See the Beamer over there?" she asked the passenger. "He's going to cut me off when he makes his left turn."

The passenger scuttled forward, peered over the edge of the front seat. "He's going to turn in front of you?"

"Yep." She goosed the gas just enough to move the cab over the crosswalk lines.

The BMW inched closer into the turn.

"He is!"

"Not if I can help it." She looked over her shoulder at the passenger. "The Law says through traffic has the right-of way over vehicles making left turns."

The BMW had its wheels cocked and had moved another inch forward and to the left.

"He is going for it!"

"As soon as the light changes." She gestured at the Beamer. "He's going to cut that corner as close as he can, as fast as he can, and flip me off when he does it."

The passenger looked down, then up Kearny. "You're going to warn him, aren't you?"

"Oh, yeah," she said. She flickered her turn signals and flashed her headlights several times at the BMW, who moved another inch left and forward.

"I don't like the Beamers," Naomi said. "Not a cabbie in town does. Those arrogant yuppie pups think just because they can buy a high performance car they know how to drive one."

The BMW moved another inch.

"He's gonna cut me off, blow past me faster than sin, and flip me off while he does it."

"He'll flip you off?"

"Guaranteed!" Naomi barked. "Hey, just 'cos you got a fifty inch dick doesn't mean you haveta use it on people. But hey, try and tell the Beamer people that."

The passenger had no idea what she was talking about.

"You shouldn't own a high performance car in San Francisco, anyway. Where you gonna drive it? I mean, you get two green lights in a row, it's a miracle. Now a car like that, it's a wonderful car, but you gotta live back east somewhere to enjoy it, Nevada, Utah, maybe Montana, where you got an open road and you can open 'er up!"

She kept her left foot on the brake, and her right held the gas pedal down. The cab rumbled with power.

The passenger grew nervous, wondering what his driver was going to do.

Naomi couldn't see the Beamer driver's face, but she could see his fender throbbing, and she knew by that he was riding the brakes and goosing the gas, too.

The passenger was impressed. "Is this a new cab?"

"It's a month old, a Crown Vic with the biggest V-eight Ford makes, with a double overhead cam shaft. It can carry six adults up the steepest hill in the City, and it can leave rubber at a green light."

She checked her mirrors. Still no one. As far as California Street was concerned, she and the Beamer were the only cars in the world. Out of the corner of her eye, she watched the traffic light flash the cautionary yellow for the Kearny-through traffic.

"Really embarrassing if when the light changes, he throttles down, cuts me off, then stalls in mid-curve. He knows I'll lay on the horn and make him feel like a jerk."

"Maybe he'll wait and go around you."

"He's got a BMW," she scoffed. "Beamer babies figure they can get away with murder." She started snickering, a most godawfully sinister sound in her passenger's ear.

More nervously: "Do you have to cut him off?"

She grinned. "It's my civic duty. It's the least I can do, and I always do the least I can do." She realized his concerns. "Hey, what's the point of living if you don't try to make people live by the rules?"

"God, this is a long light!"

She agreed. "But it has to let the Kearny traffic through." She looked down Kearny. No traffic coming.

The BMW cut his wheels far left; he could go no farther till the traffic light changed.

Naomi Lewandowski was getting edgy. She gripped the steering wheel with her right hand, and poised her right thumb above the horn. Her left hand was on her turn signal lever, ready to flipper it for the flashing headlights. Her left foot held down the brakes, and her right foot was juicing the gas. The cab rumbled and thundered.

"As soon as the light turns green," she mumbled.

She massaged the gas. The passenger could feel the cab pulsing and throbbing with her gas pedal. He gripped the top of the front seat in anticipation.

She backed off the gas and the brakes.

The light turned green.

She slammed the gas pedal to the floor. The cab lunged forward, left a patch of rubber. The Beamer popped his clutch, squealed left, leaving rubber and smoke where his tires had been.

She went at the BMW to T-bone it to hell. She went thumbs-down on the horn and held it down, laid on it like she could push it through the firewall. She flippered the turn signal lever, flashing her headlights non-stop and frenzied.

The little German car spun its butt around, its tires caught fire, and the car jumped ahead like a pouncing kitten and tore off up Kearny Street.

Naomi saw fleetingly the driver inside, youthful and tanned, goofy sunglasses hiding his eyes. He flipped her off, contempt on his face, and he was gone in the blur of his own making.

As soon as he had passed her, as soon as he had committed himself irrevocably to Kearny Street, she backed off the gas, gave up on the headlights and backed off from the horn. Effortlessly she flowed around the tail of the BMW and cruised down towards the foot of California street, unpressured.

The BMW was now committed to Kearny, going the wrong-way up a one-way street, with three lanes of traffic coming right at him.

She felt good. It was a bright sunny day. A shame she had to work, but, hey, she thought, we all have things we don't like doing. She thought warm thoughts for all poor unfortunates who had to work Sundays.

"By any chance," she asked over her shoulder, "didja hear how the Niners are doing?"

Ohio farms © Rebecca Colon

THE SWEEPER

INGENUITY & PERSISTENCE

DEBRA BENKO

Gypsum, Ohio 1937

Mama told me to keep the little ones
out of the best room after I'd said
I wouldn't set foot in there myself. Let
Martha pose dressed better than Sunday best,

paying respects. John, Jamie, and Liza took turns
swinging on the tire we'd found at the junkyard.
Until Mary begged to play Ring around the Rosy,
I was her horsey. After the sixth time

we'd reached "Ashes, ashes, we all fall down,"
Mary tucked her legs under and wouldn't get up.
"Where's Daddy? I wanna play with Daddy."
Reaching for her hands, I said she'd be with Daddy

in heaven someday, but she squirmed
out of my grasp, balling her fingers into fists,
rubbing her eyes. Then she punched my knees
again and again. "Now, take me to heaven, now."

Crouching, I stroked her sweaty hair, showing
her how to chalk her name on the baked ground
with a gypsum rock. Suddenly,
she was completely still. "I gotta go.

I gotta go now." I told Liza to take Mary
to the outhouse. Liza got down from the tire
with a frown that didn't change until
she took Mary's hand and pointed

out the Monarch, Mary's favorite color
orange. John and Jamie looked glad
to have the tire to themselves. Three years ago
we used to walk the tracks, piss over boxcars

from the railroad bridge. They still did,
but I was too old for that now.
I hadn't said a word about the window.
The room was almost empty.

As they were closing the coffin,
Uncle James and Uncle Johnny looked up,
each dressed in the only suit he owned,
the suit he'd be buried in. Uncle James

mumbled something to Uncle Johnny
about the best going first, just loud enough
for me to know he wanted me to overhear.
I saw my uncles dressed in coveralls

returning from the mine, coating
my daddy's coffin with layer
upon layer of gypsum dust,
covering everything they touched.

Lobby Teller Ballad

The FBI agents say observe
the lobby at all times,
know your customers. Look for strange
clothes, winter in summertime.

It's the end of April. The man
near the lobby door thinks he needs
a winter coat. But the time
and temperature clock reads

forty degrees, 11 o'clock.
I wore winter clothes, too.
Such a slow day, everyone
looks suspiciously blue.
The FBI agents say watch

your older customers.
Ask them about large withdrawals.
As a good lobby teller,

I should notice if they're upset.
I haven't waited
on this crinkle-faced woman before.
She writes the wrong date

on her sizable check, but I only ask
her to change it. I'm glad
I didn't ask questions when she says
two of her sisters passed

away in the past two weeks.
Next in line, an old man,
another stranger, pulls something
from his pocket. I plan

my m.o., think pistol
or revolver? What was
the difference? I fix one eye
on his bald spot, his wallet.

Observe him from the top down. Change
for a hundred. Check for
counterfeit. Red and blue threads.
He complains the weather

is controlled by politicians.
Sixty, eighty, ninety.
It's a conspiracy, he says.
One hundred. Hand the money

to the customer. One deep breath.
I look him in the eye.
I don't hold with conspiracy
theories generally, I say.

Thank you, he says, putting the money
in the wallet that could
have been a gun. Have a good day,
I say to the potential fraud

victim or robber. The line's gone.
Nothing to do but think
about yesterday in the bank vault
and the loan officer's wink.

He and I hand counted the money,
ample time to talk about him—
his divorce, his favorite
play *Camelot.* Due to his ex's whim,

he missed seeing Richard Harris
as Arthur, he said.
Poetry's practical uses
are not obvious, I said.

Are we balanced now, I asked,
his hand close to mine
putting back the last green bundle.
He added both lines

of numbers. Later in the day,
he asked me if I'd truly
rather be in the vault with him
than on the teller line. He

doesn't know I'd rather talk
to anyone than do
nothing, imagine a robber.
I said I was busy tonight.

He's the persistent type. He'll ask
me again and again,
hoping no turns to yes, and maybe
he's right, my mind could change.

I could cover the drive-thru at noon.
They're short on help right now,
so it's busier than usual.
I might have a view, notice

peach blossoms blowing off the tree
in the churchyard next door.
The flashes of pink and the tulips.
Maybe I never knew before

today how they open to sun and close
against rain, like a woman's legs.

Protest march of Steelworkers' Unions, Cleveland, Ohio
© Charles Cassady, Jr.

JEANNE BRYNER

Our Fathers

The day Joe Brodie fell into the acid pit
they say he screamed bigger than Texas.
When they pulled him out, his legs slid
off his waist like melted red candles.
He was crazy—yelling for his Mama,
his wife, Martha Jane, and his kids
all at once. Just before he blacked out,
he clutched his foreman's stiff white shirt
and said, *Help me Tom, please...my legs.*

Joe Brodie died on the way to the hospital.
Our fathers finished their shift.
That night, my Dad and his best friend, Ted,
went to Tony's Bar and got slop-the-hogs-
falling-down drunk. They talked about school
days back in Bobtown, Pa. and how yeast dough
smelled rising in their Mama's kitchen,
how many bales they could toss in June,
and how they missed those sweet, lazy,
West Virginia nights.

And how hot Ohio was, hot and flat, and people
here called us hicks and ridge runners,
but by God, we knew how to work.
And our fathers never missed a shift;
salt stains scribbled lines on coveralls
like small boys print their names in dirt.

Coal Miner, Caples, W.VA. 1938

Consider this coal miner, who is still young
and blue-eyed, how he rests his jaw
in timbers of his palm, face dusted over
with what most shafts exhale.

Down the road you know there's a shot hole,
the place where he drags his hope like a sledge
past the sun's pajamas, and pulleys lower
him in a wire basket.

Inside dark caverns, lessons begin.
His common hands follow glistening layers
of pigment to the middle ear of the mountain.
What does he hear in this immense labyrinth?

Does his heart complain that this shovel holds
no ruby, that air dances, a full-breasted
woman who spins her ether, drips juices over
him, a siren's song to make him stay?

He carries a silver pail, jam bread, yellow
cheese, coffee, cold in a jar, the memory
of screech owls in the hollows of his boyhood,
where he runs, fearless, and magnolias hang

in pink ruffles, warm yarns stick to his fork.
He tastes all of this, smells brown manure
falling from his father's mules. His vision
persists, a grail filled with morning stars.

Think of the way we are all porters, the weight
of picks slung over out shoulders, leaving
in darkness morning after morning, the shimming
up of our thigh bones to hold us in stanchions.

Isn't this is? The fatigue, days of garrets
furnished in quiet grumbles. Yet, we are rich

as this miner who scoops black honey
from a nettled ridge. We become the bear, rein
supreme in the starless land of tunnels,
where men with lanterns are kings.

Breeding

In the seventh grade, we studied England,
learned about early coal mines,
children crouched in cramped tunnels.
Men bred horses to be tiny
so they could pull heaped coal carts.

I watched my Father grow smaller
every summer at the mill,
until the only sound I heard
was his dapple phlegm
dragging dirty lungs up winter's hill.

PAOLA CORSO

Between the Sheets

My job was to shake sheets in a basement laundry at Citizens General Hospital in New Kensington. So I shook them and that's it. Somebody else washed the sheets and wheeled them to me in a big bin. Somebody else folded and stacked them on shelves when I finished shaking and feeding them into the press. Somebody else delivered them to the wards, and Catholic school taught me that somebody else would decide if life or death would be tucked between those sheets. But I ended up knowing this anyway even though it wasn't supposed to be my job. I was paid to shake sheets.

The morning low was 92 degrees. But the temperature in the laundry room started to rise as soon as steam escaped from the open lids of washers faster than smoke out of a chimneystack. It spread when the wet loads were carried over to dryers, and the laundry was floating in the middle of a cloud it seemed. A cloud that kept moving and yet it never finished passing through. It felt as though we were all playing a game of hide and seek. I saw little patches of the room but mostly just a hint of what was there--Bonita's brown eyes looking down. I knew she must have been reaching into the washer to pour detergent but I didn't see any of that. Only her eyes surrounded by a veil of steam like a bride before the husband lifts it up to kiss her. Or I saw just her hands as she folded pajama tops and bottoms. From what I could see, she was pinching at the air over and over again and nothing else. Everybody in the laundry room looked as if they were going through the motions, miming their jobs because the whiteness of the sheets and the pajamas and the bandages disappeared into the puffs of steam. Even the industrial-sized washers and dryers hid behind the pauses in the mist.

The laundry room had no ceiling, no floors, nothing ahead of me and nothing behind. Just the feet I stood on laced up in my navy blue Converse with worn out treads from gym class and a cloud that never stopped passing through. I imagined I was in the heavens standing on the wing of an airplane because of the jet-engine sound the washers and dryers made. I wanted to feel the breeze from being in flight, to fly away from the rows of dryers, each one a rotating circle of heat as if one sun in this world wasn't enough. Although I couldn't see, I knew exactly when Bonita took a load out of the dryers. I felt the current of air, lava-like molecules gushing through. The fact that it had just escaped gave it the momentum of a herd of elementary school kids stampeding through the doors to the playground when the recess bell rang. The dryers were so hot you couldn't touch the metal snaps on pajama tops with your bare hand unless you wanted to burn your fingertips. That's why, as hot as it was in the laundry room, Bonita wore garden gloves when she folded pajama tops.

By late-morning, the room broke 105. I wrapped my hair up in a tighter bun, changed into another cotton top and pulled at the frayed edges of my hiphugger jeans so they'd stop sticking to me. Still that didn't stop me from sweating where I never sweat before—in the backs of my knees, behind my ears, on my spine, in my bellybutton, between my toes. Wherever skin met skin, I sweat, and after there was enough to start dripping, it felt as if bugs were crawling all over me. Everyone in the laundry carried hankies to mop themselves up when they got too wet. Our supervisor said she didn't want us dripping sweat on clean clothes. She said that would defeat the purpose.

The steam and heat combined took my breath away. I had to fight to get it back by inhaling as if I were diving underwater to the bottom of the deep end of a pool. I watched my waist expand and contract. I didn't like to breathe through my mouth in the laundry room because it made my throat so dry. I tried it once. It felt like a cotton ball was stuck down there and I couldn't swallow it. No matter how much water I drank, the cotton ball came back.

Just as I managed to suck in another breath, I saw something strange happen. The color of the water that a load of sheets was washing in turned from a sudsy white to red. Pure red.

"Did you see that," I asked my shaking partner, Pina, short for Giuseppina.

"What?"

"What just happened to the sheets in the washer?"

Pina said she couldn't see that far. I pointed to show her but by then a cloud of steam had covered the washer.

"They turned red."

Pina reached into the bin between us and grabbed another sheet. I had to follow or else I'd leave her waiting with her back hunched over. I wanted to glance back at the washer but had to focus on picking up the same sheet Pina did, which wasn't easy since they all looked alike.

"The color of blood," I said, thinking about the washer. We were used to dirty sheets with blood or urine, hair clinging on them and the smell of someone's breath or body odor or disease. But never would it be enough to change the color of the water like that.

I could tell by the way Pina was shaking that she wasn't in the mood to talk about something as serious as blood. Her husband, Gus, was sick on the third floor of the hospital, and that was serious enough. We shook the sheet hard enough so it opened and yet didn't jerk it out of one another's hands and fed it into the pressing machine so it was centered or else the sheet would crease. We had to be extra careful not to get our hands caught between the two giant rollers. I left Pina to her thoughts as we fed sheets into the press and pretended I was a lion tamer setting a crumb on the tongue of a hungry animal or a priest offering the host to nervous second graders who shut their mouths too soon on their First Communion even though they practiced for weeks with Necco wafers.

My mind kept wandering back to the sheets washing in blood. I knew that pretty soon they'd be wheeled over Pina and I to shake and I'd be afraid to touch them. I was never afraid of sheets before. When I was in fifth grade, my two best friends and I used to make our Halloween costume, a three-headed ghost. We went trick or treating for only a half hour before we ripped the sheet so much from stepping on it that we had to take it off and run back to my girlfriend's to put stockings over our heads so we could go back out and get more candy. Even then I didn't think of sheets as spooky. I changed my mind though. My mother got mad at me every time I stripped the sheets off my bed at home, but I didn't want to sleep between them after I saw what happened in the laundry room.

Sheets started out this wet ball of confusion in a bin, too much for one person to handle. It took two wills, four arms and 20 fingers to equal the force of a single wet sheet. It was Pina and I against dead weight before we opened it up. We shook it back to life, out of its fetal ball so it could spread itself out, a pioneer in search of territory for its four corners to cover. A sheet was almost invisible when it took the shape of the surface it covered, like on a bed, so it could sneak up on you because you've forgotten it was there. Until the middle of the night when you tugged at the sheet—your body went one way and it went another. You figured out that even though the sheet took the shape of your body, it had a will of its own.

I was sure the sheets wheeled over beside the others were the ones that changed color in the washer, but it was break time. Pina unwrapped the cloth around her forehead and the strips around her wrists, wrung them out at the fountain and rinsed them in cold water. She practically took a sponge bath. She washed her face, neck, chest, arms and stomach with a washcloth before rinsing it in cold water again. I knew she was done when she set the washcloth on the back of her neck and then wrapped her forehead again. The last thing she did was open a thermos and fill her glass of water with ice.

Pina, who had brown curly hair which reminded me of an upside down bird's nest, was a lot faster than I was even though she was almost three times my age. But I got so used to her and couldn't imagine shaking sheets with anyone else. When she picked up her glass and squeezed in some lemon juice, I let go of the sheet in my hand and said to her, "I bet you if you added sugar to that you'd have lemonade."

She looked at me and saw I was thinking hard about what I just said. "How else do you think lemonade is made?"

"I don't know. I never thought about it before."

"Didn't your mother ever make you fresh squeezed lemonade on a hot day like today?"

"No," I said. "She buys Lemon Blend. The same kind they sell at the swimming pool snack bar."

"No, *limonata. Limonata.*"

Pina reached over to her pocketbook and pulled out a packet of sugar. She poured it in the glass, squeezed the rest of the lemon and stirred quickly.

"Take a sip," she said handing it to me.

"It tastes like real lemons."

"Now you know."

I took another sip of lemonade and sloshed the sweet and sour juice in my mouth as long as I could, wondering what else I didn't know because I didn't take the time to think. Some things I'd never figure out no matter how hard I thought about them, like the sheets. They were white and then red.

Pina said she didn't have a lemon tree growing in her backyard but she had almost everything else. She and her husband, Gus, were gardeners. Since he was in the hospital, she didn't have time to keep up with the weeds. She said her whole backyard was a garden and mapped it out for me. On one end was Swiss chard, beets, broccoli and eggplant. On another, pole beans and basil and fig trees. In the middle were all Roma tomatoes and hot pepper plants. Pina said her fruit cellar was full of canned goods Gus made. They didn't have children, she said, so he always had time for his fruits and vegetables. But she didn't expect Gus'd be able to do that anymore. Pina told me they had to amputate his leg. He was a diabetic now and had to get insulin shots every day.

We shook extra fast because Pina wanted to get through a bin early so she could have more time to see Gus during her break. After lunch, we'd be ready for the bin with the sheets washed in red water. Pena brought out a jar of Gus' peppers. She forked a slab and spread it on a piece of bread the way you do jelly.

"Try some."

I already bit into my banana and peanut butter and was the kind of eater who had to finish one thing before I could move on to something else.

"Thanks. Maybe when I'm finished."

"You never finish anything you eat. You always leave something behind. We could feed the birds on that crust of yours."

"I get full."

"What's one more bite? You don't know what you're missing." Pina closed the lid of the jar.

"Aren't you going to bring Gus some?"

"He doesn't want food. He wants clean sheets. He's always complaining they don't change his sheets often enough. I said to him, 'Gus, we're shaking them as fast as we can. We don't have a motor up our hind end.' He don't care. He wants his sheets changed. He says the nurse's aides don't like changing them. They have to lift him up off the bed and then put him back on it again. He says the next time they'll change the sheets under him is when he dies and the'll have to clear him and his sheets away to make room for somebody else. Then they'll put on clean sheets."

"What's going to happen when he dies?"

"God will forgive Gus for his sins."

"Then what?"

"He'll go where all good Catholics go."

"Where, Pina?"

"You're Catholic."

"Yeah."

"You went to Sunday school then."

"The nuns always played scratchy old records. They skip a lot."

"Then you tell me where," Pina said.

"I want to believe the church. But sometimes I think it doesn't know for sure where either."

"God forbid. You come this close to death, you believe," she said.

"My grandma is the most religious person there is. In all of West Tarentum, at least. Let me tell you in every single coat pocket of hers, she has at least one rosary, two holy cards and a safety pin with a string of holy medals. Even a scapular is folded up in there. It looks so old and worn, it could be the same one from her confirmation. Kleenex is stuffed in there too. But you know what else she puts inside? As if all that religious paraphernalia isn't enough, she throws in a buckeye."

"That's just for good luck. They fall off the trees. Can't eat them, even though they look just like a chestnut," Pina said.

"It's more than luck, Pina. I know. My grandma gave me a buck-eye. I lie awake in my bed in the middle of the night, and I rub it on its smooth side. And count enough layers of brown until it stays with me."

"You might as well be praying."

"I hold it in my hand and wish on it and believe something can happen. I keep it under my pillow for when I need to feel it through the fluff, for when I need to feel something solid."

"I don't know what you believe, but it better be something," Pina said.

I got up and walked over to the cart filled with clean sheets and picked up the whitest pair I could find when nobody was looking. I handed them to Pena.

"You're going to get fired if they see you doing that."

"No, I won't. Give them to Gus. When they're dirty, I'll get more."

Pina was about to finish the last bite of her pepper sandwich when our supervisor approached us.

"Your husband would like you to be with him, Pina."

"Pina stood up and hurried out the door so fast, the washcloth around her neck fell off. I ran after her with the set of sheets.

When I returned to the laundry room, I asked my supervisor if Gus was okay.

"I don't know. That's all they told me. When lunch is over, you'll be working with Bonita from now on."

"Isn't Pina coming back," I asked.

"We'll see. Go slow with Bonita today. She's not feeling well. She's got a bad stomachache. The heat's getting to her."

Bonita walked over to the sheet press and waited for me. I looked down at the last bite of Gus' peppers and was ready to throw it out then ate it without thinking. It was juicy and tender enough to just melt in my mouth, but I chewed it slowly so many times I lost count. I didn't have to swallow. It was gone.

I approached Bonita. Even though I watched her everyday at the dryers, I had no idea what it'd be like to shake sheets with her. She seemed my age. I knew that didn't mean she could shake as fast as Pina. I couldn't.

"I never did this before," she said.

"I'll show you." I knew I wasn't going to be at my best since I was worried about Pina. And wondering about the bin of sheets we were about to shake.

"It's nothing like what I do in the dryers."

"Pina had to show me when I first started."

"You and her together look like one person doing it. I watch you."

"Her husband's real sick. I don't know when she's coming back."

"That's what they say."

"She's with him now."

"Sure she is. Every woman wants to be at her man's side when he's in that condition," Bonita said.

"I'll go slow because it's your first time. And you're not feeling well."

"Don't you worry about me."

Since Bonita was closer to the washers than I was, I asked her if she saw the bloody water.

"You mean the stains? I see my share of those."

"No. The whole sheet. And the water was red too."

"Nothing like that." Bonita held onto her stomach as we reached into the bin. The sheets all looked white.

"My friends think sheets are boring because you shake the same ones over and over again," I said, wondering if the next one in the bin would be different.

"I don't think they're boring. No more boring than pajamas."

I told Bonita what I wanted to tell my friends but didn't. "You know what I think? A sheet is everything to someone stuck in a hospital bed. Their world is flat. And square. Beyond that sheet is just atmosphere. A place they can't reach so it might as well be outer space. Besides, they're afraid of falling off. That's why doctors and nurses push patients smack in the center every time and then put the metal bars up. That's why a sheet wears out first in the middle because they all rest in the same spot, no matter who they are. Everybody's afraid of falling off.

"You know your sheets," Bonita told me.

"Pina's the best shaker here. She can shake and talk at the same time when she wants to. Doesn't slow her down like it does us."

"How does she do that?" Bonita asked, struggling to reach another sheet. I moved slower than usual too, thinking each sheet was the one I saw in the washer.

"One day she told me everything about how she and Gus got married from the time they met to the time they marched up the aisle. She said his family knew hers and paired them up. Arranged for them both to go shopping down the Strip District on the same train from Tarentum if you can imagine. They didn't actually talk to each other until they got to Benkovitz's to buy fresh fish. She said they found they had a lot in common. They both thought Benskovitz's crab cakes put Isaly's to shame, even if Isaly's was just down the street. Isaly's was mostly bread crumbs and Benkovitz's was mostly crab. That was the difference. They both thought Isaly's made the best ham barbecues though and the best Klondikes too. Better than Eskimo Pies any day of the week."

Bonita said she had a boyfriend. I figured I didn't know him because she went to Valley and I went to Highlands. We were rivals in basketball, so fights always broke out in the parking lot after the game. It turned out she was good friends with a classmate of mine and started going out with her brother. She said her friend was Darlene Guffy.

"I know her. She has a brother who's a junk collector."

"That's him."

"He's not in school anymore, is he?"

"He quit that. He's in business now," Bonita said.

"I see him peddling up steep hills with scrap metal in his basket. I don't know how he does it on a coaster bike. He must be in some kind of shape."

Bonita smiled. "He wears me out."

"What do you mean?" I guessed the answer but wanted to hear Bonita say it.

"You know. Doing it. He wants to marry me as soon as we make enough money."

The next time Bonita bent over it looked like she was about to vomit. I walked over to her but she stopped me. "Please. I don't want my supervisor to send me home. I need the money."

A new load was taken out of the washers and made the place real steamy again. I went to the fountain and got Bonita a drink of water. The laundry reached 110 degrees. No wonder it felt so hot. I grabbed some clean hankies for us too. If Pina were here, I thought, she'd rinse her washcloth in cold water and take a quick sponge bath.

Bonita stood with one hand leaning on the bin and one hand on her belly. Each time we reached down for the sheets, she was hurting so I told her all she had to do was hold it while I shook it. I shook extra hard so it opened her side. Otherwise it would go into the feeder all wrinkled and be a reject. The sheet slipped out of Bonita's hand and opened up into the air, floating above our heads. I was ready to stop it coming down on us because I knew it had to be the sheet that had changed color in the washer. I felt something wet and saw the sheet already had covered Bonita. I pulled it back and there was a man with gray hair, wearing pajamas and a tube in his nose. He only had one leg. It was Gus.

He was lying in bed with his eyes not quite closed because his top and bottom eyelashes didn't quite touch. Pina was right by his side. She held onto his hand tight like he was a child crossing a busy street. He grabbed at the sheet with his other hand, crumpling it in his fist. He kept telling Pina it was time for nurses to change the sheets. Call the nurses to make his bed over again. Pina told him not to worry. They'd come when he was ready. She watched as he slowly let go of his hold on the white cotton but not her hand. She tried to hold his other hand too, but it was already frozen in time, so she covered the hand that already held hers. They rested like that for a long time before Pina pulled the sheet over Gus, making all the imprints of his body disappear like a fossil buried in the sand. You couldn't even tell he only had one leg. She could pretend that underneath he was the man she met at Benkovitz's.

A nurse came in to change the bed, and when she pulled the top sheet down, Bonita was lying there instead of Gus. They were the same sheets because I saw the place where Gus had wrinkled it with his fist was not over Bonita's stomach. Guffy was sitting in the chair instead of Pina, holding a baby barely big enough for two hands. Guffy, who was usually covered with soot, was all clean and even had his hair parted down the middle for the occasion. The nurse changed the sheets when Bonita got up to go to the bathroom. She brushed it a few times and patted the pillow before Bonita climbed back in.

I reached to pull the sheet down. Bonita was back in her work clothes, holding her stomach. "This is the sheet you're going to have your baby on," I said.

"What baby?"

"You're going to have a baby."

"How do you know something like that when I don't even know?"

"It's the same sheet Gus died in."

"What's wrong with you, girl? The heat must be getting the best of you today."

She kept looking at me as we struggled to shake the next sheet. With each one, we got a little further behind until another bin full of clean sheets from the washer was wheeled over to us just as a new batch of dirty ones from the wards arrived, waiting to go through the cycle.

SEAN THOMAS DOUGHERTY

The Sweeper

> *the one who sweats, the one who passes by, the one who shakes*
> *his self within my soul*
>
> -Cesar Vallejo

1

Into the warehouse you go,
wiping the sawdust from your eyes,
lifting the largest barrel
a man has ever tried to shift
to his shoulder. What was the name
of the guard who marked
down your time at the gate,
who argued the picture of you
was not you? Who was his father,
his mother? What did they say
that drove him to point his finger
the way a soldier is trained
to point a gun?

2

You try to gather yourself, your shirt
at the waist to wipe your face,
to rub your eyes full of sawdust
and tears, tiny oceans and trees,
to forget the years spent sweeping
the oil stained floors, sweeping
around the machines, sweeping around
the boots of workers leaning on boxes.

3

That evening your wife waits for you,
as always, in the kitchen, a dish
rag around her hair striped
with grey, setting the table,
the fork beside the plate. What does
she love besides you? What do you love
besides her?

4

When does the moon behind the clouds
resemble a horse before it storms,
before the tiny hands of the leaves
are applause, the garbage cans
drumming a beat like the beat
of a cop's feet, thunder a nightstick
against the hood of stolen car?

5

The noise shakes the sleep from your brain;
you look at your wife, at the alarm clock
staring 2:14 A.M. Have you dreamed
it was morning, have you dreamed
you were sleeping, have you dreamed
you were dead?

6

Beyond your window
the rain and thunder
are gone,
the stars are beginning
to speckle the sky
like a handful of sawdust
God has scattered across the night.

Tiny Griefs

1

Mist
  ghosting over the peaks
    of West Virginia.

2

Into the coal-mining dawn,
  I stumbled bleary-eyed
    from cheap Motels

to roadside diners: toast, grits,
  eggs asked, *how-you-want-em,*
    honey? By the waitresses

named Bobbie, Anne-Louise, or Mabel,
  as miners lifted stark, white cups
    with dust, darkened hands.

3

What to say of hope
  I wondered that first week
    in towns where no one worked,

or mined the earth for ore?
  I spoke *teacher* to those men
    who asked in every bar;

they understood
  I saw their children
    running in their eyes,

& more than once they offered,
  "Have a beer on me then, friend."
    Before walking away, quietly,

into the safe talk of the mines.

4

In the schools
  I saw those men
    in the face

of every child,
  and still I sometimes dream
    of that tiny third grade girl

who lifted her head
  to drawl so softly
    I almost couldn't hear,

"This is a poem for my daddy
cause I loved him.'
(then she cleared her throat)
'His skin was dust

when he came home.
He never hugged me

before he washed his hands.
The bible says I know

that when we die
we go to dust.'

(she looked right up at me)
It makes me think of him."

Then she gave a little bow.
    I reached to touch her palm,
        and she shook my hand.

                5
That evening I drove
    toward another dying town;
        the glare of headlights

caught the rain
    of insects
        against the glass

like tiny griefs
    we seldom feel.
        My hands,

still shaking,
    gripped
        the wheel.

THOMAS G. FAIRBAIRN

Welcome to the Pit

Mounds of shot slid off the steel beams coming through the blaster, and had to be shoveled off the floor and back onto the conveyor belt. The shovel was a crude instrument. Nothing more, really, than a four-foot length of inch round bar for a handle, welded to a square piece of steel flat plate for a blade.

The jagged spurs on the unfinished handle ripped through his work gloves and dug into the soft flesh of his hands.

To think that less than a year ago, he had stood in the center of Lauren's gallery, and bragged; "I've never actually worked with my hands. Done physical labor, I mean."

Lauren was having a party to celebrate the opening of her new show, a series of thirty-five portraits called *Working Men*. It bugged him, this mythologizing. His father had been a working man, earned his living with his hands. There was nothing noble, in Andy's eyes, about the subject. He blurted out his statement, feeling an urge to distance himself from the characters in her paintings.

He remembered, as a boy, living in the tiny, two-room house beside the tracks. At night, the house rattled from the thud-thudding of trains bounding over the steel rails. In late fall, before the snow came, his mother would take burlap potato sacks and walk down the tracks, collecting the pieces of coal that had fallen off the boxcars rumbling by in the night.

"That shot ain't gonna crawl up on the conveyor belt by itself!"

He'd end up in the pit! Dan, the foreman, hated to catch anyone standing around. He caught you standing around, you had two choices: walk down the road, or clean the pit.

Two men, working either side of him, worked silently, without complaint. Neither wore gloves. Stern faces, concentrated, intense on the rhythm: shove, lift, throw. Swish, scrape, shwoosh!

"Damn!" Andy screamed, jabbing his thumb on one of the metal spurs.

There were two steel wide beams, fifty-footers, rolling out of the blaster.

Swish, scrape, shwoosh!

Andy threw down his shovel, pulled the lever to stop the conveyor belt, and jumped up to sweep the shot off the beams.

"Get those things off there!" Dan hollered. "They gotta be taped and prepped. Morons!"

The guy shoveling to his left, broke his rhythm reluctantly, threw his shovel down, and grabbed the control box for the ceiling hoist as if it were the head of a thrashing snake. He stabbed with his thumbs at the eyes of the beast, the control buttons; and the two, beak-like hooks of the hoist, dangling from inch-thick, braided steel chains approached the two wide beams in frenzied thrusts, jumping and jerking violently.

Andy danced along the rollers of the conveyor belt and grabbed the hoist chains and held them steady. He had watched this done, and he was a quick study. Holding the chains in his left hand, he motioned with his right, arm extended, hand stiff, and fingers waving downward. The hook came down too fast and over shot its mark. There was no safety on the hoist to stop it automatically when the grappling hook hit anything solid, so it banged down onto the steel beam and the chain followed, unraveling with a clamorous din that would have disturbed the dead—if that were still possible.

Dan, face coloring with anger, grabbed the control box out of the befuddled operator's grasp and repeatedly punched the Stop button.

Andy hopped off the conveyor belt, and took the hoist control box from the foreman. "I got it," he said, patting Dan on the shoulder, and yanking on the hoist chains to move out of the foreman's reach.

The control box had eight buttons in two rows. At one time, they had been marked North, South, East, West, Up, Down, Stop, and Off, from top to bottom, left to right. The whole unit, box included, however, had been coated so many times with primer and paint overspray that only the vague outlines of the buttons themselves remained visible. Andy had tried to watch the operator's hands and memorize the directions, but it was clear that being able to manipulate the hoist was an advantage, and this was job-protection information. The operator invariably found some reason to turn his back so that you could not see which buttons were being pushed.

Andy found a small platform, the top of a bin used for storing barrels of nuts and bolts, that gave him an overhead view of the operator. It had taken him less than ten minutes to memorize the button positions.

This, however, was the first time he had actually used the controls. Top right, South: the hoist moved over the outside fifty-footer on the conveyor belt. Third button, left: the chains uncoiled smoothly, the hooks moving upward. With plenty of chain still hanging, Andy hit Stop, and moved in to wrap the chains around both beams. Growing more sure of himself, he remembered to bring the first hook over and catch it on its own chain, so that it would choke itself as the hoist moved upward. He brought the second hook and chain under and over, in the opposite direction of the first. He did this with one hand, moving smoothly, the other hand, holding the control box, jammed and held fast up against his hip, his thumb jabbing, making small adjustments: Up...North. Need a little slack...Down!

Dancing now, Andy shook off the leather work gloves, cupped the control box in both hands, and, jabbing with this thumbs, lifted, moved south, and then east, smoothly, no jerking, the two fifty-foot steel wide beams off the conveyor belt and down onto the triangular stands on the first paint bay. Foot-square flanges stuck out on one end of the steel beams preventing them from lying flat, so Andy hit the Up button on the control box and lifted the beams high enough in the air to swing them around. Still holding the box in his left hand, he grabbed the beam with his right and pushed hard enough to cause the beams to swing smoothly end for end.

He lowered the beams back down onto the paint bay and, without looking at the foreman, left the box dangling in the air and half-ran back to his shovel and began scooping up the shot and throwing it back onto the blaster conveyor belt. Shwish, scrape, shwoosh! Shwish, scrape, shwoosh! An ancient rhythm. Shwish, scrape, shwoosh!

Underneath the noise, Andy half-whispered, half-prayed: *Not the pit, Dear Lord. Not the pit!*

Shwish, scrape, shwoosh!

The five or six people standing around Lauren turned with raised eyebrows to catch her response to Andy's attempt to distance himself from the pathetic, suffering figures in her drawings.Everyone who knew the two of them had predicted the break; maybe this was it. Lauren's wrath was legendary, and the crowd waited like children expecting fireworks.

"But Dahlin' Andy," Lauren trilled, waving her long, artist's fingers through the air as if she were working another canvas. "You are misaligned. Look at your hands. You were bred to work in the mills, the factories, on the bridges and roads that stretch across this land. Your blood was meant to mingle with the rust and iron and steel-meshed infrastructure of this great sprawling industrial junk yard we all know and love!"

The group following her, spontaneously breaking into a chorus of *America the Beautiful*!

Lauren reached back for Andy, tugging on his coat sleeve. "Look at them. Do you not feel some inner affinity?"

Andy resisted her tugging, shaking his head. Lauren led the group away from him along the back wall of the gallery, stopping before each painting and continuing her working-man monologue.

"Here! This man, pulling on that chain to free that man's half-severed leg from under the concrete block. Why, in the fourteenth or fifteenth century, that man's great, great, great, grandfather probably was his Lord's overseer and lived off the harvest of others; probably had his own horse! Now it would be mythologizing (and she said this loud enough for Andy to hear) to pretend that this man, the overseer's progeny, would be anything more, in our century, than a foreman on a road construction gang."

Moving onto the next painting in the series, Lauren turned back to see Andy heading for the side exit. Waving her mocking hand in dismissal, she shouted, "Four hundred years and they exchange their horses for Hondas!"

"I demythologize," she shouted at Andy's back.

Shwish, scrape, shwoosh....

Andy stuck the crowbar into the slots of the metal grate and lifted the cover off the stairwell leading down into the pit. His little show in front of the foreman had not gone over well with the rest of the men in the paint shop. It had made them fearful and hostile. Who the hell did he think he was, anyway? He read the fear in their eyes: *After my fucking job!* they were thinking. The fear transformed to triumph when the foreman told Andy in the break room in front of them all that he could spend the afternoon cleaning the pit.

The steel that rolled through the blaster was cleaned with minuscule, metal ball bearings that were shot out of a forced-air compressor. The wide-flange beams, having sat out in the open yard, went to the back end of the blaster brown and rusted and rolled out in the paint bay shining silver and white. The shot hit the beams so hard, it left a splattered salt-and-pepper pattern on the surface of the naked steel.

The blaster had to be turned on when the pit was cleaned so that the conveyor belt would be rolling to carry the shot back into the sprayer.

Andy went down the metal stairwell to the first level of the pit and began to shovel. Shwish, scrape, shwoosh!

He ran and hid between the back of the coal stove and the wall, a small space that everyone pretended to overlook when searching for him.

Shwish, scrape, shwoosh.

Using a shortened version of the shovel used up top, he shoveled the metal shot into a five-gallon pail, then carried the pail and dumped it into a bin at the back of the pit, where the conveyor belt continued its circular loop and took the shot back into the sprayer. He took ten pails of shot out of the first level.

On the second level, the bottom of the blaster bulged downward to house the gears and compressors. It was a crude aluminum, makeshift housing and, as Andy bent over to scoop up the shot with his half-shovel, he was pelted with the shot coming right out of the bottom and sides of the blaster. It felt like being stung by a swarm of yellow jackets.

Bending, he swept up the shot into little piles, little black mounds of oil-stained sand... Shwish, scrape, shwoosh!

The gallery rocked with laughter as Lauren's Honda remark made the rounds, and Andy slipped out the side entrance of the gallery. He made his way along the graveled walkway that led down to the ocean and walked aimlessly along the beach. The tide had just gone out, and Andy walked along, kicking at the rippled mounds of wet sand that the tide had left in its wake.

Misaligned. That is what Laurel had said. *Was he?*

He stopped kicking at the beach sand, and turned toward the ocean. He turned his hands palms upward, and stared at them. They did not seem to be attached.

Why had he hid between the back of the stove and the wall? What had his hands to do with it?

That had been on Sunday. On Monday, without telling anyone, without saying goodbye, without even quitting his job, he drove to the airport, left his HOnda in a no-parking zone, with the keys still in it, and boarded the first available flight for the east coast. Since that time, he had lived in cheap hotels and rooming houses, taking on menial labor jobs or factory line jobs to survive.

He never went near his bank, and he refused any construction work if the site was on a university campus.

He began to have vivid dreams, in color, that he remembered on waking; he was able to sit down and read tediously long and wonderful theories; and lately, staring into the mirror, shaving, he had noticed a smile tugging at the corners of his mouth. In the middle of the night, he would wake up and touch, with wonder and delight, the wet tears at the corners of his eyes.

He dreamed of those days walking down the railroad tracks with his mother and his two brothers picking up pieces of coal from the railroad bed. He read long and boring books about the industrial revolution, the labor movement, the migration of industry toward the nearest, cheapest labor source, the rise of the white-collar worker, the death of unions. Showering, he would remember his rail-walking competitions with his brother, the happy tranquility it brought. Best in bare feet in the hot summer sun. How his brother loved to win, Andy remembered, smiling, while soaping his armpits. In the middle of the night, he would wake up startled and, staring into the darkness, he would see his father strapped to the white hospital bed, his limbs crudely organized and held together with plastic tubes, invisible wires, and gossamer mesh netting.

Shwish, scrape, shwoosh!

His hands ached with the work and, at night, tingled with memories. The harder he worked, the more he dreamed, suffered time, laughed at himself, cried for others.

Shwish, scrape, shwoosh!

Hands bleeding, his hair matted and full of metal shot, Andy climbed down into the third and last level of the pit. It was a cavern about four-and-a-half feet high, so that he had to hunch down to work. One naked light bulb flared and sparked as it swung on its blackened and frayed cord. On his hands and knees, working now with a wire brush, Andy swept the shot up into little piles and, with a dustbin, scooped them into a small pail.

Shwish, scrape, shwoosh!

His father was in the living room in a brown box. They had wanted Andy to kiss his shrunken, glassy face. "Like this," his mother said, lifting two fingers to her own lips, kissing, and placing her fingers on the orange lips they had sewn onto his father's face. Andy refused! His mother had taken his hand, forcing. The lips felt like wet paper.

He squeezed into his space between the coal stove and the wall and, after an hour or two of trying to coax him out, they gave up and pretended not to know where he was.

Sometimes, they forgot to censor themselves.

"The bastards killed him!" his Uncle Rolly said over and over. "The bastards killed him!"

Andy pressed the two fingers that had touched his dead father's lips against the hot back plate of the stove, thinking to burn off the memory.

Shwish, scrape, shwoosh!

It seemed to Andy that he came out from behind the coal stove and never did look at his father in his coffin, and never did say goodbye, and never did sympathize or try to understand anything, but went from small space to small space...any safe place where they would not be able to get at his hands, force him to reach out, touch something!

Shwish, scrape, shwoosh!

On his eleventh pail, he stood up too suddenly and hit his head on the bottom of the gear housing.

The white glare of the swinging light bulb blinded him. He turned away from the glaring white light.

Hanging on the wall directly in front of him, bathed in the softer light that came over his hunched shoulders, was the first portrait in Lauren's show.

One man, muscles bulging, pulled on a steel-linked chain. On his back, a second man squirmed in pain. One leg went off at an impossible angle, and the other disappeared, just below the knee, under the edge of a giant slab of cement. The man's mouth was open, as if screaming.

Andy could hear the man's scream echoing in the pit.

Andy swung to his left. There was the next portrait. He shuffled around the cavern, hunched over, sliding sideways like a crab, keeping his back toward the glaring bulb to diffuse the light, and staring intensely at each portrait.

Glaring at the third painting in the series, he staggered backwards, actually feeling the shock of it: she had used his face, his hands in the paintings!

When he came to, he was on his back staring directly up into the white light blazing from the swaying naked light bulb. Not sure how badly he had hurt himself, he raised his arms slowly, tentatively. There was no pain and, at the ends of his arms, his hands seemed well-formed and harmonious. They seemed entirely connected.

ROBERT FOX

Searching for My Father: A Working Man's Life

Throughout my adolescence, as I grew away from home, I occasionally encountered my mother or father far from our apartment. These random meetings anticipated my adulthood, how we would relate to one another cordially from a respectful distance.

Though my father was home nights and weekends during my childhood, he remained distant, aloof, his past something of a mystery. Unlike my mother, whose angers and joys were immediate, whose history, frustrations and hopes were laid out on the kitchen table like her rich meals, my father's life remained unspoken, elusive.

When I found him alone on the subway, I felt as if I'd been searching for years. In an unexpected moment away from home, away from my verbal mother, clues about his identity might emerge, windows into the 42 years of his life prior to my birth. He was seated, having boarded in midtown Manhattan, and he glanced about at other passengers, sketching their faces in the margins of his newspaper. When his glance found mine it stopped. I wondered if he felt caught, disappointed that his brief creative privacy was disrupted. However, he welcomed me, creating a seat with the cooperation of other passengers. I squeezed in and persuaded him to resume sketching, trying to guess the subjects of his caricatures without appearing conspicuous. I contemplated the chances of finding him among hundreds of commuters, a recapitulation of the genetic mystery that made us father and son, that bound us through random biology.

We got off at the Utica Avenue station and walked past the white-pillared homes and expensive apartments on Eastern Parkway. He worried about my future. I dismissed the apparent confusion of my late adolescence, declaring my distance from the troubled children my parents compared me to because I knew what I wanted. My self-confidence and determination as an artist, qualities Dad may have lacked or not been permitted to explore, seemed enough to satisfy him.

He was uncomfortable discussing my future, as if he agreed that his life was not a relevant example. I took his silence as a tacit wish for me to create my own life, fulfill all that he couldn't. I felt that he was a secret ally against all obstacles, including my mother, who while not a philistine, read the biographies of Van Gogh and Beethoven and concluded all artists were crazy. She wanted to spare me from eventual madness, but also feared I might already be crazy—a genetic defect I inherited from my father's side of the family.

Dad accepted the gap in our experience as more than generational. My mother disagreed. She universalized her own desperate childhood. To her, Europe was a cesspool of wars, poverty and persecution that culminated in the Holocaust. America truly offered hope. I would not be here, she argued, if she and my father hadn't fled. She was not amused by my smart response that they lived too far apart to have met in Russia anyhow. She raged that I knew nothing of starvation and war and didn't appreciate the material bounty of the postwar boom.

In my own way, I coveted and then rejected the American Dream. For a while I wanted nothing more than a ranch home in the suburbs, a light-haired wife named June or Linda, boys who played Little League ball, a dog, and a model railroad in the basement. Like my brothers, I was embarrassed by my parents' accents, their lapses into Yiddish when they couldn't find the right words. Unlike my brothers, I experienced a prosperity they never knew as children. They systematically wrecked my new toys and I made do, just as they had settled for the amputated soldiers and wheel-less trucks passed on by neighbors and cousins. As we grew older and they held me captive to Bach and Bizet, I rejected their idea of culture as an acquisition. I discovered a life in the imagination and dreamt beyond material security. In my teens I gave up my Disney-movie ideal of a suburban future for the life of literature and country blues. At the very time I should have been plotting a profession, I was being impractical. Attending to spiritual needs was what poet Menke Katz called true practicality. "It's like when you're on line at the supermarket and it comes your next," he told me with boyish enthusiasm. "It's your next to live."

The closer Dad and I got to home, the quieter our conversation became. Although I hadn't chosen him, it was enough that he cared—despite his difficulty articulating his concerns. It was okay for me to walk side by side with this proud, handsome man who happened to be my father. I knew such moments would not be repeated often. If I was going to pursue art I would have to do so away from the small apartment I had lived in since birth. It was my next.

I left home and its surfeit of static comfort, and while exploring the San Francisco Bay area, my parents died in an arson fire at a Catskills hotel. It was reported that Dad was a hero, returning to the burning building to rescue much older guests before the roof came down. It was typical of him not to think of himself first.

Once, when I admired a new button-down Oxford shirt he wore for the first time, he took it off, despite my protests, and gave it to me. I no longer have that shirt but have other odds and ends: a handmade Italian mandolin, a small bent pipe which I smoked for years, two EverReady shaving brushes, a can of Mennen talc. There are other things I recall: his handball gloves and black ball kept in a kitchen drawer; his helmet, gas mask and police whistle from service as an air raid warden during the war. These unrelated bits of paraphernalia are dots of a puzzle that don't make a complete picture. I wonder how he saw himself.

Had you seen my father walking home from the subway, you might have thought him a civil servant, like a neighbor of ours who worked as a clerk for the city. Dad dressed for work in sports jacket and tie, topcoat and fedora in the cooler weather. Once at the shop he changed into old clothes, stripped down to an undershirt in the summer, for he operated a steam iron in factories that made ladies' dresses. He changed back into street clothes for the trip home. How unlike middle America, I later discovered, where the workingman identifies himself by a "uniform," cotton twill shirt and matching pants of gray, blue, or dark green, with a name embroidered on the chest.

Pressing was a trade Dad learned while attending Washington Irving High School in the evenings. The diploma earned him respect but never enhanced his income. Colleagues described him as an "educated" man because he read. Diplomas and skills meant little when there were few jobs. Dad pointed out neighborhood letter carriers with college degrees. They were an envied elite, having found a lifetime of security during the Depression.

My parents married the week of the stock market crash. My father had saved $900, to be used for a downpayment for a house. When the run on the banks began he asked his local teller if the money was safe. A man of his word, Dad believed the teller's assurances. Next day the banks closed. My parents fell on hard times. There were weeks of nothing but boiled potatoes. They accepted relief from the State of New York, a welfare program initiated by Governor Franklin D. Roosevelt. My mother was humiliated.

Those who did not witness or experience the Great Depression find it difficult to comprehend the vastness of the poverty, how close this country came to revolution, a true revolt of the poor, the dispossessed. The devastation was so widespread, so profound, many saw it as the death of capitalism.

Dad fought for unionization of the dress trade. He struck, battled scabs on the picket lines, was thrown in jail. When not fighting scabs he and his colleagues combed the streets returning furniture of the evicted to their homes. Sheriffs and goons soon returned, billy clubs raised. My mother consulted zombie-like penny fortune tellers in Coney Island arcades whose tickets promised romance and riches, and she wondered why Dad couldn't be like the husband of a girl she had crossed the ocean with, a furrier who owned their small apartment building.

Twenty years later, during the prosperity of the mid-1950s, my father made decent money, about $100 a week when he had a steady shop, working a half day on Saturdays. He was still paid by the piece. It was a seasonal trade, too. Shops frequently folded or changed hands. Often he was back in the union hall looking for work.

One summer Saturday when I was 11, my mother was unable to accompany us to the beach. Dad was a self-taught swimmer, doing a powerful combination of breast stroke and frog kick. He disappeared beyond the jetties, and when I was sure he was a victim of undertow, cramps or sharks, he reappeared, a gray and wizened sea god ready for the challenge of land. We left the beach early to visit his current shop in Coney Island. We strolled along the boardwalk, past the smells of caramel corn, cotton candy, hot dogs, towards the still operating parachute jump and the defunct Steeplechase park, past a clam bar where the Oklahoma Kid, a cowboy-suited man with loose dentures, strummed a guitar and sang about drinking and losing to a sparse gathering hunched over dime draft in the dark. We arrived at a shabby warehouse building close to the boardwalk.

Inside, paint peeled from the walls and I could smell the sour odor of steam though the presses were cold. Even with the tall windows open to the ocean breeze and the fans running, Dad said it was still hot as hell in there. He tried to instill in me a sense of his demeaning working life, nasty foremen, vindictive colleagues. "Do well in school like your brothers and become a professional. Not a slave like me."

"I am doing well in school," I said, shrugging my shoulders. I looked out the window at an empty lot, the perfect size for a Little League diamond. I pictured myself drilling line drives over the fences. Neither of my brothers took such interest in things American. One was a Francophile, the other became a Zionist.

On occasion Dad found work in a building with elevators. Air conditioning hadn't come to many shops and when it did, the pressers' steamy work wasn't alleviated. Still, he wished he could end his working days in an air conditioned shop in a building with an elevator, in easy reach of the subway. Instead, his last shop was in a five-story walkup in Williamsburg, reached by changing buses on a circuitous route through downtown Brooklyn.

His boss, however, was a decent man broken-hearted about his only son, who couldn't stay out of jail. Dad described their conversations with a father's empathy, implying how easily and unwittingly a teenage boy might misstep. I was offended. Later, I came to understand that it was not a lack of trust when two high school friends of mine, talented young men with bright futures, died thousands of miles apart, overdosed on drugs.

How could my father, my ally, think I might go astray? What had I done, or what omniscient knowledge did he possess? Could it be true that beyond his apparent support for my enthusiasm there lay a vast cynicism? I gained some insight when I returned home late one night, describing to my mother how a folk music concert I produced in Brighton Beach was raided by the police. A raid to her conjured an image of police kicking in the doors, Tommy guns raised. She sent Dad to talk to me.

"So little of what I fought for in the thirties has come to pass," he said.

"You have a strong union," I said.

"Taken over by crooks. It was hardly worth it."

I explained that the concert was not political, though one of the performers wrote topical songs. A satirical promotional piece in the local paper upset some residents. A neighborhood once considered the hotbed of socialism now feared an invasion by two black men, one young singer/songwriter, and an old blind preacher who might set himself on fire with a coal from his cigarette.

How could Dad, who still maintained hope for the future of his homeland, be so cynical about his own past? Didn't he appreciate the benefits of the New Deal, the WPA? I knew my mother had put him up to it but I knew he wouldn't lie to me, either. I caught a glimpse of an abyss where he seemed unable to reconcile his ideals with reality. I later encountered adults of his generation who disowned their activism as the frivolity of youth. Dad's commitments ran too deep. I would never know the extent of his disillusionment, or if it could ever have been resolved.

When I turned 50, I sought pictures of my father at that age. I remember him at 49 growing a mustache that came in red. He let me watch him shave, trim his mustache, darken his silver hair with Darkay at my mother's insistence. Her hair remained jet black. In the pictures he looked so much older than me. I could never know the hardships he endured, what it was like to flee his home and learn the ways of a new country. I could never know the frustrations of his working day, his unfulfilled talents, what it was like to give up art school to stand long hours raising and lowering a steam iron.

Until late in my adolescence my parents were aliens to me though they won citizenship long before I was born. Their origins, reiterated in their taste for pickled herring, gefilte fish with horseradish, borscht with sourcream, spelled a distance between us greater than the ocean they crossed. I was an American, drawn to the sweet drawl of cowboys and baseball players. I was embarrassed that my parents said "kom" instead of "come," and that Dad could not teach me to swing a bat like the native born dads of my friends.

Before I ventured among the kids on my block, he was my weekend companion, taking me to Lincoln Terrace Park. He pitched and I swung a bat cross-handed for lack of correction, and ran imaginary bases in an invented order while he chased the ball. Once he strained an abdominal muscle and my mother thought it was a hernia. "If he has to miss work because of you..." She threatened tortures straight from the streets of the *shtetl.*

Once Dad brought my brother's basketball to the park. We went to the grass baseball field where he punted the ball with his head, caught its descent with his heel, passed it to his elbow, then back to his head, then to his knee. I was both awed and dismayed, the display of energy and agility unlike anything I had seen apart from the rubbery antics of baseball clown Al Shacht. Despite his dazzling skill it was foreign. I hoped none of my friends saw. "This is what they call football over there," he said. "Here, you try." It might as well have been a medicine ball he passed to me. I had as much use for soccer as I had for Yiddish.

Dad was raised in a *shtetl* near Kiev, where his parents owned a granary and general store. It was a rural area and he played in the woods among peasant farms. The family business included a stable. Except for pogroms, it was a sleepy rural village until World War I and the Russian Revolution. The stables were often commandeered by White Russian soldiers; gaily dressed Cossacks with drawn machetes terrorized Jews on the streets. My grandmother once talked her way to safety with a machete pointed to her throat. My uncle recalls a gunfight between Cossacks and soldiers, victims tumbling from windows and rooftops like a cowboy movie.

My grandfather and his brother survived a pogrom by hiding for a day in a pile of corpses. They led the emigration. The family fled a few at a time, traveling by night. My uncle, the youngest in the family, described crossing the Dnieppe River in a rowboat at night, escaping gunfire from Romanian soldiers as they headed to the Carpathian Mountains.

Dad was 19 when he arrived in this country, his name Kalman changed to Charles on Ellis Island, settling with his family in East New York, a once Irish East European enclave where he and my mother met. She was a shy, skinny girl, educated in a "mockey" class with other immigrants and the mentally and physically disabled. Her schooling ended with fifth grade.

She attributed my father's idealism, his inability to earn a decent living and provide for his family, to his older sister. Molly preached a messianic Marxism foretelling a second coming where the working brothers and sisters of the world would rise from their knees, holding hands in the sunset of capitalism.

She continued to view Stalin as a respected leader long after he signed the non-aggression pact with Hitler, and after Stalin's gulags became well-known. The regressive thinking of those who still believed in the Soviet future has a superficial counterpart in the religious fundamentalism of today's radical right, with its revisionist readings of the Constitution and the Bible. Both share the critical blindness of extreme Romanticism. While the Communists were armed with dreams of international brotherhood, right wing extremists stockpile assault weapons to protect their parochial visions of the American dream.

Dad and Molly's political naiveté was a form of nostalgia, a Romantic yearning for the Ukraine of their childhood incorporated into Mother Russia, symbolized by the large photograph of their mother hanging in Molly's bedroom. Grandma Sarah had a faint smile like the Mona Lisa and her portrait glowed like the Virgin. They sighed as they looked up at the picture, speaking in hushed tones about this wispy, white-haired saint who died of heart failure in her fifties, an old woman. My mother spoke reverently of her, having helped with laundry and ironing on weekends, "while her own lazy and vain daughters wouldn't lift a finger." Her picture evoked in my mind the green-handled spade Dad kept with his tools, with which he tended flowers at her grave.

Dad and I visited Molly's musty apartment on Saturday mornings on the way back from my piano lessons. Grandpa Joseph lived in a small bedroom hardly larger than his bed. Dusty stacks of books in Russian and Yiddish rose from the floor. The shafts of light slanting in around the drawn shades were palpable with dust. My mother once asked Molly why she never cleaned. "I should clean the landlord's property?" Molly replied indignantly. Though my mother was not a student of economics, she knew this was not what Marx had intended.

My grandfather, who survived pogroms, who in one family account, swam for the Czar, was a remote man whom my mother addressed as *shver*, father-in-law, rather than by name. I came along late in his life, barely within the periphery of his vision. My father was still a boy to him, whom he kibitzed for wearing reading glasses.

Grandpa's death came so far away it could have happened across the ocean in another time. The word stroke hung in front of me like a flash card. Did someone strike him? Had he been mugged on the street or the dim hallway of his building?

Dad's reaction challenged my sense of masculinity. Men weren't supposed to cry. Was he less of a man? Was this a weakness? Would I cry when he died? Would he live to be as old as his father? Would I be a father with my own family? Would my sons want to visit their elderly grandfather? The futility of my questions, like the meanings of eternity, infinity, the size of the universe, made me giddy. In private I would shiver with fear at how puny, temporal I was. In company my reaction was the opposite. "Stop laughing," my mother said. "Show some respect for your grandfather."

In my earliest recollections my father towered in his topcoat and fedora. I rushed to the door when he came home from work sweeping in the smell of winter and the cold air. When we walked together in spring, he lifted me to budding branches so I could observe the miracle of leaves poised to unfurl. When he set me down his face remained up in the swirl of the trees.

Though they were almost the same height, my mother seemed smaller. She bent to tell me to say thank you and to wipe ice cream from my face. She stooped to collect fall leaves, rediscovered years later pressed in wax paper in the pages of encyclopedias. We had several sets, purchased from young salesmen my mother pitied, concerned also for the education of her sons. Instead of well-used references, these complete and partial sets became time capsules of her boys' art, and tokens of fall days of years gone by. She was not one to reminisce—she had no good old days to mourn. Yet, she was sensitive to the fleeting nature of time, how quickly our lives pass. Dad complained about the money she spent on snapshots. She left a rhyme in her cosmetics drawer, "When this you see/Remember me."

From my father's shoulder I not only observed the birth of spring but sang as well. From that high perch he showed me off to all who would listen: a kid who couldn't speak but could carry a tune. The singing may be why I called him La-la instead of Da-da until I was four. When I heard him unsnap the mandolin case he stitched together from scrap felt, I went to the living room to watch him practice. He came to life when he played music. He and his mandolin were the center of attention at parties, and after some schnapps he could be coaxed into doing the *kazatchka*. Landsmen called him a true Cossack.

He taught me how to sketch a face and brought me scratch pads on which I drew incessantly: scenes from *The Lone Ranger* and *Tom Corbett, Space Cadet* radio shows, a stream of cowboys and spaceships. After a time, the throw-away pads from printers or stationers gave way to artist tablets with a picture of a beret and palette on the cover. Eventually, I became more interested in stories than pictures and declared in no uncertain terms I would be a writer. He respected my self-confidence. Or was it arrogance. But he didn't want me to suffer as he had, and urged me to find a profession which would support my writing.

How serious had he been as an artist? Did marriage and the Depression rob him of his dream? Did the stability of a profession rather than a trade protect one from the economy? It seemed that just the opposite became true after I joined the workforce, teaching at a small college in New Jersey. My cousin, a chemical engineer, lost his job with DuPont, and consequently his career, his home and family in the suburbs.

To what extent did one manipulate as well as navigate in order to survive? How had Dad's family managed to flee their homeland to come here? I wish he had stayed long enough for me to ask these questions. Did he mean I should not become dependent upon writing as a way of making a living so I wouldn't suffer, or become a slave to the marketplace? Did he mean that an artist should be rooted in the working life to produce meaningful art? Louis Wilks, the sculptor father of a high school friend, gave me more specific advice—he espoused the proletarian ethic of art connected to labor for it to be valid. Louis was a carpenter by trade who bought a piece of land in upstate New York to create a studio. Instead, carpentry became his weekend obsession, and his few attempts to return to sculpting many years later were the work of a talented novice. Dad, like Louis, seemed tied to a work ethic rooted in the Hebraic tradition as well as the Marxism fashionable in the thirties. The great Talmudic commentators were scholars only after their toil at other labor. Hillel was a porter, Rashi a vintner, and Maimonidies a physician. Neither Dad nor Louis were able to accommodate both art and labor.

My father traded off art for security. Louis became obsessed with carpentry, building bungalows on his land for artists to rent during the summer. Though neither one practiced art, both embraced in spirit the esthetic of social realism. During the thirties, the WPA recognized art as legitimate work and sponsored art in the service of labor. All across the country, public buildings are decorated with spectacular, period murals: highly stylized celebrations of the workingman, agriculture, and the promise of technology. These remain as quaint reminders of a brief optimism, partially supported by the federal government, a future where art, labor, and technology were united.

While the dichotomy between art and labor seems to have ancient Judaeo-Christian roots, other western countries have managed to recognize and support the arts generously. In this country we continue to regard the production of art as dreaming or idleness rather than legitimate, productive work. We fail to nurture the imagination in our schools and remain blind to the importance of art in building and binding communities.

What kind of art, if any, would Dad have created with Louis's freedom? What would he have done with his own place in the country? Answers to these questions don't exist. I get a blank stare and his image fades.

Though he could chat comfortably with truckers at roadside restaurants, he was unsure of himself in the new world he never fully adopted. I was child of the new world and he was confident I would find my own way. He became a spectator at my life just as I was of baseball. The one time I managed to get him to Ebbets Field, he announced to the first father attempting conversation that he was there only because I was a fan.

My father was honest and undiplomatic, and while he may have played a key role in his family's emigration, he was not an entrepreneur. It was better, he felt, to tell the truth than get caught in a lie later. Throughout my childhood I resented my mother's transparent attempts to manipulate me. At every opportunity to lie I heard my father's voice repeat, "Honesty is the best policy." Telling the truth to my teacher on the first day of fourth grade got me exiled within my classroom for the entire year—she did not want to hear that the reason for my lateness was my mother's attempt to transfer me out of her class.

Though no longer an activist during my childhood, Dad never abandoned his basic beliefs. Greed equaled evil and caused social inequality. Capitalist government was manipulated by the wealthy, who got richer by taking advantage of the worker. Wealth could not be produced without labor, but labor was not getting a fair share of return on its investment. Unchecked by government, labor was exploited. Government could act for the good and impose a moral, ethical imperative by regulating the workplace. Examples of how government could act for the commonweal were at hand. Lincoln Terrace Park, where Dad spent much of his weekends, was constructed by the WPA during the New Deal; so too was the main branch of the Brooklyn Public Library, its bright, modern facade facing Grand Army Plaza—he boasted of it with personal pride. Both projects exemplified government for and by the people.

As I try to reconstruct and understand my father's life, I realize my older brothers have sharply contrasting views. They do not remember the same person. Sol, the oldest, remembers the Depression and Dad's activist days. His father "was out running around with his comrades" and denied him time when he was home. Yet, Sol admits his own concerns for social justice come from Dad.

Marty denies his relentless attacks on Dad's ideology and their repetitive arguments about politics. He accused Dad of denying the failures and posturing of the Soviet government. He believed that somehow Dad would suddenly reject more than 20 years of dogma and listen to reason. Yet, he shares Dad's ability to reduce politics to ideology and believes today that were Dad alive he would embrace Zionism.

I was raised by a man different than the one my brothers knew. I saw him more often. He was in his late forties when I was waking up to the world. Did my youth inspire a sense of his own mortality? He played ball with me in the park, but also abandoned me to terrorize elderly strollers with my speeding scooter while he and his cronies waved their hands in the air and condemned Truman as well as MacArthur. Still, I received attention from him he never afforded my brothers.

The relative security of postwar prosperity allowed me to demand more, too. I insisted that he play baseball with me. I insisted upon bedtime stories, which put him to sleep as he talked. His tales came from his childhood in the Ukraine countryside, snow up to his waist, where he learned to build snow ovens which could truly hold fires as he occasionally demonstrated, and where he ate icicles snapped from pine boughs.

His rural childhood was an idyllic, brief dream, just as my few summers in the Catskills came to be, a parallel loss in our lives. He passed on to me his bucolic longing; he was at heart a country boy, never at home in the urban environment. He cherished working on the land. When he joined us for weekends in Woodridge, he cleared brush with a mowing scythe despite his hayfever. This was meaningful labor, a service to others, as opposed to dress pressing, where his sweat contributed to the wealth of bosses.

Had he lived to know my farm, he would have picked up the scythe once again, helped me clear brush and build fence. He would have been the same age as my neighbor Johnny Morris, who survived the Depression on that farm. Dad would have gotten along with my neighbors if he didn't talk politics. While Dad manned the picket lines, Johnny raged drunkenly about "That Jew, Roosevelt."

I used to imagine Dad on a visit dividing his time between hoeing corn and potatoes in the garden and painting watercolors, Traveler, our coonhound, curled up not far away. He would have painted life as he felt it should be lived, close to nature. Occasionally, while working outdoors, I'd stop to observe a hawk circling in the blue sky and feel his spirit close, as if this was his way of letting me know he was there. While I laugh aloud at Marty's suggestion of Dad embracing Zionism, maybe it's not so far from my own belief that he would have enjoyed my farm. Perhaps these are simply our ways of carrying him forward in our lives.

Robert Fox and his father c. 1950

DIANE GOODMAN

Jewel, On Her Way to Work

Jewel lets her tired hips round
the grocery turnstile, swivel to
the new green melons; she touches one once,
fingertips falling as she moves on.
In Mrs. Cannon's kitchen Jewel flowers
chilled oranges, plugs strawberries
inside the skinfolds, and lays sugar slices
around the curves like stars.

Jewel likes the way the summer
plums are stacked in nearly black rows
round as eyes, their skin as sweet as babies.
Sometimes she slivers the yellow fruit,
fans it out on silver plates, and pipes
whipped lime cream between spaces.

When Jewel joins the Louisiana ladies
petting heads of Georgia peaches,
her skin prickles below the stares; inside
the difference of her touch, her dark hands
paw frightened minds whose own hands
then go home to wash and wash the sun-blessed
fruit in hot detergent water. When Jewel's hands
hold fruit under the spray of Mrs. Cannon's sink,
it sticks to the softness of her palms
like steamy ready coals.

Love Stew

Mrs. Cannon named it "Love Stew" thirty years ago,
the first time Jewel served it to the Garden Gals
because they both loved the way the peppery stew
crinkled the prim white faces like unironed sheets.

When the Gals learned Jewel had made it
from a recipe in *her* family for generations,
they turned their nervous faces to
Mrs. Cannon's starry prized magnolias staring
back in full bloom, and Mrs. Cannon bragged
how Jewel could run a French chef's knife
over a line of hot chili peppers the way
a concert pianist trips down the row of keys.

Now Jewel settles flecks of garlic and dime
tin leeks into the sweet butter melting
remembering the young Mrs. Cannon's surprise
at the way her puffy guests then ate,
stuffed in their pastel suits
ready-to-burst as party balloons.
They examined the stew like an experiment
lifting morsels out and seeming to place
them right back in, yet when they left
every single plate was clean.

The grilled yellow tomato skins flatten along
the bottom of the copper pot, their scent
twirling up into the quiet kitchen air.
While they bubble, Jewel chips the jalapenos
and adds sliced lettuce and crisp white onion
she pulled from her own garden, nestled
in the steamy city lot behind the metal cans.
She knows how just how they will arrive—Miss Rue
and Miss LaVelle still stout in patterned dresses
bent over themselves like flower baskets,
and the silent Madame Jessup, dull and sturdy
in her uncreased lined suit,
the color of cooled ashes.
Even after all these years they pass
under Jewel's hello as if she were a ghost.

The fish stock has been cleared and strained,
bones and glassy eyes discarded,
the fat squeezed from the slippery skin.
Jewel pours it on the sizzling tomatoes

and swirls in some of the dry white wine
Mrs. Cannon's guests will sip slowly,
until it's too warm to enjoy. That first time,
Mrs. Cannon offered martinis
and was the only one to accept,
the Spanish olives laying in her glass like eyes.
But when the first bite of the shellfish stew
passed their lips, their mouths popping
open like corks from champagne,
they rolled savory items to their throats,
and reached for wine, trying not to gulp.

Year after year they've continued to come
still complaining the cayenne turns their stomachs,
the wine weakens their thinning minds,
still certain the recipe must call for voodoo tricks.
Jewel drops in celery crescents, whole black olives,
tiny broccoli flowers, and capers mixed with chives.
At the last minute she will lay in
little neck clams, shredded scallops that rise
up like threads of moon, and opaque prawns
that turn the color of new rose blooms
yet the ladies will move their spoons
like archaeologists on a dig,
looking for something rare, foreign,
that could exonerate them.
When they leave they are full
but convinced that something evil
has transformed them, a black spirit
moving through their systems like smoke.

Jewel stirs in the raw rice; just before
the doorbell rings she adds nutmeg and beaten eggs.
Mrs. Cannon, in a deep blue silk shift
wheels herself in like the coming of dusk,
clasping a martini in her gnarled hand.
The ladies wait for Jewel to push them
to the table and believe they're moving
on possessed air, that the pale silver
napkins float down like steel gates
to lock themselves on their trembling laps.

Late Lunch in the Museum Garden

Although Jewel is old and small, she can scoop
Mrs. Cannon from the car and set her
in the chair like a pile of folded linen;
today she feels her lady's bones
have grown even lighter, thin
as the limbs on a brand new tree.
When Jewel wheels her toward the garden,
Mrs. Cannon raises her hands to her head
using the inside of her blue wrists
to settle the bright red beret.

Famous statues take up the air
below drooping old willows
and full black walnut trees; the sun weaves
a sparkling light through all the leaves.
Jewel in her white maid's uniform finds
a table in the shade below the marble angels
blessing garden with their scalloped wings.

Mrs. Cannon no longer speaks
but her eyes are crowed with words.
Jewel knows she craves time
where history and etiquette demand
the silence and stasis
these great figures proclaim.

Jewel orders one meal to feed them both,
cold chicken poached in lime
with wild rice salad vinaigrette,
because Mrs. Cannon can still swallow and smile
and feel the need for nourishment.
Between small bites they sip
from the same glass of dry white wine

and rest in the peace of this kind of stillness,
the enduring statues rising toward the year's new leaves
and Jewel and Mrs Cannon's clasped hands
settled against a common grateful heart.

Construction workers 1996 © Peter Favorito

WHERE YOU GO WHEN YOU DON'T WORK

STRUGGLES & GETTING BY

DAVID AXELROD

In the Spirit of Free Enterprise

Roscoe Crow studied rusty car parts
we heaped up by the hurricane fence:
"If I had a truck load of them," he said,
"by God, I'd have something then."
But it was my junk to sell, my fortune
to make, not his. He collected his own
in the evenings, in an ancient Ford
flatbed with plywood sideboards.
Roscoe Crow worked for my family
30 years, wearing a new change of
my grandfather's hand-me-downs
for each of those years, making maybe
five dollars an hour, dragging around
a cart with acetylene and oxygen tanks
and a cutting torch, dismantling cars
piece by piece, sorting into piles
of sheet metal, cast iron, and aluminum,
anything we couldn't burn, but could sell
as scrap. With seven retarded daughters
to feed, each named for a flower—
Daisy, Iris, Fawn Lily, Daffodilly,
Tulip, Violet, and Rose Crow—
Roscoe was one slow, hardworking man.
Evenings, I'd see him out, creeping
cross-eyed through the streets, his truck
loaded high with junk he'd sell
at Hymie Munitz's scrapyard,
during his lunch break the next day.
He worked like this for seven years,
grimly sizing up the profit of every random
piece of scrap metal he found:
"If I had a truckload of them, by God,
I'd have something then." And finally,
he did: $5,000 cash on the barrelhead

to buy a decrepit house a mile from town
between the squatter camp and the fenced
acres of Sacco Brothers Wrecking:
two stories, with plumbing, a big apartment
upstairs, a storefront grocery down,
complete with stock. A Sunday in July—
we worked half-days on Sunday—
before he planned to move
his cross-eyed clan, we drove by
in the wrecker: believe me,
if you can read or listen to this,
you never would have lived there.
And neither, at last, did Roscoe
or any of his kin, when, of course,
it burned to ashes the following week.
I don't think Roscoe missed work that week,
though the spirit of free enterprise
withered in him a bit, and over the years,
he only sold enough junk to make ends meet,
which seems a ridiculous phrase to describe
the economy of his life, hard-fisted
and mean as it was, a life that ended
the last I saw him sprawled under
the rear end of a Buick, using his torch
to cut the metal straps that held in place
a leaky gas tank still full of fuel.

The Gift

His mother, a recent widow, lost her job
and left him with her folks, moved to a slum
in Akron, where she gained a hundred pounds,
bleached her hair orange, waited small tips,
and cashed his Social Security checks to get by.
He visited her twice: they went to a lake,
a museum, but mostly she just slept.
In his other life, he made wealthy friends,
blonde boys who golfed at a country club.

He scrounged wooden-shafted irons
from the attic and golf bag his grandmother
sewed from burlap sacks and an old belt.
A fool, he hadn't anticipated what great fun
his friends would have with those clubs.
Hiding in the woods in order to sneak
onto the private course no one
bothered to invite him to as a guest,
he joined them on the second tee,
where one boy, bigger than the rest,
took one of those sorry old clubs
and broke it over his knee. Everybody thought
that was riotous fun, and wanted to do it again.
So did he. When the old people asked,
he explained the clubs were too feeble
for someone with such a powerful swing
as his: he wanted a set of alloy-shafted clubs
with a deep-pocketed leather bag.
Though his grandfather's union
went out on strike that summer,
for his birthday they bought him clubs
from the barren couple across the street,
but these were the wife's set of clubs,
and though the irons could pass casual
inspection, the woods were powder blue,
an obvious feminine touch he tried to mitigate
by wearing a matching blue shirt.
The bag, too, presented its own problem:
scotch plaid cloth trimmed in naugahyde.
One Sunday after dark, his mother roared
up to the house in her Ford Galaxy
with its fenders and quarter panels crushed.
She waited for him to come down
the drive to visit with her: she'd brought a gift:
a new golf bag. What do you think?
Was she proud? Hopeful? Delighted
to make this gift to her already lost son,
whom she hadn't seen in six months?
Or was she ashamed, knowing that
it wasn't the right bag, and that

he'd be disappointed? She told him,
Get out. He pushed the sprung door,
but it stuck and wouldn't budge.
Then she slapped him, and next time
he tried, it swung wide on its hinges,
She roared down the block and he ran
after her taillights, but she didn't stop.
He crossed two streets, cut through
backyards, met her at the stop sign
at the top of the next hill, where she kicked
the door open and threw out the bag.
He kept it, used that bag, even after it cracked
in the cold one day, even though his friends
mocked the trash his mother gave him,
he kept the cursed bag until he quit forever
playing that stupid game. There are few
absolutes you can trust, and you'd prefer
to avoid a moral now, but count on this:
the wealthy, who you'd think could best
afford to act otherwise, are often the cruelest
human sons-of-bitches. Or this: the angel
is just outside your door. Hear her knocking?
No matter what gift she offers, say it's no
more than a poor woman's shame,
you will always accept it as if it were
your own true desire, the only gift
ever given to you with kindness, a love
unlike any other you will ever know.

DENISE DUHAMEL

The Factory

The Canucks made Christmas balls at Coby Glass, a Santa on the roof twelve months a year, looking over the parking lot, like Big Boy or the Pillsbury Dough Boy, someone everyone in Woonsocket recognized as a famous logo, even at the end when he started to get worn, when his red uniform faded into pink under years of summer sun and strips of his beard were plucked away by birds making nests. Inside were the conveyer belts where women in bandannas inspected the balls for crooked decals or mis-shapen globes. If the balls were defective, they were thrown into a rusty trash barrel on the other side of the belt. Although the women asked for goggles, they never got them and had to rely on their own glasses or the power of a quick sprint against flying glass slivers. Most of the women had swollen hands filled with what looked like a million paper cuts and tiny scars like bird footprints on their faces. Some had eye patches and smoked, using only the skillful maneuver of their lips, their hands busy with the Christmas tree balls. The ashtrays were rinsed-out tuna fish cans.

The plus was that everyone in Woonsocket could decorate their Christmas tree for free. Everyone either worked at the factory or knew someone who did. There was a lot of stealing, especially after a messy accident. The women down where the conveyor belt ended arranged the balls in sixes or twelves, decals up, into cardboard boxes with slits that made separate compartments, like those boxes they give you when you buy a lot at the drive-in, with little fences to separate your drinks and popcorn. There were elaborate schemes—how to get a few boxes out during lunch and into the trunks of station wagons and Dodge Darts. Sometimes the maintenance guys took out a few cartons at the end of the night and nestled them safe on top of the dumpster so workers could pick them up the next morning.

During breaks, almost everyone smoked pot, which was recently introduced by the young Portuguese guys from Providence who came to Woonsocket for work. Young wives smoked it, grandmas took an occasional toke, until things slowed down and the conveyor belt inched along like a traffic jam and everything awful was funny. Some people eventually left for the American Tourister factory or the Tupperware factory where at least there were things to steal that you could use all year round. The

young guys belched, the closing-a-Tupperware-lid sound, and the middle-
aged Canucks, who hated their husbands for the same such noise, suddenly found these Portuguese guys sexy. The foreman yelled, *Get back to
work.* The foreman held a ball up to the light and screamed, *Does this
snowflake look straight to you?* The women giggled into their hands while
the young men nodded slowly, over and over, exotic music playing in their
heads.

Selling Shoes

You have to kneel before the customer and take off the shoe she
already has on, unlace it if it was tied or slip it off gently. You'd be surprised how many people have runs in their stockings or holes at the toes
but you have to pretend not to notice that or any bad smells. That's your
job. You place the foot on the scale, even if they tell you they already
know their sizes, because if the boss catches you going to the back without
measuring first you'll be yelled at or worse, fired. The scale is black and
silver with a U to cup the heel and people are stiff when you try to slide
their foot into place like they are dancing for the first time not knowing
whether to follow or lead. You can find their length size by pressing down
their longest toe to the nearest white line. Sometimes their big toe is the
tallest, other times it's the second toe, all lanky like a growing boy. Sometimes those two toes cross like fingers wishing for good luck and for a
moment they might strike you as silly or amusing but you can't laugh because the customer takes her toes seriously. Then there is a lever that
slides to the ball of the foot, the chubbiest part right above the big toe and
that tells you how wide her foot is. Some women won't want to believe
what the scale says, even if they should wear a size nine they say no, get me
an eight and a half. In the back room the shoes are swaddled, toe to heel,
yin and yang, in tissue paper which you have to put back exactly how it
was or else you could be yelled at again. The shoes are lined up by style
names: City Girl, Day Break, Country Romp, and by brands: Ettiene Aigner
which only the rich people buy, then Mootsies Tootsies, Hush Puppies,
Sperry. Even though you've taken all that time measuring her foot on the
scale that looks like a shiny blackboard with white chalk, the boss says if
the size isn't back there offer the customer the next half-size smaller of
bigger, explaining not all shoes run true-to-size, or make her try on a similar style. Don't ever let her put on her old shoes and walk away when you
could have made a sale. Because people want to buy something once you've
taken off their shoes and you've seen the state of their feet—their bunions
and corns, their ingrown nails, their dry calloused heels. It would be wrong

to expose them like that and let them leave in their old shoes with the warped soles and scuff marks. They'd feel taken advantage of, like the girl who gives herself to the boy who never calls again. Slide the new shoes on with a shoe horn, like it's a production, like you're serving parsley as a garnish, like you're a game show host's model assistant motioning to a beautiful refrigerator the contestant can win. Your customer is a reluctant Cinderella and you are the footman convincing her of the prince, the fit, the improved life the shoe will offer. If she hobbles about saying no, no, it's too tight tell her it will stretch. If she complains it slips in the back put in a pad that will tighten the shoe up. Remember that she and her shoe form a marriage and marriages are always more suitable for one partner than the other. Shake your head affirmatively with compliments that seem genuine. If she wants to try on more, let her. When you walk to the back room, climb the ladder up to the shoes as though you are trying to get to the sweet-smelling scalp, the roots of Rapunsel's hair. Or pretend you are in a glorious library where each shoe box is a draft of the same book by your favorite writer and the more you work the more you will understand the nuances of his voice. Once she makes her decision and she wants to buy, try to sell her polish, mink oil, suede spray or heel protectors you can put on for her with the giant stapler in the back. If a customer tells you shoes aren't made as good as they used to be, and describes her needs in great detail—the walking trip she's going on, the important dinner—let her. Keep nodding. Keep falling to your knees, the sole of each new shoe cradled in your palm. Just make sure she stays on the carpet when she tries it on.

Killing My Father

My father can't walk too fast, now that he's seventy. Sometimes when I ask him a question he looks through me because he is going deaf. The TV blasts from the rumpus room upstairs to the kitchen and onto the street.

When he's late for work in my dream, a thug drags him back to the ovens, but because he's seventy, my father can't keep up. He's tripping and falling, and finally the thug carries my father in his arms, my father collapsed as though he were war dead or a fainting bride.

"Where is the union representative?" I demand as I follow the thug and my mother pulls me back and says, "Please, your father never wanted you to see this," and the thug clears his throat, gathering saliva to spit at me and someone says, "Don't do it. She's been to college," and I wake up with a start, my heartbeat clicking fast: *dad is dead dad is dead dad is dead dad is dead.*

Then I realize no, not yet, but I understand why he left work, why he retired on his birthday, that very first day he was eligible and came home from the bakery in the supermarket and sat with a bowl of chips in his favorite chair, where no one could hurt him.

I worked in the same supermarket chain as my dad for a few years in high school. The higher-ups demoted old gray Ed (since the union said they couldn't fire him) and put him in the parking lot to get carriages every time it rained. Or handed him a greasy bucket and mop while the sixteen-year-old kid took his time stacking blue Progresso soup cans so that all the front labels were even and faced the customer—minestrone, vegetable beef, corn chowder. Ed was once a manager and they wanted him to retire rather than get the top scale pay. Union rule: you can require any employee to do any job as long as he gets the same salary.

"The unions are almost useless now," my dad would say at dinner.

"He *ran*," my mother said, when she went shopping in the store where my dad worked, "all I did was see him running from the ovens to the displays. He never stopped. He was too afraid to stop and say hi to me."

In my dream I kept feeling my pockets for a gun to kill that man who was bullying my father, that man who wore ratty jeans and boots with chains. But my mother kept pulling me back, telling me not to watch, telling me that my watching was what was killing my father.

GLORY FOSTER

Footprints

The heavy, humid air was lazy with the sound of cicadas humming their wings dry. Frogs croaked by the flooded stream—a stream my Dad had convinced me originated in a walnut shell way beyond our property. The swampy, tantalizing smell of the creek promised cool swimming, but Dad said no, and so we worked feverishly putting up hay in the nearby field.

In the middle of the hayfield was a knoll covered with poison ivy, bracken and stunted trees as though something evil or sinister fed the twisted growth. And indeed Dad said that a troll named Grendel, descended from Cain, lived in the core of the hill, so we never explored any farther than the blackberry bushes. Those fat and juicy berries that Mom made into luscious pies grew tenaciously around the perimeter.

The rain had come out of the northwest from Canada, turning the sky yellow with an eerie, foreboding glow. From the fierce whirling wind preceding it, we had thought it was a tornado. But soon the acrid smell of lightning and swollen clouds raced over the land and broke into a Minnesota thunderstorm that drenched the hay already raked into rows. It lasted almost two days, causing the creek beds to overflow and ponds to form in the lower hayfields, where muskrats now worked patiently rebuilding their washed-out homes near the bridge.

It had taken several days for the alfalfa to dry in the moist air, but now it was ready and the forecast of more rain lent urgency to our labors. My brother Eric, bits of alfalfa stuck in his sandy hair, drove the tractor. He jumped down at every stop to help Dad load hay. "Get that goddamned junk heap moving," Dad shouted at him, and Eric's sun-reddened face flushed deeper when he killed the motor. The long wooden rakes left over from my Norwegian ancestors grumbled over the stubble as Sarah and Leif raked the hay into piles. "You waiting for the cows to come home?" Dad chided, and Sarah's eyes narrowed as she hurried to stay a couple of rows ahead of the tractor. Being the runt of the litter, though my brother Leif was younger, I had the job of riding the hay rack, packing down the hay as it was pitched up on the rack.

It must have been 110 degrees in the shade. Everyone said it was the worst heat wave in Minnesota since Calvin Coolidge had been president. I didn't even know who he was, so I guess it had been a long time. Even the Dakota Indians stopped fishing in the Mississippi because it was too hot to smoke fish. Sweat drenched our bodies, bare under the cutoff overalls that we all wore, and the chaff clung to our skin, rubbing salt into the scratches left by the stickers. My old winter shoes were split and filled with hay, and through the scuffs you could still see some of the red leather. They no longer looked like the bright new shoes we had bought from the Montgomery-Ward catalogue last fall when I entered second grade. Still they offered some protection from the thistles and burrs. Breathing that spicy stagnant air cauterized my throat, and my yellow braids scratched my neck like rope and gave me the courage to ask Dad again, "Can't we go swimming, just once?" Dad scolded, "Stop daydreaming. That's how you got hurt with the pitchfork." And Dad's warning muffled the sound of the running stream and withered my dream of swimming in deep cool water.

I thought about that accident. We had been rushing just like we were now, and when my brother threw the pitchfork up to anchor the load, like you use hairpins to hold hair, I missed and it stabbed my leg. It didn't hurt, but blood spurted like a punctured garden hose, and the golden hay was spattered a bright crimson. I clamped my hand over the wound, but it wouldn't stop, and there was a raw smell that reminded me of butchering. I was afraid to tell Dad; he might get mad. Eric saw the blood and called Dad. He yelled at me, "Slide down off that load," and I landed in his waiting arms. There was blood all over his blue shirt as he quickly tied his handkerchief around my leg. That was the end of haying for that day when he took me to the doctor.

Now Dad stopped to mop his forehead with his sodden blue work handkerchief. He used it for everything, from a baling wire bandage for the tractor's broken carburetor, to a tourniquet for my wounded leg. He pocketed his bandanna and stood looking across the field at the work still left to be done. He looked like he was daydreaming, but not about swimming. Maybe he was thinking about the accident too, or the two men, working stiffs Dad called them, who had wandered into the yard looking for work this morning. When Leif called them beggars, Dad told us all, "Don't ever call them bums, they're just working men down on their luck." My mother fed them as always, and they went on their way, but still there was a residue of anger that imprisoned my father. After they left, Dad talked to Mom about the Depression, cursing Hoover and a country that he said "had enough food to feed the whole world."

We knew he had been a Wobbly when he was younger. Our supper table was alive with stories of political strife from his younger days. He had been thrown in jail in Missoula with a broken nose because he defied the mayor's law against free speech. The lumber companies, in cahoots with the employment sharks, had pressured the mayor into passing the law. Suppressing free speech prevented the citizens from telling other workers about the illegal hiring methods the companies were using. It was a way to get cheap labor and set worker against worker. But it backfired—"So many Wobblies invaded Montana that the jails couldn't hold them all, and the town women brought homemade pies and clean clothes to those in jail.

Finally, because of sheer numbers, they had to repeal the law."

Back in the twenties, because of the railroad strikes, my father had been on the road like those two working stiffs this morning. He worked with harvest crews in the steaming midwestern summer, earning a dollar a day and meals for a sixteen-hour day. They washed in horse troughs or streams, and for shelter they slept under hay racks. Now as he stood there leaning on his pitchfork, his face drenched in sweat seemed to relax. maybe he was thinking about those days, like I was, because when he started to pitch hay again, he didn't work as hard as he had earlier.

We had already put up two loads of hay. It was too hot to go up in the loft, so we built another stack behind the barn. I longed to ask him again about swimming, but just as we finished loading the rack, Dad tossed his pitchfork into a hay pile and motioned to Eric to move over. He climbed into the driver's seat, and Leif and Sarah hung onto the back of the tractor as he drove over to the side of the field and parked in the shade of an elm. Then he smiled at each one of us and swore, "Judas Priest, it's hot! We're too close to that Devil's hill, he'll get our goddamned souls if we don't cool off," and he jumped down, heading for the creek and yelling "Let's go swimming!" Eric was already halfway to the creek, shoes flying. Sarah, running even with him, called, "Beat you to the swimming hole!' And I kicked off my shoes, jumped from the hayrack and tumbled after Leif. My Dad loped along with Leif and me, pretending to be old. He knew we couldn't keep up with the rest. The tall cattails stood guard, ducks scattered noisily, bullfrogs were jumping everywhere, and our footprints made great sucking sounds in the mud as we ran through the marsh. Sarah and Eric were already in the creek, clothes and all, when Dad, with his blue work shirt and pants held up by green and red suspenders, dropped into the swimming hole like a falling tree.

I slid down the clay bank into the stream with the rest of them, into the great pool that Eric and Leif had damned up with rocks a few weeks before. They had anticipated that heavy rains would fill it. It was like going into our damp, dark, spicy smokehouse, dormant now in summer, or like Detlefson's root cellar where cool cabbages and potatoes waited. How strange Dad looked as he smiled, floating around with all his clothes on, while I lay in the crux or his arm. Sarah and Eric started a water fight, and I fled upstream to the big granite rock under the willow tree. As I sat in the sun with my knees tucked under my chin, a jade green frog, tiny as a jewel, lit on my ankle and glittered. Motionless, I sat, pretending I was a rock— eternity was that instant.

After swimming, the rest of the day didn't seem like work as we put up hay in our wet clothes, and we got done before more rain came. We even had time left over to raid the blackberry patch on the troll's hill, all of us strong enough now to defy Grendel.

The Mechanic

I dream I am in a school play.
At the end of the first act
a woman wearing my dress says,
"All of your costumes are mine."
My hair is wrapped up in curlers
and I do not know the plot or script.
The audience laughs.
Then the stage lights darken.
I search for other actors
but the dressing room's a machine shop
with smells of gas and oil.
There my father calibrates
a metal sculpture
welding a house to a picket fence.
I wear a wedding dress
waiting for a second act.
The generators throb.

In the church my mother smiles,
"Marriage is just a babysitter,"
she calls from the sidelines.
In a rented hall
above Dunaway's drug store
we dance a polka;
my father says,
"Don't marry a man
who doesn't know
what's happening
under the hood of a car."
He shows me
how to clean the points
gap the plugs.

The curtain rises.
A woman in red asks,
"Will you dance with me?"
I wail about my scabby knees

and cutoff jeans. She says,
"let your hair down."
Then we wash our dirty clothes together
but we have so many costumes
we run out of clothesline
and have to drape them along the picket fence.
Somewhere a voice is singing,
"Falling in love with love
is falling for make believe
Falling in love with love
is playing the fool."
In a half-lit scene
the leading man has abandoned
four x-wives, I marry him anyway.
Four different times
his Chevy has broken down.
On Portsmouth Court, my father
shows him how to set the timing.
Then he turns handing me the gauges.
I walk down the aisle,
get lost in the audience.
Lost in the audience.
Lost...Lost...

The third act
I am wide awake,
the scene is a crooked highway.
The moon is full. Sitting
in a stalled car on the way
to her graduation
the leading lady calls for a mechanic.
There is no understudy
the role must be ad-libbed.
House lights dim, then darken
and I step from the wings
with a welder, a tool kit
and fuses for footlights
and a grease cap on my head.

Glory Foster's father, front row right, railroad machinist and mechanic

JIM DANIELS

All Packed

Andy had no idea where they were. It didn't matter. He stared out the window at the dark houses. The blue streetlights poured their pale light into circles on the street. Detroit copied itself over and over--this street was the same as a street five miles over—Eight Mile Road, Nine Mile Road, Ten Mile Road, all the way up to 32 Mile Road. The flat, square houses, schools, grocery stores, the cinder-block bars, tool-and-die shops, and the factories.

He turned back toward the three women in the car. Cindy and Debbie were in the back seat lighting up cigarettes. Linda was driving. He leaned over and put his head against her shoulder. She shoved him away, laughing, "You can't be tired now, can you big boy? What do you think, girls, looks like we picked us up a deadbeat."

"Five years ago, he wouldn't be pooping out on us like that," Cindy said.

"Five years ago, you would've kicked my ass out of your car by now," Andy laughed.

"Five years ago we wouldn't have let you in the car," Linda said.

"Five years ago," Debbie said, and trailed off. He'd danced with her earlier at the reunion. They'd joked about kissing each other at a party in junior high.

"Ain't that the truth," Andy said. He reached into his pocket, flicked a couple of tums from the roll and popped them in his mouth. They passed two teenagers standing near the curb under a street sign sharing a cigarette or a joint. They stared at the car with that scared defiance Andy remembered so well.

They were driving to Debbie's for coffee—no one wanted to go home. Stan Edwards had planned a post-reunion party in his new house, but he'd gotten sick on the drive there, so his wife sent everyone home. They used to call him "buy six—drink two" Edwards, though the whole thing about who could drink the most didn't make a lot of sense anymore. Now who couldn't measure up? Andy closed his eyes. He didn't even have a job. Tomorrow, he was leaving town to look for work down south. His car was at his parents' house, all packed.

He'd gotten a ride to the reunion with his old pal Zack, who had left early, so he mooched a ride off Linda, with Debbie's help. He was sure Linda and Cindy thought it was funny having him in the car with them— Andy, the old burnout.

"Sure you don't want us to take you home?" Linda asked.

"No, no. I could use some coffee," Andy said. He was embarrassed to still be living at home. He'd never really moved out, except for his half-hearted attempt at college. Besides, he was in no hurry to get home with his head swirling the way it was. He wasn't up to facing his parents, facing the morning's move.

Andy leaned toward Linda to turn up the radio. It was an old Bob Seger song, "Ramblin' Gamblin' Man."

"Wasn't our class song a Seger song?"

"Yeah. Not this one. It was 'Turn the Page.'"

Andy turned toward the back seat to look at Debbie. "You're right. I think I voted for some partying song—I don't remember."

"I'm surprised you remember anything from senior year," Cindy said.

"Hey, c'mon, I wasn't wasted all the time...."

Andy thought it might be time to go home after all. He tried to stick to beer as a rule, but tonight all the old fears crept back, and he'd needed to beat them off with some stiff drinks. He was stuck with how people saw him five years ago, and stuck with five more years he wasn't proud of. He hadn't told anyone except Zack that he was leaving town. As it was, he'd ended up answering too many questions about flunking out of college. When it happened, it was almost a joke to him, but now, when asked about it, he swallowed hard and shrugged, "I guess I just wasn't ready."

"Despite tonight, I don't drink much anymore. And I quit drugs. Even pot."

"It's okay, Andy, we believe you," Debbie said, and patted his shoulder from the back seat.

"I bet some of those guys are eating their hearts out right now, wishing they were single again. And me, here with three beautiful women...."

"They can always get divorced," Debbie said. She'd married pregnant the year they graduated. Had two kids now and was divorced. He turned to face her.

"Sorry." He rolled down the window and let it slap his face. He was playing the fool again, but he didn't know how to stop.

"No need." She smiled at him. He'd gotten a girl pregnant in high school, but she'd had an abortion. A secret he'd told no one. She'd showed up tonight with her husband. Andy had meant to at least say hello, but every time he moved toward her table, his heart jerked in his chest. They'd both been drunk. Getting married and keeping the kid was never an option. Her parents took care of everything. She probably had no interest in saying hello.

Debbie had been quiet for most of the ride. She really didn't fit with Cindy and Linda, college grads, professional women. They pulled into Debbie's driveway. She'd gotten the house in the divorce. And the kids. The principal had made her leave school when she started to show. Later, she took night courses to graduate.

The father of her children, Richard Wood, had been a basketball star two years ahead of them at school. His father was a school board member, a barber who called himself "the drug buster" in his election materials. They were both known as Woody. Debbie confided to him at the reunion that Woody Sr. had made trouble during the divorce. "A real mess," she said, shaking her head slowly through the smoke from her cigarette.

Andy followed the three women into Debbie's house. The kids were with her mother for the night. He bounced up the steps, buoyant with the strangeness of this group, something different at last in the sameness of his life.

Debbie held the door and said softly as he passed. "I don't remember much myself, since they threw me out."

"What?"

"Senior year. I don't remember much myself."

"How'd you end up with those two?" Linda and Cindy were already in the house ahead of them.

"We grew up on the same street. I'm their charity project. Their mothers probably made them ask me. I didn't want to go, but then my mom offered to take the kids. I don't get many chances to get out. I think they were all in on this together."

"Are you glad you went?" Andy leaned toward her.

"Let's go in. I'll get that coffee going."

A strange combination of passion and compassion surged through Andy. The other two women were both headed toward success. Debbie was stuck here living on child support, her future tied down by two strong ropes. In high school, she was as smart as any of them.

They sat at the kitchen table while Debbie showed them pictures of her kids. The absence of music, after a long night of it, settled uncomfortably into the air. Andy slurped down two quick cups of coffee till he felt his heart starting to pound. He had a headache. He chewed a couple tums, then went into the bathroom and searched the medicine chest for some aspirin. He found some asper-gum and popped a couple pieces into his mouth.

"This one's Katie, my oldest." Debbie smiled, pointing to a somber girl alone on the porch. "And here's Katie with Bobby." Two years apart, they stood with their heads leaning into each other, a man's hand on their shoulders.

Cindy was talking about her job, her transfer back to the city, the condo she was buying. Andy remembered when condo wasn't a word. He felt Debbie's foot moving up his leg. He looked across at her, and she smiled. He flipped off his shoes and stretched his legs out under the table. She squeezed his feet between her thighs as the others talked, their words fading into rising and falling sounds, a dull song Andy had no patience with.

Andy wasn't dumb. At one point, he'd been college prep, until he cut so many classes and did so poorly they bumped him down. He had nothing as tangible as Debbie to point to as an excuse for his failures, yet she herself offered no excuses, took pride in what she had, her children. He'd clearly wasted the last few years.

He wondered why Zack had left early. He'd seemed excited about the reunion, talking about it for weeks. When they'd arrived together, some guys had kidded them about being a "couple." Old reliable Zack, still living at home, just like himself. Zack lived for bowling, and bowled on three other teams besides the one he and Andy bowled on together. Zack had more seniority in the plant than Andy because he'd started in directly from high school, so he still had a job. Zack liked living at home, and his parents liked having him. He weighed close to three hundred pounds.

Andy was glad they hadn't gone out to breakfast with the others. He felt like enough of a failure right here. Cindy would be moving home to clerk at a local law office. Linda had an extra room in her condo. They were making plans. His plan was simply to drive away. He had two thousand dollars saved. It would have to do.

Debbie caressed his feet, which had stopped moving. He began moving them again. He felt like he was at someone's house whose parents were away for the weekend and he was worried they'd come home early.

"When I get out of law school, I'm gonna kick some ass. Big bucks." Cindy laughed at her own display of bravado. Andy was sure she'd make a good lawyer. She did everything right, all through school. The teachers loved her. Andy had always been intimidated by her. In high school, they were miles apart in every way. Now, it was light years.

"Where were you when I needed some ass-kicking done?" Debbie asked as a joke. It silenced the others.

"Well, you got the house," Linda finally responded, exchanging glances with Cindy.

"How come you're not a lawyer, Linda?"

"You wouldn't believe how many people ask me if I'm a lawyer yet. Shit," Linda held a cigarette to her lips, stamped it red with a kiss, "the assholes don't even know how long it takes to become a lawyer....The kind of money I'm making now, who needs it?"

"How long does it take to become a lawyer?" Andy asked. Debbie smiled across from him.

"Hey, are you two playing footsy?" Linda said, incredulous.

Andy reddened, despite himself, despite being drunk, despite knowing he shouldn't care.

"Safe sex," Debbie laughed. "It's been a long time. I have to start somewhere."

"Maybe we'd better get going."

Debbie moved her foot up Andy's crotch. He was humming to himself. He wanted more coffee, but his gut was hurting.

"Coming, Andy?"

Debbie squeezed his feet. "No...no, I think I'll stay awhile. Debbie will take me home...I think."

She laughed, "Eventually."

Cindy and Linda looked at Debbie, then at each other. Cindy shrugged. "Okay."

Debbie quickly locked and chained the door behind them. Andy kissed her immediately with wet, hungry kisses. They were starting to undress each other when the doorbell rang.

She froze. "Go in the other room, quick." Now someone was pounding hard, and Andy knew it wasn't Cindy or Linda. He hurried into the bathroom and sat on the edge of the tub. He heard a man's voice. He locked the door and wedged his feet up against it.

"There's someone in there with you, isn't there?"

"Woody, it's none of your business. We're divorced now, remember? What do you want?"

She emphasized *want*. *Want*, Andy said to himself. He wanted to pee, but he was too scared. He hadn't been in a fight in years, and Woody was a big dude with "drug buster" blood. He must've been watching the whole time, Andy thought—probably has a gun—saw us come, saw the others go. Andy looked at the Flintstones bandaids in the medicine chest. He tried to open the bathroom window. They were arguing. He heard the chain rattle, tried to remember a prayer. He hadn't been with a woman since forever, and now this. He spat out the asper-gum.

"See, there's no one here. Now will you leave?"

Andy breathed into his shirt and shut his eyes.

"Okay. But I'll be back."

The door closed again. The chain rattled again. Andy couldn't believe it. Woody never had been very bright. Maybe he hadn't see them after all. He heard Debbie sigh, then heave into tears. He was sober.

He stuck his head around the corner, then awkwardly put his arms around her where she was sitting on the floor. After she calmed down, he asked her how long she'd been divorced.

"Six weeks...Oh, we've been separated over a year. I don't know what his problem is. He must've found out the kids were at my mother's and suspected something. I mean, he doesn't love me anymore, he's told me that. He's just not ready for anyone else to love me I guess."

Love, Andy thought, oh man. She wiped her eyes and pulled Andy down to her, kissing him fiercely on the mouth. They hurried upstairs, stopping on the landing to shed their clothes. She tackled him onto the bed. The phone rang. She let it ring, but her kisses slowly faltered.

"I have to answer it," she said, pulling away. "It might be something about the kids."

It was Woody.

"Why won't you leave me *alone*? Just let me live my life," she spat, one word at a time. "We'll talk about it later." He called three more times. She ignored it, and finally, he gave up.

They made love wildly, clumsily, like high school lovers, and it was over quickly. Afterwards, they lay still and quiet in the bed.

"What do you want?" She asked.

"To do it again."

"After that?"

"I don't know." Andy rolled over onto his stomach. At the reunion, he'd only make jokes when anyone asked him what he was doing. The sky was gradually graying into light. He closed his eyes—the long drive, to who knows where, filling his brain, an expanding egg. Then he blurted out, "I'm leaving town tomorrow. Driving south to look for work. My car's all packed up."

Debbie looked at him blankly. He went on explaining, "There aren't any jobs around here. My unemployment's just about run out. I still owe money on my student loan...." He let his face fall forward and he groaned into a pillow. She put her arms around him tenderly.

After flunking out of college, he'd gone to work in the plant with his father until getting laid off a few months ago. College was his own fault—just like high school, he tried to party his way through. His own fault, his parents often reminded him. Wasted their hard-earned dollars. After a few years in the factory, Andy had no doubt that they were hard-earned. He was tired of hearing it.

"Do you ever think about leaving here?" he asked suddenly.

She laughed. "Woody's dad would track me down. Besides, I got my kids...I love my kids...Do you ever think of going back to school? Once the kids get a little older, I'm going to try."

"That's a great idea," he said, ignoring her question. "You were always smart."

"Not always," she said. "You were pretty smart yourself, till you started getting wasted all the time." She punched him hard in the shoulder.

He kissed her then, and they made love again, slower this time, almost sad. They both stank with the smells of a long night—whiskey, sweat, smoke, coffee. Exhausted, he buried his face between her breasts. They slept for such a short time, he wondered if he had imagined it. She shook him gently—the sun was up.

She got up and went downstairs to make coffee. It was morning, and there was no way of getting around it. He dressed slowly, then followed her down. He had the shakes. She held him against the kitchen counter, staring out the window over his shoulder. He slumped in a chair sipping coffee while she showered and dressed.

"I have to pick up the kids in an hour," she said.

"I gotta leave town today," he said. He'd put off leaving until today because he'd promised Zack he'd go to the reunion with him. Seeing everyone getting on with their lives was just what he'd needed to harden his resolve. His uncle had written from Houston to say he could find work there. It sounded as good as anywhere. He wondered if getting laid off might turn out to be a good thing. In the long, horrible months living at home and watching bad tv while his parents nagged him, he realized he had to get out of there. And the factory work, well, maybe he could do better.

He knew his parents must be ready to kill him. Staying out all night another example of his refusal to take responsibility for his life. He figured they expected him not to leave today, to come home and sleep it off, to blow off another day of his future, and he had to admit, that sounded good to him right now. The night with Debbie was something to sleep on. He'd be lucky if he made it as far as Toledo, the way he was feeling now.

"Are you glad you went to the reunion?" he asked.

She smiled and kissed his neck. "Yes," she whispered in his ear. "You?"

"The reunion, I don't know about, but these last few hours. I'm glad I came here."

Andy looked for signs of Woody before emerging from the doorway and hurrying to Debbie's car. Even though Woody still had his factory job, Andy felt sorry for him. He had a family to support and was living, Debbie said, with his parents for the time being. Andy thought of his father's bitter laugh, the factory embedded in his hard stare, and his mother's weary silence, her sighs of disappointment. Goofy from no sleep, he felt hot tears welling up in his dry, burning eyes.

The leaves were turning, some falling. His stomach was on fire. Toilet paper hung from some tree branches, that old high school prank. They passed from subdivision to subdivision, past their old school, the corner store he used to work at. He tried to shake off the tears with a sharp laugh. Debbie held his hand, her eyes holding to the road. He wanted to break out, leave the rotten children of his past on all the doorsteps of this barren town. He wanted to skip winter and drive off toward spring.

Andy rubbed his eyes and took a deep breath as she turned down his street. He saw his parents dressed for church, getting in their car. His hand trembled a bit as he wrote her phone number down. His parents ignored them. Debbie reached across the seat and buttoned a button he'd missed. They both smiled. He kissed her again as his parents pulled out of the driveway, then he slipped out of the car.

"I'll call next time I'm in town." Debbie squeezed his hand through the open window, pulled him to her again. "You'd better," she said.

"You've got it tough, Debbie. Hang in there." Even as he spoke the words, he realized how lame they sounded, how much he suddenly felt toward her. "I *will* call," he said. "From Houston, or wherever." She had to pick up her two kids, then have it out with her ex-husband, but now, she was smiling. He let go of her hand, then walked up the steps, turning to watch her drive away, then heading into the house. He showered, changed, wrote a note, ripped it up, wrote another, longer note, then walked out the door. He started his car and drove off. At the expressway, he turned south. A light rain fell. He drove on for miles, then, finally, turned on the wipers.

Laborer digging for sewer line © Charles Cassady Jr.

MAGGIE JAFFE

In a San Diego Sweat

shop
wedged between massage/
tattoo parlors
Chinese women sew
piece work.

At their bone-tired
feet, "camo" cloth
become uniforms—
become soldiers slain
on alien fields—
become money in the bank,
that you can bank on.

For luck & prosperity,
a red wax Buddha lights
up the shop's dark corner.

For lunch: rich with
shrimp speared on chop-
sticks, gaudy & plastic.

I think of red-crowned
cranes (*Grus antigona*)
hunched up in chemical waste.

Cooked

americium-95
When Rosemary got cooked
by plutonium
they had to scrub down her skin
with a steel brush & chemical wash.
Karen, this means I got cancer!
Karen made them take
a nasal smear.
This way they'd know
how much she was
cooked.

berkelium-97
Though Rosemary's glovebox
was only fractionally torn,
her rads were way over
the permitted body
burden. Plus she's young
& kind of scrawny
making her more susceptible.
Karen writes this down in
her cribbed, child-like scrawl.

californium-98
In less than two years
Karen's made the union rep,
aches to bust it wide open.
How the Company's shipping cracked
fuel rods to their fast-breeder
up in Hanford.

einsteinium-99
"It's a job, someone's got to do it,
Karen just *cunt* shut up.
She ought to know that in Oklahoma
McGee & Kerr own your ass.

They own your sorryass first born,
if they want it."

fermium-100
That night, Karen works
the graveyard shift, chain-
smoking Kools
tired as shit,
already "married" to it.
> *At Kerr-McGee*
> *plutonium's something special!*

nobelium-102
In the parking lot
her battered white Honda Civic
ticks in November frost. *

[*From 1972 until her death in 1974, Karen Silkwood worked for Kerr-McGee Plutonium Corporation. Her growing concern for workers' health compelled her to contact the *New York Times*. She died, suspiciously, in an automobile accident; the crucial notes for the *Times*' meeting were never found. According to the autopsy, her body was "riddled" with cancer from exposure to plutonium. Silkwood's family contended that she was intentionally contaminated by someone at Kerr-McGee. She was 28 at the time of her death. Americium-95, berkelium-97, etc. refer to the nine atomic elements discovered after the initial bombardment of uranium-92 in 1940. The same year, the first industrial production of plutonium-94 (which has a half-life of 27 million years), began in the laboratory of Enrico Fermi. Uranium was used as the core for the Hiroshima detonation; plutonium, which is far "dirtier" than uranium, was used for the Nagasaki denotation.]

LISA MARTINOVIC

Killin' Snakes

I been killin' snakes all my life
copperheads and water moccasins, mostly
and every so often, when I'm ridin' in the brush
a rattler'll slide on out and spook my mule
Don't matter what kind, a'course
I shoot 'em all with my sawed off shotgun
or use whatever else might be handy
shovel works just fine
I kill them snakes without a thought
Man's got to protect his family

They's always killin' to be done on a farm
killin' you got to do
killin' you don't ever want to do

I been killin' dogs all my life
Folks on this here mountain call on me when their old hounds go blind
or get the rabies
they can't bear to do the killin', so they ask me
some folks call me the executioner
but I don't mind
it's a job needs doin'
Hardest thing for me is when my boy has a dog
what won't quit chasin' cows
can't keep a dog like that
can't risk the livestock
I saw a dog one time run a pregnant cow through a pasture
with a calf a'comin out of her
calf died
I been killin' dogs like that all my life

sometimes the killin' don't have no purpose
other than sport
I been killin' deer all my life

best time for that's in winter
if you hit a buck, but you don't drop him
you can follow his trail of blood through the snow
ain't nothin' like followin' a blood trail to a kill
Last buck I got this season came in after dark
I strung him up in the old blackjack tree beside the pond
gutted him by the headlights of my pickup truck
I tell my boys
never kill a deer lessen yer gonna eat it too
God didn't mean for us to waste
I been killin' deer all my life

Last week I was out workin' on my new barn
I felt a strange wigglin' under my boot
sure nuff, it was a big fat writhin' copperhead
I flew backwards bout as far as a man without wings can fly
grabbed me a rock
and scored a direct hit on the bastard's head
Now, I been killin' snakes all my life
and this was the first time I done felt sorry
Seems like ever since I got saved, I been seein' things different
that old snake wasn't hurtin' nobody

I stopped my work
and said a prayer for God's creature smashed to pieces at my feet

later on, my wife asked
did this mean I wasn't gonna kill no more snakes
Hell no! I said
If I see one in the yard tomorrow, I'll shoot it sure as rain

I been killin' snakes all my life
caint even God stop me now

I Was Hitler's Secretary

But it's only a day job
really I'm a poet

but damn I gotta make notebook money
so here I am knocking on one more alien door
to yet another monstrous mindless mystery job
The outgoing temp sez her boss is a total dictator
name of Hitler
yes, *the* Hitler
Like any sensible writer I figure
this will make great material for my muse
I accept the job
we meet
and some how the father of all fascists
seems as ordinary as white toast
but his files are a mess!
I sort and collate, label and alphabetize
Whew!
How did he manage to take Poland without me?
Hitler is so impressed with my crisp Aryan efficiency
he gives me his personal briefcase to manage
Boy, am I important!
I commence Operation Sort
never thinking what I might unearth
then I see it
there--
mingled amongst Luftwaffe bombing patterns and
swatches of Auschwitz uniforms
there lies a crumpled condom
stiff with Fuhrer cum
good god he's human!
this scandalous artifact raises a specter more terrifying than
your average bulging rapist—
if I'm any more zealous a secretary
boss-man might yearn to learn of my hidden talents
and wind up making me a Nazi by injection!
any miscalculating the death counts and I'll be sporting a numerical tattoo
Hey, God, don't make me choose!
I'm just a perverse poet who wanted to tell the world
in precious prose or vulgar verse:
I was Hitler's secretary!
und nothing worse

PETER MARKUS

Sissies

I am not the type of guy you'd cross the street to avoid. You might say—my father used to say so—that I'm a sissy, a wuss, a fairy. That's okay. I don't mind. I am meek and mild and scarecrow-skinny, all the things Jesus was said to be, and if you and I were to meet, even at night, in the darkest hour, walking down a dimly-lit Detroit side-street, the city where I right now live, my appearance would not—or should not, I should say—inspire fear.

My father, on the other hand, he is another story. He is a big man —not big in the way that body-builders get big: muscle-lumpy, awkwardly stiff—but big from working, with his hands clenched, back bent, muscles constantly flexing. In the words of a liquored up buddy of his, my father is built tough, like a Ford truck. Which is true. But not only is my father *built* like a pickup, my father used to *build* them at Ford's Michigan Truck Plant in cross-county Wayne, a twenty-minute drive from where both he and I were born and raised, in River Rouge: a town of hard-hats and steel-toed boots built along the slag-duned shores of the Rouge and the Detroit River —a dirty, tooth-and-nail type town where you wouldn't want to visit, much less live.

My father liked to fight. I remember times when he would come home from work—or from a night spent at some bar—with bloodstained hands: sometimes blood still dripping from his fingers, his knuckles cut raw, skin hanging off in strips. I used to think that this—my father's fight-ing—made him a terrible man; but now I understand that fighting was the one thing he knew he could do better than most of us. And I can't hate him for this.

My father always said the same thing when he came home after one of his fights. "That sons-a-bitch so-and-so," he'd mumble out the side of his mouth. "Teach him a thing or two. Telling me I don't know what I'm talking about."

We lived in a house, a two-bedroom, shingle-brick bungalow, that seemed especially small on the nights of my father's fights. He'd pace the hall in his steel-toed work-boots, his hands balled into fists, chuffing out air through his nose. He looked like a man who felt as if at any minute he could be jumped in the privacy of his own home. Though after a while he'd settle down with a fifth of whiskey on the couch, where he'd fall asleep to the sound of a test pattern hissing on the TV.

My mother never said anything about my father's fights. My guess is that she simply got used to them, the way that you get used to and finally accept the fact that you will always be poor. My mother is not the type of person who believes life is what you make of it. And luck isn't something you can change. In all of my life, I never once saw my mother buy a raffle ticket or play the dollar Lotto. I suppose once she married my father she tossed out all her dice.

Only once did I ever see my father come home nursing a wound of his own. It was also the only time I ever saw my mother comfort my father in a way that made me realize that, at one time, it was possible my parents had actually been in love.

I was in bed at the time, but I wasn't sleeping. I'd just gotten up from a bad dream and was sitting upright in my bed. I was staring into the dark, afraid to close my eyes, trying not to think about the dream, when I heard my mother's voice say, "My God, what happened, are you alright?" all in one gasping breath.

At first, I thought that my mother was speaking to me, but when her silhouette didn't appear in the doorway to my room, I thought maybe I was still dreaming. I got out of bed and stepped quietly into the hall. There I saw, in that gauzy half-light, my mother holding my father's chin in her hands: his right eye swollen completely shut, blood—my father's blood—blackening his hands.

My father didn't say anything. He just nodded his head as if to say that he was okay, and then he slowly raised a finger to his lips, as if he didn't want anybody else to hear.

"Richie's asleep," I heard my mother whisper, though before I could back-step into my room, my father turned his head and looked down the hall to where I'd been standing, hiding halfway in the darkness, halfway in the light.

Nobody ever said anything more about that night.

For a week straight my father wore mirrored sunglasses, even inside the house.

Nobody was going to call Russell Simms a sissy, at least not to his face.

He took the week off from work: personal days. Sick days. Days he'd been meaning to save for summertime. My father liked to sit in the sun and fish. For walleye, catfish, white bass.

At dinner, one night, I sat across from my father so I could try to get a look at his busted-up eye. But all I could see was my own reflection staring back, a little crookedly, at times, when my father realized what I had in mind.

Eventually, the eye healed. And my father went back to his fighting ways.

My father thought it was his duty, as my father, to teach me how to fight. I was in junior high at the time—the age when kids begin to fight with their fists. I was tall for a seventh grader, though I was built like a barbell without any weight. It was time, my father told me, I started to pump some iron. Build some muscles. God knows, when he was my age, even he was as thin as a stick, he said. But it took time for a boy to grow into a man.

I nodded my head, went along with it.

"Stick out your arm a minute," my father instructed. "Straight out in front of your chest."

I did like I was told.

"I bet you got the reach of a goddamn gorilla," he informed me. "A goddamn gorilla," he said again.

"And that's good?" I asked.

"Good?" he said. "You combine that with a little hand speed, you'll be alright."

That afternoon, down among the dust and the musty smell of wet boxes and dried up cans of paint, I learned how to fight: how to shuffle, how to bob and weave, block and spring, bouncing light on the balls of my feet.

My father cut all the lights except one. Suddenly my shadow appeared on the side wall. It was like a side of myself I had never before seen.

We fought. It was more like dancing. I'd never known fighting could be so much fun.

My father made it a point to tell me that there are several ways to hit a man. You can hit a man to hurt him—to physically cut or leave your mark on a man's face; you can hit a man to insult him, rub his nose in his own shit; or you can hit a man to kill him—hit him *that* hard. I didn't want to know about that.

I kept my fighting life indoors, down in the basement, with nobody around, just me and my twice-my-size shadow.

Every day, for a month, when my father got home from work, he'd ask me if I got into any fights.

"Did you get into a scrap today?" he'd ask. "I'll bet you made them bleed?"

I'd watch his eyes get big, then shrink back into his brow when I'd answer, "No."

At the end of that month, my father looked me in the eye and said I was a goddamn sissy.

I felt ashamed. I hated my father, hated him so much I went out the next day and picked a fight with Bruce Holbrook, a sixteen-year old eighth grader with the beginnings of a beard, a kid who drove to school in a 1969 cherried-out Mustang 302: a convertible with mag wheels, duel-exhaust, not a pinch of bondo or rust—the kind of car my father would've died for. So I snuck up from behind Bruce Holbrook's back and I shoved him, and I called him a fag. He turned around, suddenly, with a stunned look on his face, a look that said, with his head cocked, his eyes cut to slits: 'You better not be talking to me.'

So I called his car a puss-mobile, a shit-magnet, a bondo-bucket of rust.

It was all a bunch of lies.

But it didn't take him long to drop me in a puddle of my own blood. One punch. I never even saw it coming my way.

That night I couldn't wait until my father got home. It felt like I was wearing a boot on my nose. I could hardly even breathe.

I met my father as he was coming up the walk. I could hear him humming a country & western song. I think it was "Coward of the County."

"Look," I said. "I fought Bruce Holbrook."

Those few words hurt so bad it felt like I'd been snorting nails up my nostrils.

My father knew Bruce Holbrook. He'd worked with Bruce's father in town for a time over at Great Lakes Steel, back when he was a "hot metal man."

He didn't say anything at first. His yellow hard-hat sat perched on his head, backwards, like a catcher's cap.

"So you got in a scrap with the Holbrook kid," he said, and nodded his head.

"That's right," I said.

"Bruce Holbrook's a pretty big kid," my father said, like he had to remind me.

"The biggest kid in school," I told him.

My father stuck his tongue in the pocket of his cheek, as if he was trying to loosen up food from his teeth. "You shoulda dry-gulched him," he said.

"What?" I didn't know what that meant.

"Next time you kick that bastard in the balls," he explained. "Hit him right where it counts."

I shook my head. "That's fighting dirty," I argued. "Fighting dirty isn't fair."

"He's bigger than you. *That's* not fair. The whole goddamned *world's* not fair."

My father turned then and he disappeared, without another word, into the house.

A few years later, in the winter of 1980, my father lost his job. I was fourteen, a freshman in high school: a kid going through my own set of losses. I'd just begun to understand what was meant by the phrase 'growing pains.' That winter I had shot up seven inches and was now tall—six-two, and thin, too thin: a hundred-and-thirty-five pounds. I was nicknamed the Scarecrow Kid, a name I didn't fight. In fact, I liked it; liked it better than some of the other names I'd been called as a child: names like Itchy, Dickie, Dick Face.

That same spring, from out of nowhere, Bruce Holbrook re-entered my life. I hadn't seen the likes of Bruce Holbrook's face for over two years, since the time he dropped out of school and dropped out of my sight. I was with my father at the time, driving west on Jefferson, along the river, on our way home from a baseball game I'd just finished playing in against the Wyandotte Indians, our biggest rivals. My father seemed in some way upset, though I did not know if this was because of the game or not. We'd lost by a run, though I'd had a pretty good day: two-for-four at the plate, a bunt single, plus an R.B.I. double off the leftfield fence, and I didn't commit a single error at first base. My father drove on in silence, though every once in a while I'd see him shake his head, almost as if he was talking to himself.

"I don't know why Coach MacDonald left Schultz's kid in as long as he did," he finally said. "I mean Christ, by the seventh inning that looping curveball of his was hanging like a goddamned weather balloon. He gave the game away by leaving Butchy in like that. That's a sign of poor coaching."

I could smell whiskey on his breath. Ever since he'd been laid off, he had a habit of drinking first thing in the morning. Kessler's had taken the place of Maxwell House.

"Your mother could've coached a better game," my father went on. "I don't know about that cop-coach of yours. He better learn to keep his head in the game if he knows..." He didn't finish his thought. His voice trailed off into silence.

I wanted to defend Coach Mac. I wanted to explain to my father that Couz, our ace reliever, could barely raise his right arm. But I figured it wouldn't do any good.

I knew my father was beyond the point of talking. He'd already made up his mind.

"Motherfuckers," my father then cussed, laying on his horn with the heel of his right hand, pounding it, punching the accelerator pedal to the floor.

I didn't see what'd happened. I was busy looking at the river where a row of fisherman stood, shoulder to shoulder, casting huge silver spoons into the wind out toward the Canadian shoreline shrouded by a thickening ridge of dark marbly-looking clouds that were coming our way.

"What is it?" I asked.

"Cocksucker cut me off."

My father locked the brakes to a skidding halt at a redlight on the corner of Jefferson and Outer Drive, across the way from the blank marquee of the boarded-up Harbor Theatre.

A jacked-up Mustang 302, shined up red like a wax apple, its engine chugging heavy beneath the hood, sat idling, waiting for the light to turn green.

My father edged up, lined up the side-mirror of our pickup with the mirror on the passenger side of the Boss 302.

He hit the horn, twice.

The guy in the 302 looked over, and then he smiled. And that was when I recognized Bruce Holbrook's face: looking older, covered by a thick beard.

My father elbowed open his door and got out. He stood there, in the middle of the street, his hands clenched. He walked around to the driver's side, and I heard him say, "Come on," waving at Bruce Holbrook to come out of the car. Then he hollered, "Teach you how to drive that piece of shit."

Bruce Holbrook stepped out of the car, then. But it was no contest.

My father dry-gulched Bruce Holbrook, a grunting knee to the groin, that dropped him to the street, doubled in on himself, like somebody who'd just been shot.

But my father didn't stop there. He kicked him, twice, in the ribs, with his steel-toed boots, then once more in the ass. Then he back-kicked, like a donkey would, the front quarter-panel on the passenger side of the 302. It was as if my father was saying, 'Look who's boss now.' Though all I knew was that this was more work than those boots had seen in two-and-a-half months.

My father got back inside the pickup and drove off without saying a word.

And he didn't say anything the whole rest of the way, until we pulled up in our driveway, which was when he turned to face me and matter-of-factly said, "Don't ever say your old man never does nothing for you. That was payback for the broken nose." We never talked about Bruce Holbrook ever again.

That summer, though, something happened that I haven't been able to stop talking about. I tell people about it all the time. Just like how I'm telling you.

My father got in a fight and he killed a man. I'm telling you. It's true.

It didn't happen the way you might think. The fight. For one thing, it didn't take place in a bar, or outside some bar in an alley: those settings where most of my father's fights did, in fact, occur, at one time or another. The fight that I want to tell about now came about at home, as if trouble had walked right up and rapped its knuckles on our front door.

It happened in July, on the weekend of the Fourth, though the way I saw it, my father didn't have much to celebrate. He'd been out of work now for close to six months, and I know that I was beginning to wonder if he'd ever go back to working at Ford's. I'm sure my mother was thinking some of these very same thoughts; though I never heard her say a word about it one way or another.

My mother did say this. On the Wednesday before the Fourth, I heard her ask my father if he wouldn't mind if she invited her brother, my uncle Tom, and his wife, my aunt Mary, over to grill up some hot dogs.

Then maybe later we could all head downtown to see the hydroplane races. My mother knew that my father wouldn't say no to watching those fancy-finned, three-hundred horse-powered outboard boats scoot across the rough waters between the Windsor-Detroit channel, shooting roostertails to cool off the crowds.

It was not a secret that my father did not like my uncle Tom. Uncle Tom was my mother's older brother, and although he and my aunt Mary didn't live but a half hour away, up the river in St. Clair Shores, where he owned his own business—a print shop, I think it was—we only saw them maybe three or four times a year.

I understood why my father did not like my uncle Tom. Uncle Tom was a know-it-all. He gave advice free of charge, even when you didn't ask for it. Once, when I was ten and I told him that I wanted to be a fireman when I grew up, he shook his head, crossed his arms at his chest, then said being a fireman was dirty work, that I was a smart kid and I shouldn't waste my time working with my hands.

My father was in the living room at the time, watching TV, though I knew that Tom was talking loud enough for him to hear our conversation. But on that occasion, my father didn't say anything to me or to Uncle Tom. Though later on, after everyone had gone, I heard my father tell my mother that one of these days, if he didn't watch what he said, he was going to put that cocksucking, cocky, Republican brother of hers in his goddamned place.

I was out in the backyard helping my father get the barbecue ready, filling the grill with chunks of charcoal, soaking the coals with lighting fluid, when I heard the doorbell ring and heard my mother's voice warn us, "They're here."

I glanced up at my father and he looked at me and rolled his eyes, and he did not have to say what he was thinking. When I heard my uncle Tom say, "Happy birthday to a great country," I thought my father was going to draw blood from his bottom lip.

"Let's get this over with," he finally said. "Wish me luck. I'll be needing it." And what I felt, then, at that moment, was that my father and I were in this fight together. I knew that it was going to be a long, hot day.

A few minutes later my uncle Tom appeared on the back steps holding two bottles of Stroh's and a can of Mountain Dew.

"Martha told me you two boys were out here trying to set the neighborhood on fire," he said, "so I thought I'd bring you out a cold beverage to cool things down a bit."

I couldn't help but smile at the stupid grin Uncle Tom had plastered on his face. He was dressed in a way that seemed like he was on his way to play golf, ready to step up to the tee in his lime-green slacks and his yellow polo shirt with the little alligator sewn on above his left breast.

But it was true: it was hot. The thermometer nailed to the trunk of a hemlock tree read that it was already eighty-eight, in the shade. It was not yet noon. The big boats upriver weren't scheduled to hit the water until two o'clock.

"Thanks, Uncle Tom," I told him, and my father said, "That sure was thoughtful."

"So, what's cooking?" my uncle Tom said. He handed my father a cold beer. My father took it and then he took a good long drink, the muscles in his throat working hard to swallow it down. I could tell from the way sunlight hit and lit the brown-tinted glass that my father'd drained half the bottle. Then my uncle added: "We sure as hell know the auto industry ain't burning up nobody's deck. Isn't that right, Russell?"

My father made a grunting sound as if metal shavings had been mixed into his beer. But he didn't put what he was thinking into words. The look on his face was of a man who'd just struck his thumb with a hammer. "Times have been tough over here on this side of the river," my father said. "But we're not worried. Things'll pick up again. They always do. Though I guess we'll just have to wait and see."

I'm sure my father wanted to seem optimistic, though I wondered how he truly felt about things.

"Yeah, well," Uncle Tom shook his head, "I saw in the Detroit *News* the other day how the mill down the river a bit in Trenton, McLouth Steel, I read that it's this close to shutting itself down." He pinched his thumb and his index finger together like someone who was about to thread a sewing needle.

"Who really knows what's gonna happen," my father shrugged. "It's a touch and go time everywhere." He shoved out his big bottom lip.

"Yeah, well, I don't know," Uncle Tom went on, "I think it's a sign of things to come."

"Is that so," was all my father said.

"I think you should start thinking about a move," Uncle Tom told my father. "You're skilled. You're still young. How old are you again, Russ?"

My father didn't say anything. He acted like he was busy tending to the grill, to the fire that wasn't yet lit.

"Dad's thirty-six," I said. "He'll be thirty-seven this September."

I was still at an age when you believe the older you are the better off you will be.

"You hear that, Russell?" Uncle Tom asked. "Richie here's counting off the years for you, aren't you son?"

I smiled, though my father looked like he'd heard just about enough talk for one day.

"I'd be worried," Uncle Tom said. "If I were in your shoes. I mean, boots. Excuse me." He made a sound in his throat like he was clearing away the phlegm.

The can of lighter fluid fell from my father's hands. When he bent down to pick it up, I could see his lips moving as though he was muttering something to himself. I wanted to hear what he wasn't saying. But I had an idea.

When my father finally spoke all he said was, "Don't. Don't worry."

My uncle Tom said, "You know, Russell, if ever I can be of help. It wouldn't be like a handout."

"Don't," my father said again. "Don't you talk to me that way." And I thought, for a moment, that my father was about to hit my uncle Tom in a way that would say, 'Smell this,' that he was going to rub Tom's nose in a pile of shit.

"Okay, okay, okay," Uncle Tom said, and he raised his hands. "I can take a hint. Don't say I didn't offer though."

And my father said, "I won't."

"What's the hold up," my mother said, a little while later. "Are we having some trouble lighting the charcoal?" She sounded more cheerful than she had in the past two or three months.

"No trouble," my uncle Tom answered, and I knew he wished this were true.

My aunt Mary came outside then holding a sparkler in her hand. When she lit it she handed it to me, like she figured I'd get a kick out of it, though in the midday light its shower of fire seemed as dramatic as a fire drill at school.

Somewhere in the neighborhood, though, it sounded as if someone had set off a bomb—a boom so loud I think all of us raised our hands to our heads.

My father seemed especially unnerved by the explosion. He'd been in Vietnam in the mid-sixties, the years right before I was born, though this wasn't something he liked to talk about. He'd been on edge all week, since the sound of firecrackers blowing up had taken the place of cicadas flexing their wings. Even the paperbag snap of a Ladyfinger—a type of firecracker you can hold in your hand without fear of losing a finger—caused him to hunch his shoulders and flinch and look behind his back as if somebody was approaching.

"Goddamn hoodlums," my father said. "It sounds like a goddamned war out there in the streets." He looked around then as if he was going to put an end to something.

"There's no harm done, Russell," my uncle Tom said. "It's just kids being kids." He swigged off his beer then and he scrunched up his face the way I did the first time I drank a too-big sip of whiskey from my father's canteen while we were ice-fishing out on Lake Erie's Brest Bay. I was maybe nine or ten.

Then my uncle Tom crossed the line and said something he should not have said, did something he should not have done.

"I always knew there was a softer side of you, Russell," he said to my father. "Hidden under all that." Uncle Tom smiled, poked a finger into my father's gut.

And that's when it happened. It was like a quick-wicked firecracker exploding in your hand.

My father slapped Tom's finger away from his belly and then hit him with the open flat of his hand, at the base of his palm—he hit him hard, as hard as you can hit a man, in the bony part of my uncle's chest. And my uncle Tom fell then, straight back from his heels, as if he'd had his feet kicked out from under him. At first he made kind of a coughing sound, eyes open wide as if he'd seen the rage in my father's eyes staring at him like the headlights from an oncoming truck that had lost use of its brakes. And then he fell. He fell like I'd seen boxers fall on TV—fall and then just lay there as if they would never get up again. And the sound of my uncle's body hitting the paved drive was a sound I had never heard before: a flat, lifeless sound I haven't heard since, one I don't ever want to hear again.

"My God, my God," my aunt Mary said, and she covered her hands over her mouth. She ran to his side then, and she lifted his head up off the hard ground. "Are you okay?" she said. "Tommy sweetheart, talk to me. Tell me you're not hurt."

My uncle Tom didn't say anything. He just lay there, on the ground, not moving, though his fingers and feet every once in a while would twitch the way that people do when they are dreaming, when they are trying to run away from a bad dream. But this wasn't a dream. And my uncle Tom was in no position to get up and run. Even his eyes shifted in their sockets like in a dream, rapidly, from side to side. And all I could do was wonder what he he was looking at: if he was looking up at us, at my aunt or my father, or if he was looking up at nothing but sky.

"Martha," my aunt called out, looking even more helpless than Uncle Tom himself.

Though my mother had already gone back inside, and was probably already dialing 911.

And right at that moment it felt like my father and I were standing outside alone. And what I thought then, though I didn't say it, was 'Run.'

And my father looked at me then, with his arms dangling flat at his sides, and then he moved, first one way, then another, so that he reminded me of an animal—a lion, maybe—locked up in a cage. And then he trotted down the driveway—the way that a baseball player trots off to first base when he's intentionally walked—and he hopped up into his truck. And then he drove off, though he didn't burn rubber the way that you'd think. And I didn't know what to do with myself at that point in time. I looked down at my hand, at the sparkler that had burned itself out. And then I just stood there, silently, as if I were by myself, and waited for what I didn't know what would happen next.

I knew my uncle Tom was already dead by the time the police and the EMS team had arrived. I could tell by the way that he had all of a sudden quit moving, even his fingers and toes, as though all life had left his body as quietly as a breath.

My mother wrestled my aunt Mary away from my uncle's body while the two paramedics did whatever they could to bring him back to life: mouth to mouth—those things that sometimes can make a stopped heart start beating again.

My uncle Tom was pronounced dead, dead-on-arrival, at Wyandotte General hospital. Cause of death: cardiac arrest. A heart attack. Though I knew my father'd had a hand in all of that.

A policeman by the name of Gravel took me aside and told me to tell him what happened. "Go slow," he said. "From the beginning." Which is what I have tried to do here with you.

After telling him much of what I have just finished telling you, he asked me if I knew where my father might've gone. "We just need to talk to him ourselves," he told me. "Accidents happen," he tried to assure me. But I didn't tell. Not right then, I didn't. I figured I'd let my father enjoy one last day in the sun.

They found my father, like I knew they would, just like I told them they would, later that same night. He was sitting down by the river behind the triple-towered Ren Cen building in downtown Detroit—Hart Plaza, it's called—where only a few hours earlier people fought to get a closer peek at the big-engined hydroplanes as they skimmed by, helmets flashing, fists raised in the air.

That entire afternoon—while my mother tried to offer my aunt Mary words of comfort; while police walked into our house, without knocking, as if they now lived here too; and neighbors gathered in the street, pointing fingers; and I sat inside listening to stories circulate about my father's vicious temper: how he was a time-bomb waiting to go off, a crazed vet, an out of work lunatic, and a drunk—I pictured my father standing along the bank of the Detroit River, his stomach pressed up against the steel guard-rail, shirt off, a cold beer in hand: just another face in the crowd, just another fist clenched, just another hoarse-holler voice shouting, "Go! Go! Go!"

When they finally found my father—after I finally told them where to look—my father turned himself in without a fight. I think he realized that he'd crossed a line I'm sure he never really thought he'd see himself step across, and he figured he'd be better off facing his troubles head on than he would by making a run for it.

I was there when the cops cuffed him and took him away in the back cab of the patrol car, though I didn't see him after that until after he'd been arraigned and brought up on manslaughter charges for killing my uncle with his fists.

During his trial my father didn't say more than a handful of words. When the judge—Judge McNamara, whose son I used to play baseball with —asked my father how he wanted to plea to the charges, my father replied, simply, "No contest," which was his way of admitting guilt for all of what happened.

Afterwards, as they were taking my father back to his waiting cell, I couldn't help but notice how much smaller he looked, standing before the judge in those drab-blue prison clothes—my father, who had always seemed so much bigger than life. It was as if I were seeing him now for the first time. Who I saw was a man who looked like he'd been in a fight and had lost. And now that the fight was over he didn't know what to do, which way to turn, or who to turn to.

As it turns out my father was sentenced to spend seven-to-ten years at Marquette Correctional, a prince-of-a-place if you compare it to Jackson State. It's true that a man like my father can kill a man and still be pardoned for an early parole. My father ended up serving a little bit less than five years for killing my uncle, but in all those years my mother and I only visited him twice. I don't know why we didn't go see him more often than this. I didn't give it much thought, then, back when it mattered; but now, I think about it often. I think about him—my father—and I realize this: we were afraid. We were all fighting to say the words: "I'm afraid."

I saw my father just the other day. It'd been three years since I'd last seen him. You would think that you'd recognize your own father if you crossed paths with him on an otherwise deserted sidewalk in the middle of the day. But I didn't. I was walking along Michigan Avenue down near Tiger Stadium and the old and still-beautiful but abandoned Amtrak train station when I saw a man coming my way. Keep in mind: this is Detroit, a city where even in the light of day it is common practice to cross a street, at all cost, to stay out of trouble's way. So I'd cut down Trumbull toward the two-room flat I rent in Corktown when all of a sudden someone called out, "Hey sissy." I picked up my pace a bit, but then stopped and turned around when I heard my name. "Richie Simms." And I realized it was my father. I shoved my hands, my fists, into the pockets of my pants. I don't know why I did this.

"Hey there, Dad," I said. And that was all. I didn't know what else to say.

"So," my father said. And he nodded. "It's been a while. How've you been?"

"Not too bad," I told him. Which was not an all-in-out lie. "I live right around the corner there on Bagley." I kind of pointed off to my left with my shoulder.

My father glanced that way, then shifted his gaze across the street to Tiger Stadium, which looked deserted and lonely and cold. It was still two months away from Opening Day. "How about that," he said. "You can walk to the old ballpark."

"I do," I told him.

"We'll have to go sometime."

"We will."

"Okay," my father then said.

And we both just stood there, then, as if there was nothing else to say. I wanted to know what my father was thinking at that moment—I wanted to know what he was doing here, now; though I knew this was too much to ask.

"I've stopped fighting," my father said—he said it as if he had been rehearsing it: that one line over and over again; but it still came out sounding stiff.

"Good," I said. "Good to hear."

"I just thought I'd let you know," he added. "I thought maybe you'd like to know."

"Thank you," I said. "I do."

"How about you?" my father then said. "Tell me what's new with you. I am your father. I should know these things."

I didn't know what to say or where to begin. So I told him what had *not* changed.

"I'm still a sissy."

"The Scarecrow Kid," my father said, and smiled, and I smiled back. "My son the sissy." He nodded with his chin. "I guess there's worst things to be in life."

"I guess so," I said, though whether my father thought this was so, or if he was just saying it, I don't know.

"How about it now, Scarecrow?" my father said. He raised his fists. "You and me. One last fight. Show me all you know. Everything I taught you."

"Here?" I said.

I looked around. We were the only ones standing out on the street. A cargo truck hauling fill-dirt muscled by up Trumbull in a blur of fast food wrappers and dust.

"Why not?" my father asked. "It's as good a place as any place I've ever fought."

I pulled my hands out of my pockets.

"Well okay now, alright," my father said. And what I thought, then, was he must be drunk, though I couldn't smell any liquor on his clothes or breath. He was bobbing his head, back and forth, like a boxer who had just set foot inside the ring. "Come on now, Scarecrow. Let me see what you're made of." He shuffled from boot to boot, chuffed air out his mouth. "I may be old and out of shape," he breathed heavy, "but I'm still your father. I can still whoop your skinny ass." He was grinning, trying to egg me on, to get me to fight. "That's good, kid," he said. "I see those hands. Now just curl those bony fingers of yours into fists. Oh yeah. Uh-hum. That's right, Scarecrow. That's it, boy. It's just you and me now. Just you and your old man."

I narrowed my eyes. "I thought you said you stopped fighting?"

"What's one last fight?" my father said and shrugged, his shoulders swallowing his neck. "For old time's sake."

I raised my hands, felt my fingers flex back slowly and close up on themselves into fists.

"Well I guess," I said. "Why not?" I shook my head. "But no hitting below the belt."

"Are you ready?" my father asked. "You got your fighting socks on?"

I nodded. I was ready. I looked my father straight in the eye and I said, "Come on."

I swung. I hit him hard just below the left eye: a lucky shot.

"Not bad," my father said. "I always said you had the reach of a goddamn monkey."

"It was a gorilla," I corrected, and connected again, a left jab to his jaw.

"Quick hands." He ran his tongue over his bottom lip. I wondered if I drew blood.

"Come on," I said again, and I threw a wild right, a looping roundabout, that grazed his ear.

"He's cooking now, boy," my father said. "Will you look at that. We should go down to Kronx gym. Sign you up with Emanuel Steward. See if Tommy Hearns is up for a little sparring with a white boy born and raised in River Rouge."

"You're talking more shit," I told my father, "than Muhammad Ali."

I was breathing harder than I had in months, maybe even years. Cold air drawn down into my lungs got coughed back up white, then rose into the sky. And for a moment it felt as if I was back in the basement of our home in River Rouge, boxing my shadow. Not fighting. More like dancing with myself. Dancing to music only I could hear.

"Sting like a butterfly," my father sang, "float like a goddamn bee." He grinned a shit-eating grin.

"Come on now, old man, built tough like a truck," I spit back. "Quit standing there like a sissy."

"So I'm a sissy now too?"

"That's what I said, sissy," I said. I regretted saying it the moment the words left my mouth.

My father hit me once then, hard. I could feel the bones in my nose crumble behind the force of his fist.

I fell back on my ass. When I breathed, I thought I heard laughter. I couldn't tell the difference between the street and sky.

Later, as I fought to get back to my feet, and the world gradually fell back into place, I remember my father reaching down, the sound of his voice whispering in my ear, his breath hot on the back of my neck: "Don't forget this now, Scarecrow. You hear? I'm still your father, see. And I'm still bigger than you."

GEOFF PENROSE

Where You Go When You Don't Work

A friend called it "unenjoyment"
as he rode a junkyard-saved Schwinn,
with complimentary orange and rust spots
        that colored together
            as he pedalled to the state offices.

$132.75 each and every week
smack barrel-headed by Uncle Sam
right to his house no stamp. That's
what he got I think, but 1989
is when I'm talking
                and things
                cost more
                these days.

So today when I line up,
today when I take in
safe-lifting posters
with my best deconstructionist technique
and request extra paper
and a typewriter
            for the explaining,
today when the gum-chomping drunks
recognize the tenor of my body
and wheeze insinuation,
I'll be wanting
            more.

Rubbed brown track on a red carpet.
Finger-worn worry ruts in formica.
        This money...
        This money...

I can wait through noon

and only be eighteenth in line
for the telling of my worth.
I can gaze around dumb-blasted telling
Marx to my hand. A child
smacks cheese puffs inflated of America,
his loving parents together in line,
"no Jimmy"-ing without a look when
he tugs my leg and points
out the door at the bustling
contraptions those working
resemble; to work and work
for money and money...

****

Six dollars an hour each hour worked
of that July we thought shade
a bathful of miracle. Hand by hand
with crowbars and rakes me
and other men brick by bricked
down a weary brownstone
        finding pennies
that fell through some farmer's numb hand
to his benign curse,
and through the slots in the roughed
oak floor.

Biceps of slim pride tanning.
Dust the color. Dust the mouth.

Roger boss-man knew
the building way back when,
and told a little tale for each story
we made gone: high school champs,
1936—worked at a milk farm—chopped
fence-poles for fun and work and less money
than us punks only used
for beer each 5:00 in shaded red light
and pizza the color of dust

or for gas to leave Rog, to cruise

to the beach to leave off a skin,
and new books whose authors
never labored more than Rog, never
built or unbuilt or straddled rafters
in dust-cloths picking pennies
from cracks left unhanded
for half-a-century and more of crumble.

****

The working woman
            behind the job service counter,
        like all women,
    is my lover.
Approaching her, I've known
the arcs of her forearms
and liftings of her chest for hours.

As she tells me the worth
of my services,
            I go deep into her eyes
                for how she feels
                about the circled "18"
                next to "years of schooling"
                and the "preferred job," a lie:
                "English Professor."

She's 38 at the perfect least
and from some rumble in her cheeks
I'd say two kids strong and done.
I wonder if she worked
as they built inside, her oak chair customized
for hemorrhoids, her stiff lips
daring comment
on damp evidences of milk; she'd horrify
any slackers
            in her line of work.

Production cell-by-cell plus a paycheck.
Making work making worker. Making money.
Seems I'm worth ninety-two dollars each and every week.

****

Three times teenage workers
have cornered me
while stuck for the salmon season
on a toenail of cannery land,

and disclosed seeds
working in their wombs.

Company policy would move them
out of my grabbing machinery section,
but I asked them to stay because that sort of labor
deserves pay, I thought, knowing
my want of them there
sprung more from the chance
the new mom
might touch me once

if I should smash my hand when a wrench breaks.

****

These hands,

want to shape soul
with a knotty wood
carving that becomes a doorframe.

These hands,

some mornings,
wander down to my crotch
and embrace there
work to be done.

These hands,

born tired relieve the pressure
in valves and smooth gouges
in formica.

These hands
scuff until blood
crawls to light

and reddens the whole world that
means hands,
    and red,
        and doorframes.

           ****

Eight dollars an hour independent contracted
to mold and spindle oak strips
for cushy chairs furniture executives
would sit upon:
        I believe
        I knew this job like I'd been born
to tell metal men
and the women they attract
how wood
works but

such hubris cannot mean more
than the carpet worked
under so many feet
it sparkles.

           ****

If you go down
to the unemployment lines,

if you should need to go down
with the men and women
to the unemployment lines,

if you should see a similar scene
with similar women
and similar worth,
        remember
        your hands,
     the motions
they make on a work-site
inviting an order as-yet-unfounded,
        but shaping joy
        in the simple search

that is your hands
caressing money
from a dull wood stud
or hen scratches on paper.

If you go down

passing couples
productive
of flesh, and the butcher, the baker
and the movie ticket-taker, the fireman
watching, the prostitute, watching,
and the land lawyers and marriage
brokers, carpenters, cooks,
teacher-painters and street sweeping
people who deal with trash of all...
and you're maybe appalled
at the hustle-bustle
nudge-nudge follow-me whistles,
work whistles,
direction whistles,

remember
your lungs,
and the amount of sky
they can hold.

Friend, if you go down
to that unemployment line
and leave with your worth
in hand,
and turn right with that money
out the door toward downtown with that money
and store bells chant transactions
with that money and jack hammers
prepare ye the way with
that money and a steam from lungs
wreathes it all with that money remember
work will save
when money is spent.

Los Angeles Habitat for Humanity workers, 1995 © Leigh Charlton

CLEANING STALLS IN WINTER

WORK ETHIC & DIGNITY

GERALDINE CONNOLLY

Past the Corner, Opening Gate

-Stanislaus Skavinski
(1883-1927)

Their father's memory arose
as they labored, bones of glass,
braided veins, the dark mustache.

After that carload of coal swerved
                as Number Seven Mine,
his spine was crushed, and his sons
forced to work in the glass factory.
                    They assembled
goblets and stems, cake dishes and feet,
Michael, Jiggs, twelve and fourteen
          holding the platter of the family
                      together.

In the city,
                carrying tin lunchpails
                down past the corner
                to the opening gate,

they watched dawn's fiery tongue
          devour the morning.
Nightfall, they returned
to read to their brothers and sisters
from the book
about a dog that looked up at them,
          his saucer eyes aglow.

"The dish ran away" says the youngest
who is my mother, "ran away with father."
His sons
          breathed in smoke as they worked

deafened by roaring gears
as they ground down, doubled over,
      scrolling sheafs of wheat
onto the dazzling glass.

Vase after vase
was stamped and sealed,
sent down the line,
      one to hold
flowers from the cutting garden,

a pitcher for lemonade,
  a poached egg holder,
   a brandy snifter,

for the woman at dinner
in her great house
      on Prospect Hill.

She tips it back, drinks
  from its crystal mouth,
her lips grazing
      a cold rim.

She touches
its curve of cheek
      above the linen cloth

this piece of glass
etched with wheat
before the hearth fire.

The Way She Could Disappear

Adella stepped out
from steerage and leaned
against a stair rail—
long braids wound into a knot,
her spirit rising.
The gray skirt hung,
dusty with old world dirt,
plain and foreign
among the flour sacks,
yet edged with a thin
trim of vermillion.

She liked the way she could disappear,
one face among a sea
of faces, roulette-like,
whirligigged: onion domes, slashed
crosses, children wheeling
dizzily on bicycles, a woman sweeping
the street with her broom.
From the mill, a flare of red thunder.

Beneath high buildings, she passed
windows made of thin glass,
ringing trolleycars, a blind man
with one leg, selling gladioli.
Coke ovens blasted their smoke
but she flew by, going to the edge
of where she would like to be
passing through into greenness

to the county with that name—
Somerset. She wanted a farm.
She wanted a safe place
where she could be at peace,
even though
she would pay the price,
never part of the old life now,
nor part of this.

Pears

they remind me,
the dried fruits she sent—
tart apples, cherries,
pear, of the way
her life was shrunk,
turned into some diminished thing
she was forced to eat—
chicken heart, pig's knuckle,
beef tongue.

They loaded the family
furniture into a truck
when her father died.
She stuffed her three silver dollars
into a sack and held it
on her lap. I bite
the thought in two.

Her brother lifted her
onto the stack of baggage.
She pushed down on it
to deep that knot of rope
from unravelling. "The city"
they talked of drew

a picture of concrete and smoke,
girls skipping across a sidewalk.
Holding still as she could,
she looked straight ahead
and remembered one knife,
a golden pear on its own plate.
This thought alone kept
those bags from flying off.

JO GIESE

They Shoot at Houses, Too

"I *digs* roofin'!" hollers James, a 12-year-old waving a staple gun. Straddling the peak of the roof, he takes aim at another shingle (*Pow! Pow!*), and yells, "I ain't comin' down!"

"I'm glad you want to work," shouts Ron Brunner. He's craning his head back, squinting up to the roof where society's throwaways -- gang kids, foster kids, welfare kids—have clumped themselves tightly together at the top of the ladder like slivers of magnetized metal. Cupping his hands around his mouth to be heard above the construction din of a hundred volunteers, Ron explains the new rules to the children, most of whom have worked on this single-family house on Watts Avenue for the past ten Saturdays: "As of today the insurance cut-off for kids on the roof is fourteen years of age."

Jasmin, a pudgy eight-year-older, mistakenly thinks Mr. Brunner is saying that the kids must stop working on the house completely. This blow causes the second-grader to start comfort-sucking on the yellow pacifier that hangs around her neck. Light-skinned, 12-year-old Yoyce, who has told every adult on the job site that he wants to be a doctor, is peering over the edge with worried eyes. The one-boy-crime-wave in the neighborhood, 13-year-old Van, whose Reeboks are worn so slick he has no traction for roof work, is already on a classic downhill slide to juvenile hall, jail, and prison. But right now skinny, muscular, angry Van is ripping the wrapper off a bundle of shingles, impatient for Ron to leave so he can get back to work.

A house under construction anywhere attracts kids but the building of a Habitat for Humanity single-family dwelling in South Central L.A., has pulled in a ragtag group of kids who, ordinarily, wouldn't hang together. But they are so drawn to this work that they show up early to tie on a nail apron, buckle on a tool belt, and grab a hammer before the adults get all the good tools.

"This is messed up!" pouts James. He's also disappointed that his new dressed-to-kill head scarf, which earlier in the morning had cut a menacing swath with the other volunteers (who are mostly white and middle-class) is not impressing Ron Brunner.

"It'll be really messed up if somethin' happens to you," says Ron. As a Habitat volunteer, Ron Brunner, 57-years-old, dressed in jeans, T-shirt, and sandals (because he's footsore), is trying to keep the kids from falling over the edge of the roof. But as a black man from South Central who made it out of the ghetto to west Point (class of '58), who helped negotiate the '92 truce between the Bloods and the Crips, and who currently finds jobs for gang kids, this man knows the jeopardy facing this next generation of ghetto kids is far greater than falling fourteen feet off a roof. The kids are probably safer up on the roof than down in the hood.

In most cities a rooftop view can enlarge and expand the scope of a child's vision, sending it soaring up and away beyond the realities of their daily life. Except in South Central a longer lens only furnishes a bigger view of what's wrong: the kids can see that the prairies of graffitied houses do extend forever; that Watts Tower has been stripped of its former dazzling glory; and that neighbor, who doesn't think anyone's watching, is dumping an armload of garbage in the middle of the street. Ron Brunner, who recently rented an apartment in this area and described the nights as "a mix between Viet Nam and the Fourth of July," also serves on Habitat's Family Selection Committee. Two families that had qualified for the next Habitat house refused this Watts Avenue lot that the Community Development Commission of L.A. County granted to Habitat for $1: a "couch family" of five people living on a couch in a brother's house; and a "composite family" of twenty crowded into a parent's two-bedroom house. Both families told Ron they wanted a chance at the American Dream of home-ownership but didn't want a twenty-year mortgage tying them to Watts Avenue, an area with eight gangs.

Habitat for Humanity International is the non-profit, all-volunteer builder, headquartered in Americus, Georgia, that gets high visibility from First Carpenter Jimmy Carter. Since 1976 the group has built almost 40,000 houses. With 984 affiliates in the U.S. and 163 international affiliates, in 1996 Habitat will complete a new home every daylight hour of every day. Typically, they build in high-risk areas like Hidalgo Street in San Antonio, the Lower East side in Manhattan, and Watts Avenue in South Central, because that's where the cheapest land is available in urban areas.

"Good mornin'," Ron nods to Angel Lowery, the 33-year-old black home-owner-to-be of this house. Emptying a dustpan through the studs of the kitchen, her black leggings and shirt with a ruffle around the hips are already gray from construction dust. There's something about Angel tidying up with her broom that unequivocally states ownership, that says, there might be a mess of volunteers everywhere but this here is: *my house.*

On July 12, 1992, at 5 o'clock p.m., Calvin Jerome Lowery, Angel's 31-year-old husband, a substitute cafeteria worker who also repairs bullet holes in auto bodies at $15 a hole, was giving a customer a curbside estimate in front of his apartment when a carload of South low gang bangers drove up. As Calvin ran for cover, the Hispanic gang shot him in both legs. Calvin, a high school drop-out, who says he's never done anything worse than "beat up people and take their lunch money," claims the shooting was racial:Mexicans against blacks, and on Sunday afternoon he was the only black on the street. If a home is a castle, in South Central it's also a fortress with bars on the windows and security gates across the yard. After the shooting the Lowery family (Mookie, 12, Shakeila, 9, and Latoya, 6) became prisoners in their apartment. On her application for a Habitat house, Angel, who works three hours a day in the cafeteria at Washington High School, wrote: "It's so much bad goin' on I can't explain them all."

At the Family Selection meeting Ron asked his fellow committee members: "Are we doing the Lowerys a favor? Calvin Lowery has already been shot. How will moving from an apartment into a house at such a prime drive-by shooting location be any better? They shoot at houses, too."

In the eight months since the shooting a disabled Calvin Lowery has progressed from wheelchair to walker. He says a house his family owns will be better than a rental apartment because with a house, "I can say to the dudes, 'Stay out! This is *private* property!'" Watts Avenue is also the couple's home turf: between Angel's four siblings and Calvin's seven, most of their relatives are nearby, including angel's mother who lives within walking distance at Imperial Courts, a mean, 36 acre, two-story, cinder-block public housing project where crime is higher inside its borders than outside.

However, Ron Brunner's most pressing concern this Saturday morning is still to get the kids off the roof. He could resort to the West Point command—*You must!*—but Captain Brunner was once Ron Brunner, a kid from a broken home in South Central. "Come on down," he pleads. "I'm serious. I'm gonna have a heart attack."

"I'm fourteen!" lies James. Nonetheless, the twelve-year-old in the gang scarf steps toward the ladder, and the others follow.

Slouching and sprawling down on the ground, the kids half-listen to Ron explaining construction jobs they can do. Always testing authority, James turns to start up the ladder. "Don't do that because I'm going to order you down."

"We can't work?" says Yoyce. The pain in his voice conveys that something valuable is being snatched from him. With an understanding beyond his years, Yoyce had commented to Ron: "I can look back and say, 'I built that house.' That doesn't happen to a kid. It's a once-in-a-lifetime experience."

"You can do *safe* work," stresses Ron. "You can offload trucks, keep the little children and animals off the site. Do you buy into that?"

Habitat Volunteer Saturdays are an exercise in perpetual motion, and by next week the kids will be back stapling shingles on the roof. But now they're making a beeline around the front porch, fanning out, dispersing into the horde of volunteers. Just as this house has been a magnet for kids, it has also pulled in adults, who after daring to venture into South Central once, got hooked on the feeling that they were making an immediate tangible contribution.

Los Angeles Habitat for Humanity workers 1995 © Leigh Charlton

In speaking about the Clinton administration's call to national service, Hillary Rodham Clinton has spoken about a vacuum where "we lack at some core level meaning in our individual lives...that sense that our lives are part of some greater effort." Habitat's power is that it fills that spiritual vacuum both for the adequately-housed volunteers from the suburbs who come to help, and the under-housed volunteers from the ghetto who are helping themselves. When a volunteer spews the Habitat line about "building housing and hope," a cynical listener is apt to rush to the conclusion that the volunteer means hope for the disadvantaged poor but the volunteer is just as likely to be speaking, perhaps unconsciously, about restoring hope for himself—a middle-class American who lives miles from the L.A. ghetto, who watched it burn in the '92 riots, who grew fearful of new riots spreading to his community in '93, and who is stunned by the epidemic of violent crime in '94 and '95.

Jack Davidson, who has built over 9,000 residences in the for-profit sector before his construction company donated his services to Habitat-L.A., has commented, "I'm not much of a flag waver, but when you come around the corner at Watts Avenue and see a house where a garbage dump used to be, it does somethin' to you."

Relying on volunteer labor, donated materials, and donated land, Habitat is able to produce housing cheaper than any other L.A. builder. On Watts Avenue this formula will translated into a 3-bedroom, 1 bath, 1,050 square-foot house which Habitat will sell to the Lowerys for $55,000 (for-profit housing in South Central would be 2 to 3 times); 1% down payment ($550), plus 500 hours of sweat equity; the interest-free monthly mortgage payment, including taxes and insurance, will be $343, less than half the rental rate for the area.

His puny shoulder braced against the foundation, lying in the gray-green clay of South Central, Yoyce has hooked up with Cathy Chew, an insurance lawyer. They are hammering in hold-downs, the 2-inch wide, 4-feet long steel strips that anchor the house to the concrete footings. Yoyce, whose natural curiosity allows him to make the most of every contact ("I don't meet people like these everyday."), is quizzing Cathy, asking if she thinks he should be a doctor or a lawyer. This foster child, who has "no vivid imagination" of his parents whom he hasn't seen since he was two, was adopted at five but was so badly beaten he escaped back into foster care. His only "parent" now is a weary 74-year-old foster grandmother who can't read and is barely able to write. Yet despite these heavy odds, Yoyce will be one of the quiet success stories of Watts Avenue. Because he's told everyone, "I'm studyin' and strivin' to be that doctor," before the house is finished a volunteer will open the door to a University program that tracks minority children for medical school. Even though his foster grandmother will throw out the application ("We takes care of our own."), another will be sent. By December, when Yoyce has to stay indoors to save himself from gang threats, he'll also have the Christmas gift of a volunteer-donated laptop on which to do his homework.

Each hold-down, an earthquake prevention measure, requires 26 nails, yet because Yoyce and Cathy, amateurs, have banged in the #16 nails crooked, they whack in a few extra, just in case. In 1992 Hurricane Andrew swept through south Florida, destroying 85,000 houses. Yet in homestead, Florida, the 27 Habitat houses remained, 27 sentries standing solid against the storm. Millard Fuller, the founder, has said that the Habitat houses withstood the storm because they were built by volunteers. "Most of whom don't know what they're doing," said Fuller. "So when it calls for two nails, they put in ten. A hurricane didn't have a chance." Or an earthquake. Not quite a year later when a 6.7 earthquake shook L.A., this Watts Avenue house, which the local building inspector had said is "built like a tank," and the four other Habitat houses in South Central, won't have one crack.

Van, a.k.a. Dirt, a Nutty Block Crip, the skinny gang banger who is terrorizing the neighborhood but who shows up faithfully to work on the house, is helping Jack Davidson, the Site Superintendent, set up a saw-horse table for the Skilsaw. In this area adult males are apt to be guys wearing shower caps, so disabled from shootings that they roll down the street in wheelchairs with a nasty pitbull trailing behind. Jack, who looks like a big, balding Swede, became a hero in Habitat circles when he took Van under his wing. Their first meeting was telling: Van was about to club a kid in the head with a 2 x 4, and when Jack stepped in, Van threatened to smash the windows in his truck. Later that same day, doing wheelies on Watts Avenue, Van pedalled back to the site, and straddling a rusty (stolen) bicycle, returned Jack's locks and keys. Jack, a self-described redneck, surprised himself when instead of cuffing this hoodlum, who had been robbing the site and snipping the phone wires, said, "I'm going to show you how to sheet a floor, put dry wall on, run base."

In a moment suspended in time that lingers in the mind, the six-foot tall former football player at Sacramento State placed his calloused carpenter's hand on the bony shoulder of the five-foot three-inch gang banger, and trying to narrowing the chasm between their worlds, said, "I'll put it this way, man-to-man, you work with me, I'll work with you and show you a good time." In his new role as Van's mentor, Jack told him, "It frosts my cookies when I'm talkin' to you and you have that damn Walkman on, take it off." Grinning for the first time, Van shoved the headphones down. "And while I'm preachin' to you," said Jack, "let's try to change your image in the neighborhood. It's more negative than positive." Jack offered his hand. Van put his out and looked the other way. "When you shake somebody's hand, always look 'em in the eye. Okay, Babe?" As Van turned to bicycle off, Jack added, "I'd like my beeper back, too." That was a month ago.

Today Jack has just paired Van with Dave Rasche, an actor, who is cutting filler pieces to fit under the rafters. Dave explains to Van that the plywood needs to be cut into sixteen-inch pieces. Dave asks Van, "What's sixteen plus sixteen?"

Van stops smacking his gum. His cheekbones tighten into a steelflint hardness.

"Come on, come on," says Dave.

Staring blankly at the tape, Van is lost. This truant, who should be a ninth-grader but who writes his name on the Habitat Sign-In sheet in the block printing of a first-grader, is being brought to his knees by simple arithmetic.

Shocked to learn that a 13-year-old cannot add, Dave backs off. Politely, he counts it out for Van on the tape measure, marks it, makes a clean slice with the Skilsaw, and hands the sixteen-inch piece of wood back to him. Van jumps up on a scaffold and, crouched under a rafter, confidently nails the filler under the overhang. He and Dave are "furring out" the wall, creating a smooth line for the siding. It's unrealistic to expect that ten Saturdays as part of a work crew could smooth out a fatherless kid with a rap sheet that is already pages long, but of the dozen kids working on the house, Van is the best worker; unlike most volunteers wielding a hammer for the first time, Van has a naturally strong swing and an excellent aim.

In life, when a person finds work which suits him—whether it's a dancer, a doctor, or a carpenter—there's an elegance and harmony to the fit that's a pleasure to watch. That's how Van looks up on the scaffold: his countenance has changed—his body has softened, his mean black eyes seem less so; he's smiling. However, as one of five children of a drug-dealing prostitute, with no moral compass to guide him, he uses his talent indiscriminately—to squarely drive int the head of a nail, or to casually whack a kid on the head with a two by four.

Since there isn't a restaurant nearby, and if there were volunteers would be afraid to eat out in this neighborhood, lunch is brought in. With barbecue smoke billowing over the Lowery's dusty front yard there's a companionable family feeling as everyone relaxes, eating burgers, gulping down iced drinks, exchanging construction stories. Inside the house, where workers with sun-burned noses have gone to escape the heat, six-year-old Latoya Lowery, with a headfull of pigtails bobbing, is throwing a screaming fit. *Mommeee! Mommeee! Look!* A volunteer just spilled a soft drink on *their* plywood sub-floor.

On the north edge of the property, James is leaning against the doorway of the metal dumpster that serves as Habitat's field office. His gang scarf now hangs limply from his rear pocket, and as he finishes lunch his eyes are fixed on the Lowery house, as if *seeing* it for the first time. He turns to Steve Wright, chairman of the Construction Committee, who is sitting next to him. With a longing that is palpable, James says, "They're winning a pretty house. It's *fresh*. It's way better than mine." His is a tiny wooden structure that sags from the weight of all the foster boys who have gone through, usually five at a time. Steve explains that the Lowerys are *buying* the house but this correction flies right over James: his eyes tell him that the Lowerys have won the house lottery, hit the jackpot, reeled in the big one.

Even at this early stage the Watts Avenue house holds the promise of more than barebones shelter. In a Habitat solicitation letter Rosalyn Carter was careful to stressed that Habitat houses are "simple not fancy."

Yet because lots in Los Angeles are irregular, the local affiliate can't stamp out in "cookie-cutter" style a house the way Habitat does in rural areas: so most Habitat houses in L.A. turn out to be architect-designed custom homes. Driven by the ego of the architect, the generosity of the donors, and the energy of the volunteers, the Watts Avenue house, which prompts people to say, "Is that cute, or what?" will stand out as a jewel in the neighborhood. In just six more weeks, on the anniversary of the riots, Calvin and Angel will move from a stucco box of an apartment into a home with a gabled roof-line, a 12-foot cathedral ceiling in the living room, an all-tile kitchen with disposal, dishwasher, greenhouse window, and floor-to-ceiling cabinets of such fine quality that volunteers will run their hands over the solid walnut, and say, "I wish *I* had cabinets this nice in my house." There are other touches not usually associated with affordable housing in the ghetto: a laundry niche with washer and dryer, an all-tile bathroom with a top-of-the-line Kohler tub, bay windows in the two children's bedrooms, and all rooms wired for cable and phone. In Imperial Courts, where Angel once lived, in a cost-cutting measure typical of public housing, the closets have no doors; here the architect's specs call for the three bedrooms to have sliding *mirrored* double doors. And in an area where a fresh green lawn is a rarity, the house will be framed with yards and yards of thick green sod.

Lunch is usually punctuated by the background sound of a lone hammerer: Van. Normally, he works through the meal—stripping forms, reinforcing studs, nailing trim. But this morning an 18-year-old Nutty Block Crip trespassed, unnoticed, onto the site, and has given him a gang assignment to carry out immediately. In the midst of all the lunchtime chatting—the adults comparing today's aches and pains with last week's—no one is paying attention that Van isn't hammering. They aren't aware that he's crossed Watts Avenue, sneaked behind the handsome two-story, pre-war school building, and out of view of his new friend Jack, has joined forces with three other gang bangers. They have broken into #12 kindergarten classroom. After stealing four computers, they will spray the room with the fire extinguisher to cover their fingerprints.

As this neighborhood has deteriorated into a war zone, Ritter Elementary, with its graffiti-free red brick walls and immaculately groomed grounds, has won the First Place L.A. Beautiful Campus Award every year since 1987. The despicable crime of breaking into this school gives new meaning to the term "neighborhood watch". The last time Van vandalized the school, a neighbor watched him brazenly rolling a television set from a fifth-grade classroom down the street; this time two men at Hammer's Liquor Store, around the corner, will watch Van and three others climb over the back fence in broad daylight with the kindergarten computers. Yet, as Calvin Lowery, the home-owner, said, "One thing this side of town don't like is a snitch," and the neighbors won't. "We're afraid our house will be shot up, or we'll be killed," said a neighbor with young twins. "It's a hostage situation."

This one act—of Van putting down his Habitat hammer, and with it the possibility of following a different path, to rob the school again—sets in bold relief the basic, hard question: coming up against the monumental problems of the inner city, what can a group of volunteers accomplish? Habitat, a builder of houses, has never claimed to solve all the problems of poverty, and by accident it became an employer of the young set who stumbled onto the Watts Avenue worksite and stayed. But if volunteers are busting their chops to help a neighborhood yet the parents who live there are too frightened, or too apathetic, to take back their school and their streets from the gangs, and if on Watts Avenue Habitat's expenses for an armed security guard equal lumber costs, what does it all add up to?

Richard Hicks, Executive Director, Habitat-L.A., would be the first to admit that one house on one street in one inner city will not rejuvenate the neighborhood, not make much of a dent in the local housing crisis. But Hicks, who took an early retirement from corporate litigation, has the kind of laser sharp intelligence where he sits back, listens to all sides slogging out an issue and at the crucial moment, leans forward and says: "Let me cut through this..." Cutting through the question of Habitat's value on Watts Avenue, or on any similar street in a tough neighborhood, Hicks explains that the first house acts as a catalyst. Like the foreman in "Schindler's List," who said, "He who saves one life, saves the world," Hicks believes that you build one house, you *start* to change the community. Detractors might dismiss this optimism as the charmingly naive talk of a do-gooder with a hammer, but before the year is over the squalid crackshack next door to the Lowery's will be renovated into a pink Spanish stucco by a private individual, and down the block there will be two more Habitat houses: houses Van couldn't work on because he was locked up at Las Padrinos, a juvenile facility, for auto grand theft with a dangerous weapon.

In another year, in the summer of 1995, one early morning just as the sun is rising, if the kids climb back up on the rooftop at Watts Avenue, they will see their immediate community in a new light: directly in front of the Lowery's house, in the once starkly dismal stretch of railroad right-of-way that cuts down the center of Santa Ana Boulevard, they will see a former President and a swarm of volunteers from all over the United States building twenty-four houses. In a neighborhood where the sun always seems to be shining somewhere else, that morning the sun will be shining here on a row of new Habitat houses. Probably for the first time a long lens from a rooftop on Watts Avenue will offer a vista of hope.

Newly proud of their neighborhood, perhaps the kids will remember hearing Barbara Vighi, a volunteer, say as she knelt stapling shingles onto the Lowery's roof, "There's so much that needs to be done. If we can triumph here..."

JULIA VAN GORDER

Maw

August 12, 1945 Great Pacific Cannery Our first night. Beth and I arrive at ten p.m., just after dark, having waited for the last bus. The only person up—Anna, in running shoes without socks—is setting long trestle tables for breakfast in the cookhouse. She grumbles, as she leads us by flashlight up wooden stairs and down a hall to our room, that people work hard here and go to bed at a decent time. She nods sideways at the washroom across the hall, switches on our light, and leaves.

A single light bulb hanging in the center of the room. The air alive with buzzing flies, hyped up, I'm sure, by the smell of rotting fish, which permeates the building. I tug at the window. It won't open. The floors and walls unpainted boards. Two metal cots covered with striped mattresses. Dust balls like families of mice huddle under the cots.

We go to the washroom. It has its own supply of flies. We take a broom back to our room and sweep off the mattresses before unrolling our sleeping bags.

"You and your big ideas," Beth says. She is crying. She undresses and gets into her sleeping bag.

I am too stunned to comfort her. She's the comic in our team. I count on her spirits to carry us through situations like this.

"It wasn't my idea. It was Ella's."

"So where is Ella?"

"Maybe this is her revenge for my being a bum riveter." We got our pink slips from Boeings last week. Ella didn't.

"Next war you learn to rivet fast. Okay?"

"Okay."

"And I'm not promising to stay here. Understand? As soon as Doug hits town, I'm quitting."

"I hear you." And I'm depressed. I can't imagine life without Beth. But that's not reciprocal. I must accept that. And I have to stay. I must have another month's work. Beth is not going on to do graduate work like most of us. She'll take to the woods when Doug gets his job as a forester.

"Sleep tight," I say by habit, turning out the light.

"And none of your little ironies. This is not an ironic situation."

"No, it's awful, but I still hope you can sleep."

"You too. Goodnight."

I can't sleep for wondering if this isn't an ironic situation. Do we deserve it? Is there something we, I, didn't learn at Boeings that I need to learn here? When I read Dante's *Divine Comedy* last year, I felt that I was living in Purgatory—repeating experiences until I had learned from them. But this, this feels like the Inferno. My face crumples and I cry. But crying attracts flies to my face. I slide down into my sleeping bag and try to fasten the cover over my head.

August 13, 1945 The first morning the cookhouse is full of people eating at the trestle tables. A handsome woman of about fifty comes to us. She has an orange-red gladiolus spike pinned to her white smock. Her lipstick and nail polish match the gladiolus. High rubber boots, white kerchief, fine skin.

"So you got here after all," she says. "Well, sit down and get some breakfast. We start work in..."She glances at a dainty silver watch. "...fifteen minutes."

We sit. No one speaks to us, but food is passed—orange juice, porridge, pancakes, toast, bacon, coffee. Someone hands me an oval platter of fried eggs. The eggs sit in front of me, staring like fish eyes. I can't eat. I am breathing the smell of rotting fish. I read somewhere that the nose turns off its recognition of foul smell in ten minutes. Not so.

When the bell rings, the handsome forewoman ("Maw," to the work crew) puts a hand on each of our shoulders. "Come and get a clean smock and gloves. I'm glad you've got the sense to wear boots and a kerchief." Her hand on my shoulder has become a comfort. She barks out orders, expecting obedience and hard work. But she coats the harshness with touch, a reminder of a different world.

The main canning space, a huge barn that opens to English Bay when the fish boats come in, is not the white sterile factory I had imagined sitting in, packing orange-red sockeye into tins. We stand on concrete against scrubbed wooden tables, waist high.

Maw is not afraid of getting dirty. She shows us how to gib pilchards, cutting off their heads and dragging their heads and guts in one movement across the table and into a bin. Pilchards are the dirtiest fish dead. Half of these seemed bad. I can't gut them in one movement. Maw shows me how to get my finger into the cavity to make sure they are clean. In no time my thin cotton gloves are soaked.

During the smoke break one of the piece workers says, "I stop to blow my nose when I'm on time, but when I'm on piece work, I just wipe it on my sleeve."

This place is mass production down pat. The Chinamen bring us fish and take away the tubs of guts. When they come around to sharpen our knives, they hand us another so we won't stop work. Ten hours a day at fifty-two cents an hour! The Chinese—why are they called Chinamen here and Chinese at the university?—are pleasant and distant. Is it a language barrier? No. The others are the same. Here to make money, like me. The older women seem to have stuck it longest. There are a few native women, shy, not driven like the rest of us. Two grads from Dalhousie, three kids going into first year at the University of British Columbia. The men a rough-looking lot.

August 15, 1945 Yesterday VJ Day. Did we win? Here we worked ten hours.

August 20, 1945 Yesterday I was sick to my stomach. We were back to gibbing pilchards, after a couple of days of stringing herring in the smoke house (a wand forced through the gills and mouth, with the eyes staring their pain at you.) Maw decides I am allergic to pilchards and sends me to clean the women's washroom. A man Beth calls Romeo follows me into the washroom. He has already begun to haunt us in the cannery. His shirt opens to the navel, his hairy belly loops over his pants. He leans against a wall, his bare arms akimbo, as I clean toilets. I don't like having him behind me, so I switch to wash basins.

"You sleeping with that squirt you came with?"

"That's none of your goddamned business!"

"Just thought I would give you some of the real thing."

He unzips his fly just as Maw comes in. When she is in the cannery, Maw has a cork tip cigarette drooping from her lips. Maw's cigarette glows. She spreads her hands over her hips, the nail polish glinting against her white smock. She says nothing. Romeo zips his fly. Maw turns sideways in the door, so that he has to face her as he leaves.

"You okay, kid?" she asks me.

"Sure." I go on cleaning basins, knowing she is too short of workers to fire him. When the boats come in full of herring, pilchards, salmon, she has to have a crew to unload, can, or smoke the fish.

"The jerk," she says and leaves.

She transfers me to the bloater house to pack bloater paste into tins with a woman Beth calls Diva.

I find that if you sing, time speeds up. Diva has already discovered that. She sings in a monotone, sometimes *I Will Take You Home, Kathleen* and *Old Black Joe*. Mostly it's *Holy, Holy, Holy*, just the one verse. Must be a member of the United Church. An hour of *Holy, Holy, Holy* is quite a few tins of bloater paste.

August 25, 1945 Ella from Boeings turned up on the production line. Pretends not to see us. We welcome her at lunch time, and ask her to go to a movie in West Van with us after supper. She agrees, but neglects to take a shower. People in the bus and theatre move away from us.

"They don't like our *Nights in Norway* perfume," Beth whispers across Ella.

Ella restless. Next day she begins to eat with Diva, whom she shares a room with. Pretends not to see us again.

August 27, 1945 Beth and I in the loft, rolling cans down the conveyor belt for ten hours. Like sorting letters at the Post Office at Christmas. You achieve so much in one minute repeating a motion, that time drags. We roll a hundred cans a minute. I try to figure out how many cans per hour, per day, but my mind staggers. Everywhere I work I see that the Industrial Revolution didn't free us. It made us into Charlie Chaplin machines. How can that silly economics professor say that industrialization is the answer for the underdeveloped countries? I ask Beth what she is thinking about.

"Sex."

"Sex?"

"What else?"

"The meaning of life. Why we are here."

"Here in this cannery? I thought it was your crazy idea."

"No, the meaning of our individual lives. Are we here in the cannery because we chose it, or were we sent? A part of a pattern or plan?"

"I thought we came here because the money was good."

"We did, on one level, but..."

"How many levels do you want to live on at one time, for Pete's sake? You're unreal, d'you know that?"

Am I unreal? I don't feel so. But I realize, rolling one hundred cans a minute, that Beth and I have grown in different directions. Her whole focus is on Doug. She is quitting the cannery tomorrow to be with him.

August 29, 1945 Yesterday I was alone for ten hours, packing cans hot out of the steamer, which burned through these cheap gloves. My nails are brown, the skin of my hands is rough and scaling.

Today Maw put me to work with Mrs. Petra, who gets the easy jobs and is not popular. The others say she is a stool pigeon, because she does housework for the owners. But she's okay. She has a scrubbed look, skin hanging loose on her face. She says a few words of Chinese to the Chinamen. I'm impressed, ask how come. She trained as some kind of mission worker, learned Chinese to go to China, then the war.

"Oh, are you going now the war is over?"

"Oh no! I met my husband meantime."

Would I do that? Given the choice of vocation and marriage, would I choose marriage?

August 30, 1945 Well, what do you know? Today I made money piecework. Eighty-two cents an hour instead of fifty-two. But oh, my back is bent out of shape. Maw put me to work with Roberta, the fastest worker in the cannery. She doesn't look forty-five, with her shiny store teeth, her mashed carrots hair worn with a pomp of curls in front, braids around her ears, a purple kerchief. She jokes about her smock barely containing her large breasts. "I had five kids. Breast-fed 'em all. Should have been a Guernsey cow. Had a cup of yellow cream left after feeding each one."

September 2, 1945 This week when 35 tons of my allergy came in, I worked with the men for two days in the warehouse. The men, some unfamiliar with English, watched to be sure that I did no heavy lifting. People are by nature kind, particularly when you are accepted as one of them.

Yesterday Brenda and I washed cans in the alkali bath. Brenda has a tilted nose and gentle brown eyes. She is saving for a washing machine for the bungalow she and John are building in North Vancouver. They keep chickens in the back yard, her pets, his food.

John? She points to Romeo, of the open shirt and loopy belly. He sees her point to him and comes over. Eyeing my breasts, he leans too close.

"I'm not coming home for supper," he says to Brenda. "The # 3 boat is coming in."

Maw looks over at him. He goes back to his job.

"He means he's going to a beer parlor with the crew after they unload."

This is outrageous. How can gentle Brenda ally herself with this crude man? Romeo never eats with her in the cannery, has never treated her as special.

When I work with Roberta again, I ask if Brenda and John are married. I wish I hadn't. She roars at me.

"Kid, I can't believe you. How old do you say you are? What do they teach you in that university anyway?"

Her voice is resounding, yet when she chitters to the Chinamen, I can't hear what she is saying.

She did tell me her favorite is Barney from the # 5 boat. Favorite. I bet she services them all. No wonder Beth caller her "our lady of the fish boats." No wonder she laughs at me.

September 7, 1945 My farewell to Great Pacific Cannery. On Marine Drive, waiting for the bus from Horseshoe Bay, I can look back at this little community with its green lawns, gray cedar buildings, gray smoke rising.

Tonight at supper, except for Ella and Diva, there was lots of chatter, and I was part of it. When Maw came up behind me, I captured her warm hands pressed on my shoulders.

"Well, kid, will we see you back here next summer?"

"I hope so," I lied.

She walked away. And I walk away. I am able to.

Julia and Beth outside Great Pacific Cannery bunkhouse, 1945

RICHARD HAGUE

Breaking

"Goddama you breakin em."

Saturday morning, a February mean with ice, and I'm helping unload the truck. The driver's everything I know about Chicago, talks funny, wears cowboy boots and a Stetson. He carries a gun, an old long-barreled revolver, jammed down the back of his pants so it rests in the crease of his butt. Name's Clarence.

"Goddama you breakin em."

That's Primo Guerrero, head cutter. Quick with a knife as he is with a woman. He doesn't help us unload; he comments. We're nothing but a bunch of trouble to him, high school punks. At first you can feel your hands freezing. There's an ache that runs up your fingers, the bones in them, right up the center of each one. But then that goes away. And that's when you're in trouble. You drop the hindquarter and maybe smash your buddy's hand, but he doesn't know it for an hour, and then he fucks this and fucks that all day, trying to make a fist but he can't. So maybe he punches the wall in the john, right under the picture of the naked woman, and that makes it easier for him somehow.

I used to run track. The mile, 880. I liked to get out in front of everybody, sprinting right out, the sound of the others fading behind me. Getting away, breaking out of the pack. That felt good. But this work has killed my knees. The bottom of the trailer is an inch of cold grease and running the sides and quarters down you slip about half the time and you're down on the grooves of the floor. Three or four bad ones like that and your knees are gone.

"Goddama, boys, you breakin em."

What we're breaking is Primo's balls. He stands below the rollers and checks the quarters and sides and the boxes of bacon and the barrels of Calais hams off the invoice. If just two boxes back up he grabs his crotch through his bloody apron and he cries, "Goddama you *breakin* em!" We don't work fast enough for him. He's the boss's head honcho, always in a hurry.

After we get the truck unloaded Clarence comes back from the Twilight. That's the bar next door. He still doesn't talk to us. He only speaks to the boss out front, and they only talk numbers. I mean the racket. The boss is one of two or three hotshots in the numbers here, and we all give him our nickels and dimes or quarters and our picks, straight or boxed. We write them down on pieces of butcher paper around lunch time, and he takes them down the street and comes back with the winnings, if there are any. Me, I've lost maybe a hundred in the two years I've worked here. But one of the clerks, Tina's her name, a skinny woman with glasses who takes care of the lunchmeat case, she hit for three thousand last year the week before Christmas. Threw a big party for Christmas Eve. Got every one of us high school kids drunk on rye whiskey and Coke. Dominic Antonucci, he's in school with me, spilled half a fifth down the grinder when he was making hamburger. I'd like to have seen one of them burgers hit the skillet. Probably went up like dynamite.

I suppose it's pretty good to have a job. I get out of school at 1:30—they let anybody with a job out early—and ride the bus downtown and have twenty minutes before I have to show up at the market. I hang around McCrory's, buy a dime's worth of their roasted Spanish peanuts and stand inside the glass front door and eat them while they're still hot from the roaster. There's a big radiator on the wall and it's always warm. Almost everybody in town walks by that door in a day—there's lots to watch.

Take the Chief, for instance. Story is he was a famous football player at Stanton High years ago. Scored a couple hundred touchdowns or something and could have played for the Steelers right out of senior year. But he killed a guy down on Lake Erie Avenue, just beat him to death. He got off, but something had broken inside him after that and so now he just bums around, wearing army surplus coats, cleaning windows and sweeping out bars. He's big, with a broad flat face, thick black hair. Never wears a hat. Lots of days all he does is walk Fourth Street from the North End to the South End, back and forth, panhandling cigarettes and quarters.

So I watch till two and then walk down to work. It's just a hole-in-the-wall place, really, from the outside. But inside, it's deep, the cases running all along one side for fifty feet or so and then sweeping around across the back. Behind them are the saws, two of them, beyond a counter about shoulder high where the beginners do their job, which is to wash the meat trays with the green disinfectant that comes in cardboard tubes that weigh about a thousand pounds. They come on the truck, too.

When you first start working here, you bag, out front. There's a conveyor belt under the tables behind the counter, and on a busy Saturday after payday, three or four hundred big sacks of meat come down that. The customers line up with their half of the green register ticket, and the bagger matches the numbers on their tickets to the other half taped on the bags and hands them overt. Genius work. The boss counts any mistakes and if there's too many, or if he gets a few phone calls from some old lady whose head cheese is missing, or who has ten pounds of neck bones instead of ten pounds of kielbasa, he fires you. But if you do a pretty good job out there, you can get an extra dime an hour and break in as clerk, or sometimes you go back and wash the trays.

"Goddama, Dominic, you breakin em."

Dominic is washing the trays and he's just dropped a whole stack. Sounds like a car wreck. Primo Jumps and almost cuts himself. His face gets red, redder than his apron. Cutting yourself is the worst thing that can happen to a butcher. It's bad form. When I first started a guy named Foster worked here, he was a drinker, hands shaking all morning till his vodka at lunch time. One morning he sliced the end of his thumb off, half an inch. It fell in among the hamburger trimmings. Primo cussed and made Foster call a cab, telling him he wasn't going to lose time taking some asshole to the hospital. By the time he got back, the other cutters had found the end of his thumb and they'd put it in a matchbox and wrapped it in butcher paper and written Foster's address on it. One of them mailed it on his lunch break. Foster came to work with a gun the day his thumb came in the mail and the boss fired him even before he'd gotten his coat off.

So Primo's mad at Dominic now and throws his trimming knife across the room and it sticks in the wall about a foot from Dominic's head. Dominic stands up from gathering the spilled trays and tells Primo to fuck himself and his brother and three cousins.

The lading bill's checked off now and we've got to stow the boxes of wieners and six barrels of hams in the cooler. The sides and quarters are hanging on the rails behind the cutting blocks and Primo and Tony Cline, a young cutter from the vocational school who's just starting out, begin breaking them. Primo's expert at it, can break a whole side in three swift cuts without thinking. Tony's slower, more careful. Still he messes up once in a while and ruins a piece. Primo stares at him. "Jesus Christ, Tony," he says. "You breakin em."

It's about 38 or 40 degrees in the cooler and always damp. You wear gloves and stocking caps but still you're cold all through. Just when you're starting to thaw out from unloading the truck, and your hands and feet are coming back to life and aching, you've got to spend an hour in the cooler stacking and pulling.

I knew this girl once, Carmen DeLucca. She was tall and skinny but beautiful, hair the color of olive oil. She had hard little breasts and said the Hail Mary to herself whenever I touched them. We went out all last winter, then in March, when there was black slush all over the streets, we broke up. She didn't want me touching her anymore. She said that if I could keep my hands off her, she'd think about seeing me again. But my hands were always cold, and I couldn't help slipping them up under her sweater and just cupping them there until I forgot how cold I was. But that was a long time ago.

When Primo and Tony are finished, Dominic and I have maybe two tons of hindquarters and sirloins and sides to hang. The cooler's foggy with our breath, but underneath our clothes and two aprons, we're sweating. Then our hands start to cramp, and when we're heaving a quarter up to the hook sometimes it slips and comes down on our shins or our feet. It gets sawdust all over it, and we've got to wipe it off with a rag, and that only makes the cold worse.

That sawdust. It comes in big burlap bags. A guy named Wilbur brings it in once a week in a pickup truck. He's from out in the boondocks somewhere, out there on the ridges back of the river where there's a saw-mill and people still keep pigs and chickens. We haul the bags off the truck and roll them down the basement steps. There's one light bulb, back in the corner, and we heave the bags against the wall that smells like the river. Wood chips and sawdust and the river. Sometimes we have a smoke down there, but it's dangerous. If the boss caught us we'd be fired on the spot. But it's warm, and the smells are like camping.

After we've got the meat hung and all the boxes stacked, it's time to start pulling the cases. Four-thirty, a day of cold and complaining, and you've got to finish up with reaching in and pulling the trays out, slapping a piece of paper over the steaks and chops and city chicken, and then stack-ing them in the cooler. And wait on customers, too. And when that's done, you start on the chickens. There's maybe fifty of them in the case, stiff and numb in ice. You drag them out of there, the sharp crushed ice jabbing your hands, and you drop the chickens in a box and lug them back. But there's always some customer who wants one, right in the middle of your job. "Let me see that one," she says, pointing at some measly carcass clear down in the front of the case. You reach way in and pull it out, your hands so numb you can hardly grab it, and you lift it up over the top of the counter so she can eyeball it. "Too big," she says. "Find me a smaller one." That goes on two or three times, and finally she says, "Well, I don't know. None of them looks any good to me. I'll come back tomorrow," and she leaves.

Then it's quitting time. The boss locks the front doors and Violet, the cashier, hunches over the day's receipts and the register chatters and rings for another half hour. In the back room, the women crowd the john, changing their clothes and smoking cigarettes. Sometimes I hang around, leaning against the frame of the door between the front and the back, watch-ing Violet out there, busy, humming some Serbian tune to herself, the green lamp in the cashier's cage like a light way down in the river, deep down and quiet. Then I go back. Primo and Tony sit on one of the big tables, their bloody aprons folded across their laps. They make wisecracks as the rest of us haul the last trash out to the dumpster.

"That all the faster you can go, Dominic?" Tony says. "You got polio or what?"

Primo shakes his head. "Hey, Dominic," he yells, "You breakin em, man."

Dominic and I stand by the sink later, having a smoke.

"Fucking job," Dominic says. His hands are raw, frozen half the day from the cold, scalded the other half from washing trays. "Fucking Primo and Tony."

"Yeah," I say.

But all the time I'm tuning it out, like the tiredness lets me do. I'm tuning it all out, the meaning of it, so that the words people say are just noise, a kind of music. All day's becoming a song, snow falling out of the gray sky outside, millsmoke and snow, the hard faces and dark clothes of the customers, the red blood of the cutting blocks pooling and dripping, the aching in my knees. "Goddama, you breakin em," *la la la.* "You sumbitch," *do se do.* All day's a song. "You breakin em, breakin em. You breakin em."

Yeah.

Bartender © Roger Pfingston

JOE NAPORA

NoAfterWords

ONE: The Ad

After the day after is a nothing.
A popular television show succeeded
when the government demanded it deny that nothing.
And the advertisers applauded the absence of that nothing.

And television cannot collect revenue
   (the echo: *avenue, au revior*, and in the distance
   the distance that separates the touch, the touch of our hands
   the touch of so much
      of what we need from
      from what we make bleed. It is that raven and the
whisper: *nevermore*).

Collect revenue on the real apocalypse
but it can create sequels to the fake one.
   The survivors will set new standards for fashion.
   The survivors will create new soap operas.
   The survivors will host Saturday Night Live.
   The survivors will become a new Halloween.
   The survivors will be politicians.

Joe McCarthy never died, he faded away
into advertising.

The 50s never passed on anything
but their disease.

The CIA became microbes, became carcinogens.
   The virus spread through Iran in 53.
   The virus spread through Guatemala in 54.
   The virus attacked Nicaragua.
   The virus born in the USA let loose on every street corner.

Strontium-90 made mothers fear their breasts.
     At the milk company the alchemist
     takes fallout and turns it into gold.

TWO: Cash Flow

I grew up during the 50s in the middle
of the heartland that is the ache
in the middle of the midwest
—Dayton, Ohio. I remember most

the SAC base and NCR.
The planes overhead, half of them always
in the air with their bombs. And
The National Cash Register Company's shows

on Saturdays. For a can of fruit or soup
an hour's worth of cartoons.
     The air base remains.
     The bombers come and go.

The cash register company has skipped town.
Large empty lots where factories once stood.
     Hiroshima, those pictures.
     Gold dust spread to the four corners
     hot to the touch. Strategic

         Air Command.

The men and women who filled the registers
with their worth, they are gone.
Large empty lots, they remain.

Money turned into time future,
     bits of light flashing
     at the end
         of the sewer.

THREE: The Vista

I remember school windows
I remember a time when

windows were not seen
as weapons. And

I remember the a-bomb drills.
I remember the remembering

in this fear of windows.
A whole generation in a forced leap

of its imagination turned inward
replacing the windows out into the world

with   brick,   stone,   lead.

EDWINA PENDARVIS

Cleaning Stalls in Winter

The girl pushing a wheelbarrow through the icy night
steps into a starless puddle,
cracking its silence.
She walks across the pitchdark barnyard,
frost on the grass and in the mud
crunching underfoot.

At the edge of the yard, she tips the barrow forward,
tilting it left, then right,
emptying it as simply
as a mound-builder tossing a basket of dirt.

She walks back to the barn,
pushing the empty barrow uphill, leaning into it.

Inside, she pats the mare's muscled neck and flanks—
shining and shadowed under the bare bulb—
leads her through the lulling, communal crunch
of summer hay and sweet feed
to a stall next to the palomino,
who stomps softly and snorts, blowing
a warm, whiffling cloud into the chill air.

She shovels clods of dung and urine-soaked sawdust—
with a rake picks up the smallest pieces,
flinging them neatly on top of the heap.

Bending and straightening
in motions older than history
she works through the moonless hours.
Alone in the cold she's happy.
Knowing the earth has a will of its own,
she moves with an easy stride through the icy night.

How I See the Rapture

Them preachers've got it wrong;
the end ain't goin' to be in a twinklin' of no eye.
The Lord's waited too long for that.
I bet He's goin' to set back and enjoy the show.
He'll put a deep sleep on the children first
and on all the meek—so they won't be scared.
Then the fun'll begin.

The four horsemen, on Harleys instead of horses,
will bust out of a skyscraper
like Evil Kneivel, doin' wheelies and revvin' their engines.
Gangs of angels'll ride around town
scarin' bankers and lawyers
and all them other educated fools
that couldn't get into heaven if you held the ladder
and gave climbin' lessons.

If the poor get raised up like I'm hopin'
all my friends'll be lifted right out of their foot-achin', back-
breakin' jobs
and off the couches they've sunk down in
too deep to get out their ownselves.
They'll drop their dishrags and their wrenches;
stylin' scissors'll clatter to the floor.
The blacktop'll be littered with jackhammers;
and potato chips'll be spilled across livin' rooms ever'where.

You know the rich are too greedy to get through the needle's eye.
I bet the Lord won't even let them out of their cars.
They'll have to stay inside, weighted down with furs and jewelry.
Them automatic windows'll raise, the locks'll click,
and alarms'll go off.
The rich'll sit there swelterin' forever,
listenin' to buzzers, bells, and voices
remindin' them their lights are on
or tellin' people to get away from the car.
Them that're caught out on their yachts
will sail through eternity on a sea of fire.

The Lord'll have a good belly laugh, *I* think,
before he gathers up the long-sufferin'
and breathes peace and happiness into them,
fillin' their tired lungs with a wind from Eden—
fillin' their lungs with the sweet breath of peppermint
that grows alongside a creek flowin' through Paradise.

Truck Driver

A red pick-up pulled off the road,
crunching its wide curve onto the gravel lot
of a machinery repair shop.
The driver who stopped to say hi
to my white-haired uncle
was covered with grease and oil.
Overalls dark with stains, he smiled
and stepped down, then leaned
against the truck, the dusty sole of his left brogan
over the toe of his right.
He lit a cigarette
and passed the time of day—
a scar across his cheek
and over the bridge of his nose,
a shy look out of his eyes,
sweetness and irony behind them—
and behind him the hills.

DANIEL SMITH

Down Time

In the cold crib, on my back,
frozen fingers fumbling
broken bolts, links of chain
that won't connect,
hearing the rain
on the tin roof turning
            to sleet,
cold draft of wind
diving thru the slatted sides.

I've worked four hours
under the old sheller
I cannot fix.

Late November, and getting later.
I've left two weeks work
standing in the field.

Daylight gives way, the crib
           leans silent and dark.
Tools and half-fixed iron
scattered amongst cobs
         and the husks of old harvests.

Why do they call this farming?
All we do is repair, pick up
        what we threw down yesterday.

I go out
through the dark doorway,
into a late round of chores.
I have cattle waiting on feed,
and dawn breaks
        at five a.m.

Texas, 1974

Halfway through
the first good week of harvest—
North Texas dryland wheat—
the combine snapped a shaft.

With a kick and a cuss, the boss
                    left for parts,
                    80 miles round trip.

Old Texan Harry Martin—
  wheat rancher, cattleman, oil driller,
offered a hand, so he and I
started in
tearing the big Gleaner down—
  backing off belts,
  loosening chains,
  pulling bearings.

The tools hot in our hands,
on our backs
            in the cheat grass,
shirts soaked,
fire ants at our ankles,
grasshoppers leaping in the heat.

Till an hour later
we took a break, and there
in the shade of the heavy traction wheels
he wanted to know
"What's a college boy like you
doing cutting wheat?"
I told him I'd never been this far west,
wanted to see the country.

Harry Martin.
His body brown and bent

as old mesquite, stared with eyes calm
as summer fallow
over miles of endless wheat, spit
between his boots and said,
"Ya know, kid, I really don't think
you'd have missed
a goddamn thing."

Field

I would like to have been
the man
who plowed this field,
so far back
in a seldom seen hollow
of southwestern Wisconsin's
unglaciated uplands.

I would like to have had
my hand
on the wheel,
turning the old Farmall
across the headlands
where the white birches
stand guard
before the dark pine woods.
And to have looked back,
over my shoulder,
as the moldboards
sliced into last year's crop,
turning the old under
to feed the new.

I would like to have known
what he knew,
as the breath of new furrows
followed him, round

after round,
while the world spun on
in separate orbit
far beyond the hills,
leaving him
alone with his land,
doing just what needed
to be done.

I would like to have been
the man who plowed this field.

Daniel Smith's father, Robert J. Smith, going out to 1945

ANNABEL THOMAS

Laying Ulajean's Ghost

They buried Theron's mama as if they were launching a ship.

First they scooted her downhill. Then they lowered her into the dark.

When the grave-diggers commenced shoveling dirt onto her box, their shoulders cut off Theron's view.

"Well, she's gone," Ansel told him.

Theron went home and had a beer.

"On my own," said Theron.

He waited to feel fancy-free but his nerves were unsteady. By morning he knew well enough what was wrong. His mama, Ulajean, was still hanging around.

For all his eighteen years he'd longed to be rid of her. On her burying day he'd thought he was. Now here he found her fastened inside his skull like a woodtick. Stuck in his throat like a chicken bone. For the life of him he could neither swallow her down nor cough her up.

"We got no more business to do together," Theron told her. "Let's us go our own ways."

On his friend Ansel's advice he gave Ulajean's clothes to the Salvation Army. When he moved into his own furnished room over the post office, he believed he was shet of her at last.

Ansel got Theron a job at Captina Brick lifting raw bricks off the conveyor belt and stacking them on the cars that took them to the kilns. Ansel told him the job needed muscles and brains. You had to know how to lift or you'd rupture yourself. Ansel called it 'men's work.' "They ain't a woman alive could start to do it," said Ansel.

In fact scarcely any women worked there. Men brought the shale in on the two-mile narrow gauge railroad. Men dumped it into the storage bin. A man ran the two 20 ton wheels that pulverized the shale. A man operated the pug mill that mixed the powdered shale with water to make clay. A man ran the extruder. Most of the brick was machined but some was handmade. Handmade was on the way out. Captina was one of a small number of yards in the country that still turned out the unique, multi-colored blocks.

There were a few women workers. Two sisters, Bonesy and Riva Pritt, filled the wooden molds for the handmade brick and struck them off.

It was men, though, who pushed the brick into the drying tunnel and, after three days, placed it in the round coal-burning kilns.

Theron was fascinated by these old 'bee hive' ovens. They were mysterious. Full of heat, they licked out light as if battles were taking place inside. The soft, shaped mud came out of them sucked dry. Made useful but diminished.

It was there at the brickyard his mama caught up to him again. Noon times, the workers sat around with their brown bags or their lunch buckets on their knees gulping coffee from their thermoses, joking and yarning.

One lunch period, without warning, Ulajean's voice sounded in Theron's ear.

"Look at you, Theron," she said, plainly disgusted. "You eat like a hog jest the way your daddy done."

Theron put down his ham sandwich and wiped the grease off his chin with his shirt sleeve. All the hairs on his nape stood up.

That was the first time his mama visited him at the brickworks, but it wasn't the last. She came now and again all through the summer. By fall she was still coming.

For a long time Theron didn't talk to anyone about his trouble. Finally he told Ansel. Ansel listened, whittling off a piece of plug, wadding it into his cheek. When Theron finished, Ansel took off his hardhat and stared into it as if he might find the answer to the problem there.

"Likely some wrong you done her makes her pester you," said Ansel. "Or maybe she jest wants a proper 'thank-ee' for all what she give you whilst she was alive."

"The back of her hand," said Theron, "was what she give me, mostly."

"She give you titty, didn't she?"

"No," said Theron.

Ulajean hadn't wanted to chance her boobs being sucked out of shape. He'd heard her say so. Her boobs were her livelihood. She'd worked as a go-go dancer at Ridley's Bar on Moffit Street.

Her job was one reason she'd got such a low opinion of men. They wanted to ogle her and feel her up, but they didn't want to stuff dollar bills into her g-string. And without dollar bills, how was she supposed to keep body and soul together?

"My papa left her when she got in a family way," Theron told Ansel, "and she forever tooken it out on me. All my life I felt like I'd stepped into a war I never started and couldn't finish. And here it is a-going on yet. I got to get loose from her," Theron said. "She is wringing my mind like you'd squeeze out a dishrag."

"I'll study on it," Ansel promised.

Right off Theron felt better. He had confidence in Ansel. Ansel had served a hitch in the Navy and come home with a blue spider the size of a half dollar tattooed on his stomach.

"Girl spiders eats their mates,"Ansel told Theron. "This is here to remind me no female is a-going to gobble me up."

And, sure enough, Ulajean backed off. And kept her distance. However, she didn't leave Theron alone entirely. She began to send him pictures of herself. They rose up before his eyes whether he wanted to look at them or not. Some resembled comic strips with words in balloons coming out of Ulajean's mouth. Others were like snapshots. Or like movies. A few were blurred like watercolors or like reflections rocking on water.

These pictures sought him out no matter where he was or what he was doing. They came at him like bullets from a gun. As the weeks wore on, Theron got frazzled and jangled and fit to be tied.

One Saturday, loafing in his room, heels propped on the windowsill, he was staring sleepily at the sun coming through the pane when of a sudden he saw Ulajean and, along with her, his own smaller self. He was sitting on his mama's lap, his untrimmed hair hanging down his neck, and she was brushing the bright red ends of it round her fingers making it fall in ringlets onto his shoulders.

He remembered her doing that and how, all the while, she'd give him light, funny kisses and whisper secrets against the back of his neck so that her breath went tickly down his back under the straps of his playsuit.

In this picture, Ulajean plaited their hair together. Her hair was yellow. When the braid was done, they two were fastened together by a living red and yellow chain.

Truth to tell, Theron was four years old when he got his first haircut. He sat on a board across the arms of the barber chair and jumped when the cold clippers touched his skin. When the barber lifted him down, his mama stared.

"God!" she said. "He's Marty's spitting image!"

She rubbed his head above his ear. "He even feels like Marty's chin felt," said Ulajean, "prickly as a stickerbush."

After that she wouldn't have him on her lap. Nor she didn't tell him any more secrets.

One Friday after work when Theron went into a discount store to buy a thermos bottle, Ulajean was standing in the check-out line.

She held up two brassieres with the price tags dangling and smirked at him. He could tell she was thinking about the time in the five and dime when he'd poked the brassiere strapped to the headless body set on the counter. Underneath were two big mounds like Ulajean had, only hers were soft and these were hard as stone.

"Get your fingers off them!" his mama hissed, yanking his arm. "Starting a'ready!" she said. "Looks like men's jest bound to be men, cradle to the grave, don't it? Help us, Jesus!"

All the sales girls sniggered.

After that, the pictures of Ulajean quit coming for nearly two weeks and Theron thought she was gone. Over the weekend, though, he was in the john taking a leak when she said to him in his ear, "Don't miss that toilet and pee on the floor like you always do."
He was so mortified he couldn't finish his business.
On Monday, Ansel gave Theron a wink to draw him aside from the other workers at the brickyard.
"I know a way you can get loose of your mama," said Ansel. "A buddy of mine in the Navy told me about it. I only just remembered.

"See, his wife drove her car into this concrete bridge abutment. So they scraped her off and buried her in the churchyard. Well, a few nights later, Myrtle Ann came walking into his bedroom looking jest the way she'd looked in life and grabbed hold of his dick. He swore to God that's what happened. She kept doing it, too, night after night, till he was ready to go bananas.

"He fixed her, though," said Ansel. "And here's how he done it. He tooken his new lady out to the cemetery about midnight one night and fucked her on his wife's mound. After that Myrtle Ann never came round him no more.

"Course," said Ansel, "they wasn't blood kin like you and your mama. Fact is, they wasn't even married legal but only common-law. Still, I figger what worked on Myrtle will likely work on Ulajean, beings as they're both women. To get shet of your mama," Ansel told Theron, "you got to fuck on her grave."

A week later, on lunch break, Ansel leaned over and asked Theron in his ear, "You tried that cure yet?"
Theron reddened. He squeezed his brain for a lie to tell, but none came so he told the truth.
"I don't know no girls," he said, "fer to try it with."
Ansel shifted his chew, turned his head and spat a great squirt of tobacco juice against the wall of the brickworks.
"Why the hell didn't you say so?" grunted Ansel. "I'll fix us up with the Pritt sisters. I'm already thick with Riva, and Bonesy's too thin to be picky."
Before the day was out, Ansel had it arranged for him and Theron to meet the girls at Ridley's on Friday night. Whenever Theron thought about the double date, his stomach churned like the pug mill. While they worked together setting brick, Ansel told Theron what to expect.
"Soon as them girls swallers down a few beers," explained Ansel, "they'll be so hot you won't believe it. You can tell when they're ready by

the way they can't do nothing but giggle. When you jedge what little brains they was born with has gone and leaked out their ears, that's the time to make your move."

Monday passed. Tuesday came and went. Wednesday dragged by. Then Thursday. Friday arrived at last hot and dry as the dog days, though September was very nearly over. After work, Theron scrubbed the brick dust off himself. His hide, his hair, his clothes were always stained crimson as if he bled daily from some hidden wound.

He met Ansel on the corner. They walked slowly down toward Ridley's. When they got to the bar, Ansel went though the door first with Theron close behind, craning to look over Ansel's shoulder.

Bonesy wore shiny red pants with sequins on the pockets. Her T-shirt read, "Tease me. Squeeze me," across the front in pink letters.

Riva was spelling out the song titles on the juke box, flipping the cards over, click, click, click. Bonesy was perched on a bar stool chewing a pretzel.

Ridley's was full of noisy people. In front of the juke box, couples were dancing.

They had a round of beers. Ansel paid. Then they had another round and Theron paid. Every time Riva told a joke, Bonesy dug Theron in the ribs with her finger.

Theron commenced to feel giddy and foolish. He daren't look at Bonesy, so he smiled slyly down into his beer. As they left Ridley's, the baseball game went off and a simulation of a missile launch came on.

Ansel bought two six-packs in a convenience store while Theron and the girls waited on the sidewalk. The girls whispered in each other's ears.

"Any them brickers see us, they'll drink up our beer," Ansel said. "Let's go a place can't none of 'em find us."

"Where'd that be?"

"Up behind the church."

The Pritt sisters hooted. Shook their heads. Snickered. Wavered. Shrugged. In the end they led the way.

All climbed the hill, laughing. Every time Riva moved ahead, Ansel goosed her with one or the other of the six packs and she squealed.

They sat down on the grass amongst the grave markers and Ansel opened four bottles. When Theron tried to drink, he was so nerved-up he choked and had to be pounded on the back. Afterward his hand shook and he could scarcely hold the bottle to his lips. He drew his sweaty palms along his thighs and breathed deep breaths.

At his elbow, the Pritt sisters prattled about tv soaps. Bonesy stared at him with bold eyes, but when he leaned over and laid his hand on her shirt where it said, "Squeeze," she moved away.

Ansel opened four more bottles. He chug-a-lugged his, showing off. Bonesy did the same, keeping up with him. Theron watched as the swallows of beer moved down her long neck. It was like watching a snake swallow a rabbit.

After dark, the breeze fell. The air grew hotter. The scent of flowers off a new grave was strong. Above the church, the moon sailed smartly through bits of cloud. Ansel, who had been lying on his back holding his empty beer bottle upright on his stomach, suddenly sat up.

"I know a game we can play," he said. "I learnt it in the Navy. The name of this game is 'Sunset Strip.' It's a dandy game," Ansel told them. He stared at the Pritt sisters. "I expect, though," he said, "you girls is too chicken to try it."

Bonesy stood up. She was breathing hard. "Do you dare me to?" she asked Ansel.

"I double-dog-dare the both of you!"

"I ain't never tooken no dare off no man yet," said Bonesy. She held her arms akimbo. Her sharp chin pointed at the moon.

"I bet you have, though."

"No, I ain't. Not onct," bragged Bonesy.

"All right," said Ansel. "This is how you play. Bonesy and Theron goes first. After they're done, then me and Riva. Every time it's your turn, one of you's got to name something a man's got but a woman hasn't and the other one, vicyversa. All right, start."

Bonesy drew a deep breath. "Whiskers."

"Boobs."

"Balls."

"Lace underpants."

"Hairy chest."

"The curse."

"Tattoos."

"Wimmen has tattoos," objected Theron. He was sweating like a pig. He could feel trickles of water running down his back and across his chest. His voice sounded unsteady and too high.

"Theron's right," Ansel ruled. "Tattoos don't count."

Bonesy howled and stood on one leg.

"Bass voice," she called out at last.

"Plucked eyebrows."

"Jockstrap."

"Shaved legs."

Bonesy wrung her hands. Pounded her head. Stamped her feet.

"A jawful of chewing tobaccy," Bonesy said at last, her voice coming like an explosion.

"Pointy red fingernails."

"Sideburns."

"Them's the same as whiskers," said Theron.

Ansel rolled his beer bottle over his forehead from right to left and back again. "They is and they ain't,"said Ansel at last. "I got to call this here a tie game. Them's the rules. So you both got to take off half your clothes."

"Which half?" asked Bonesy doubtfully.

Ansel produced a dime out of his pocket. "Heads, top half, tails, bottom half," he said. He sent the coin spinning into the air off his thumbnail, caught it in the air and slapped it onto his arm.

"Tails," he announced. "You'ns go over there a piece and finish your game whilst me and Riva steps behind the hedge yander and plays one of our own."

Taking Bonesy by the upper arm, Theron moved her toward Ulajean's grave.

Their business was soon over. Theron scarcely knew what he felt. Bonesy lay limp against his chest. She seemed to be sleeping. Ulajean wasn't anywhere around.

Theron watched the moon drop, slow as a sinking ship, behind a dark cloud.

After a while Bonesy stretched her limbs and sat up. They both put on their clothes. Theron looked around.

"Where's Ansel and Riva at?" he asked.

"They've went their ways."

The girl brushed dirt from his shoulder. "Looky there," she said. "Your barndoor's open."

When he had trouble with the zipper, she reached over and slid it up for him.

"Come on," she said. "You get to walk me home. Ain't you the lucky one?"

They started off, her boney fingers gripping his as if she never in this life meant to let them go.

GRANT VECERA

Driving the Senior Citizens: Jim Fain

One morning, Jim forgot his teeth.
So I had to loop back around, after picking up Emily Johnson.
This was so he could eat lunch.
Some of the others complained, of course.
Paul Trout said he was going to shoot me with his shotgun.

Paul Trout hates Jim Fain. He also hates Loyce Gullick
and me and everyone else he can think of.
Paul, who has hair growing on his teeth, can hardly walk,
even with his walker. And everyday I'm sure it burns his gut
when everyone has to sit in the van and wait while he hobbles
and grunts his fat way out of the cripple seat.

And he drools too, and knows it.

Jim Fain says, "Don't pay him no mind."

Jim Fain had a huge piss stain
streaking down his overalls today.
And no one told him, including Paul.
Even when the bus began to smell.

I thought of all the green frogs of my youth
letting go at the terror of my tiny fingers
spread so gently under their soft bellies.

Driving the Senior Citizens: Letha Hudson

Letha Hudson once found a scared kitten, and spent three days
trying to lure it out from behind a dumpster behind the high-rise.
June Dawson told me this. Said Letha used milk and bologna scraps.
Said she finally got the little critter into a cardboard box,
took it up to the third floor and threw it out the window.
"She's a mean old lady," June said.
Also said Letha used to come into the Center most every day.
But now they won't let her, June told me. Said, "She's too dang mean."

It was raining cats and dogs the only time I ever saw Letha Hudson.
She was propped up on an aluminum cane
out by the bus stop, wearing a long, floral nightgown
which stuck to her flabby thighs and belly.
She had on lime green socks and sky blue eye-shadow
smeared way up. No slippers. No jacket.
Just eyes like blue moth wings
staring at us as we pointed her out and stared back
and pulled away.

Driving the Senior Citizens: Lea Lavender

You can tell when someone's first day will be their last.
The elderly who have no money fall into the Senior Center.
Some, like Lea Lavender, have experienced
too much of the regular world,
and so the Senior Center is too depressing.

You can tell stroke victims by their eyes,
one's landed on you while the other dodges away,
like an uncaged canary. Lea Lavender
seems to have turned old just the other day.

And now she sits in a windowless lunchroom,
with no one but dying people to talk to,
like Loyce, whom she accused of getting fresh on the bus
when he reached for his seatbelt.

THE AUTHORS

RANDY J. ABEL [Youngstown, OH] writes of, "watching cement-crusted neighbor men trudge up our back steps from Croatian Club happy hour, back to small-town family life... Searching for God in St. Anthony's, finding him larger-than-life in stained glass, looking just like Grandpa Abel. At seven or eight in Bessemer, Pennsylvania, I began to question male figures and their assumed roles as my heroes; but by twelve or thirteen, I settled for what they displayed as *what men were*: late or absent, happy in bed, tired and drunk, larger-than-life. I took my search for a solid me into the Navy, looking for national and personal security with my buddies in the bars of Tokyo, or alone and sober on the Cascade peaks of Washington. It brought me to Youngstown State University—to the scrap and rubble downtown, where I finally grope, like everyone else here, for words to turn inside out and make me believe in Home." His story "Tsunami" won the Youngstown State University 1996 Hare Award for Fiction.

DAVID AXELROD [LaGrande, OR] was born and reared around the small manufacturing towns of Alliance, Ohio. "I come from a family of farmers, machinists, and small business owners and worked myself in the family's auto wrecking business in the black ghetto till I found a new allegiances in Nature and writing." He has two books: *The Kingdom at Hand* (Ice River Press) and *Jerusalem of Grass* (Ahsahta Press). He won the Carolyn Kizer Poetry Prize and is working on a new collection of poems, "Earthbound."

DEBRA BENKO [Bowling Green, OH] is completing a doctorate in English at Bowling Green State University. She writes, "I have worked as a library page, secretarial temp, student teacher, writer, and bank teller. My family tree includes immigrants who worked in a gypsum mine." She is poetry editor of *The Heartlands Today*.

JEANNE BRYNER [Newton Falls, OH] writes of, "A background of waitressing, cleaning motel rooms, and working on the assembly line at Packard Electric helped me to prepare for being a registered nurse in a busy emergency room. Growing up in a housing project taught me how to utilize negative space: empty coal bins became summer playhouses filled with white grins and one-eyed baby dolls." She graduated from Trumbull Memorial Hospital School of Nursing and from Kent State University in 1996. Her first book of poems *Breathless* was published in 1995 by the Kent State University Press.

BONNIE JO CAMPBELL [Kalamazoo, MI] teaches math at the local community college. She writes, "I grew up on my mother's small farm outside of Kalamazoo where we collected eggs, raised beef and pork, and milked a series of Jersey cows. Since flying the coop, I've lived in Chicago, Boston, Los Angeles, and Milwaukee. I write personal essays and fiction in which the protagonists hold real jobs and have to make sense of lives which aren't obviously going anywhere. (And they do make sense of them!). My husband is a sometimes union shift steward at a paper converting plant." Bonnie is completing a book to be entitled, "Gorilla Girl and Other Stories of Women and Animals."

KEVIN CLARK [Lewisburg, PA] grew up in McKeesport, Pennsylvania, near the U.S. Steel National Tube Plant. After graduating from Slippery Rock University, he worked as a radio journalist in Pittsburgh, Guam, and Alaska. He is completing a Master of Fine Arts degree at the University of Pittsburgh. He recalls, "Many of my friends' fathers worked the 3 to 11 or 11 to 7 shifts at the mill, and we had to play quietly while they slept a punch-clock 'night' during the day. My own blue collar identity comes from working a variety of jobs including newspaper delivery, dishwasher, short-order cook, pizza maker, church and barn painter." He is completing a novel.

GERALDINE CONNOLY [Bethesda, MD] grew up in a working class family in western Pennsylvania, and has worked as a waitress, a sundeck attendant, an editor and teacher. Her forthcoming "The Unexplained Territories," "chronicles the immigration of my grandparents from Eastern Europe." Her *Food for the Winter* was published by Purdue University in 1990. She has been awarded the Carolyn Kizer Prize from *Poetry Northwest* in 1989 and two fellowships in poetry from the National Endowment for the Arts.

PAOLA CORSO [Weehawken, NJ] teaches creative writing in New York City as a member of the National Endowment for the Arts-funded Writers Corps. Her short story collection *Giovanna's 86 Circles* was published in 1995. She writes, "My grandfather was so determined not to miss a day of work that when his 1936 Chevy stalled, he got out and walked to the mill, leaving the car on the railroad tracks. It's sad to say this kind of worker loyalty is next to impossible now that companies are so blatantly fixated on profits and shareholder values." She is at work on *Undercurrent*, a novel about an Italian-American working class family set in a mill town along the Allegheny River in the Pittsburgh area where she was born and raised. She won the 1995 Voices in Italian Americana creative writing award.

JIM DANIELS [Pittsburgh, PA] teaches at Carnegie Mellon University and is the author of these books of poetry—*M-80* (University of Pittsburgh, 1993); *Punching Out* (Wayne State University, 1990) and *Places/Everyone* (University of Wisconsin Press, 1985). He writes, "I was born in Detroit in 1956. My grandfather worked for Packard until they went bankrupt, and my father worked for Ford until his retirement. I worked summers in a Ford axle plant to help pay my way through college in the late 1970's. My grandmother, who lived with us, watched the children every Thursday while my mother worked [as a nurse]. I attended the local public high school, passing by rows of machine shops on my way to school every day, a constant reminder of what awaited."

SUE DORO [Oakland, CA] worked as a female machinist at the former Milwaukee Road Railway and Allis Chalmers Tractor Shop for thirteen years. Sue writes, "I was born on April 17, 1937, in Berlin, Wisconsin. I lived most of my life in Milwaukee. At the age of thirty-five, after years as a homemaker, I was compelled to make some challenging career decisions as a result of abandonment and unemployment." Her *Blue Collar Goodbyes* (Papier-Mache Press, 1992) from which "The Cultural Worker" is taken, chronicles the lives of working people in a period of plant closings and downsizing. She now works as an affirmative action compliance officer for the U.S. Department of Labor.

SEAN THOMAS DOUGHERTY [Syracuse, NY] was born in New York City in 1965, and grew up in the working class cities of Toledo, Ohio, and Manchester, New Hampshire. "A former high school drop-out and schoolyard basketball star, I worked as a warehouse manager, security guard, and at numerous other 'dumb jobs.' I write for my people, the friends I spent years beside lifting boxes, kids in schoolyards, and for my God. Poetry is the opposite of barbed wire." Sean is a popular performance poet. His books of poems include *Love Song of the Young Couple, The Dumb Job* (Red Dancefloor Press, 1995), *The Mercy of Sleep: Poems and Drawings From the Saint Catherine of Siena Project* with artist Larissa Marangoni (Basfal Books, 1995). He teaches writing for the Arts in Education Institute of Central, New York, and edits *Red Brick* magazine at Syracuse University.

DENISE DUHAMEL [New York City, NY] grew up in Woonsocket, Rhode Island, as a "Canuck" of French Canadian ancestry. Her mother is a secretary in a hosptial emergency room; her fater, a retired baker. "I have worked as a waitress, an assembly line worker, a nursery school teacher, a phone solicitor, a shoe salesperson, a cashier, a receptionist, and a college teacher. I now live in New York City with my husband, poet Nick Carbo." She is the author of four books of poetry: *Smile!* (Warm Spring Press, 1993), *The Woman with Two Vaginas* (Salmon Run Publishers, 1995), *Girl Soldier* (Garden Street Press, 1996), and the forthcoming *Kinky* (Orchises Press, 1997). A series of her stories based on working class girlhood recently was awarded a Money for Women/ Barbara Deming Memorial Grant.

THOMAS FAIRBAIRN [Winchendon, MA] grew up in the mining area of Sudbury, Ontario. "As the son of just another ground gopher, I saw very little of the glory. What I was was my father with his cracked and bleeding hands, tired and mean tempered all the time. At night I read John Steinbeck while listening to my father hack and cough until he choked. The whole house vibrated." He has worked in a furniture factory and now labors at writing as well as construction jobs.

GLORY FOSTER [San Diego, CA] has sailed a 65-foot racing schooner, lived on a geode claim in Blythe, California, and on a gold mining claim in Big Sur. She has worked as a cook, waitress, telephone operator, teacher, maid, housewife, farmer, singer, miner, mechanic, and poet. She writes, "I was born on a truck farm in Mendota, Minnesota, and am proud to be a working class poet." Glory Foster received degrees in creative writing from San Diego State University where she teaches part time and works in the poetry in the City Schools in the "Border Voices" program. Currently she is working on a long performance piece "Measuring the Divide" which deals with chaos and order.

ROBERT FOX [Columbus, OH] is a native of Brooklyn, New York, who adopted Ohio as his home in the 1960's when he and his wife moved to a farm while he taught at Ohio University. He works as literature coordinator for the Ohio Arts Council. In addition to his writing stories, poems, novels, and essays, Fox is an accomplished blues guitar and piano player. Among his credits are the story collection *Destiny News* (December Press, 1977); two novels, *TLAR and CODPOL* (December Press, 1987); and the musical cassette, *Primarily Blues (1995)*. He writes,

"James T. Farrell was one of my earliest inspirations to become a writer. He taught me, in my early teens, that the life I knew on the streets could be the stuff of literature. The proletarian writers of the thirties had a great impact on me—they spoke to my background, my roots, especially writers like Michael Gold in *Jews Without Money* and Albert Harper in *Union Square*. And, how can I forget, Nelson Algren, who's the model for writing about those without voices." Bob Fox is now completing a book of personal essays.

JO GIESE [Malibu, CA] is a non-fiction writer and teacher at UCLA. She is researching and writing a photo-essay book to be entitled "A Woman's Patch: How Did We Get from There to Here." She writes, "The thread that unites these voices of women of achievement is that they have found the song they were meant to be singing." She authored *The Good Food Companion* (Doubleday).

DIANE GOODMAN [Meadeville, PA] has published a chapbook of poems, *Constellations*, with Heatherstone Press, 1993. Two of the poems in her Jewel series appeared in the 1995 issue of *African American Review*. She writes, "These poems all revolve around a maid/cook named Jewel, who strives to be successful at maintaining a warm environment for her own family as well as for the wealthy Southern woman who employs her."

JULIA VAN GORDER [Vancouver, British Columbia] writes that when her father, a policeman, died at the age of 31, she and her sister Ruthie became Inner City Kids in Winnipeg, Manitoba. After high school Julia began working for a bakery chain making $7.50 for a 48 hour week. She graduated from the university with degrees in the arts and social work. During WWII she worked as a waitress-chambermaid with her friend Beth, and at jobs with Boeings and Great Pacific Cannery. She married philosopher D.G. Brown and worked as a social worker in London and Oxford, then as a school counselor in Vancouver. She is a past chair of the Federation of British Columbia Writers. "Maw" is taken from her journal entries of working in the Boeings and Great Northern Cannery in 1945.

G. TIMOTHY GORDON [Santa Fe, NM] began his work career through "work in piecework metalshops and paper-and-steelmills and, during sweltering summers, in construction (swinging, with a gang of four, 16-&-20-lb. sledgehammers onto spikes in concrete-like blacktop). . . . I am especially inspired and renewed by the courage, endurance and humanity of those performing what used to be called menial work, blue and grey collar employees—toilet attendants and street cleaners, construction day laborers and pieceworkers in sweatshops, miners and subsistence farmers, roadside vendors and hucksters of trinkets, foodstuffs, a whole slew of people hustling to get by, working two, even three, jobs selling their labor but rarely their talent." Gordon's first collection of poetry, *Night Company*, was nominated for the NEA Western States' Book Award.

RICHARD HAGUE [Cincinnati, OH] is a native of Steubenville, Ohio, a river town in the Appalachian coal and steel country of eastern Ohio. He writes, "For five generations after immigrating from Ireland, my ancestors worked as cobblers, laborers, stationary engineers and railroaders, occupying houses in the riverfront neighborhood known as 'the Patch.' My own work experiences have included clerk and laborer in a meat market, house painter, laborer in the Brick Department of Wheeling Steel, foreman of a cleaning crew, and for two summers in the Sixties, fireman on the Penn Central Railroad out of Weirton Junction, West Virginia." He now lives in Cincinnati where he teaches writing. His poetry, essays, fiction often explore the tensions between industrial and natural Ohio. His books of poetry include: *Ripening* (Ohio State University, 1984), *Possible Debris* (Cleveland State University Poetry Center, 1988), and *Mill and Smoke Marrow* in the collection *A Red Shadow of Steel Mills* (Bottom Dog Press, 1991)

MAGGIE JAFFE [San Diego, CA] is a second-generation America whose family emigrated to the U.S. during the 1914 pogroms in Minsk, Russia. She writes in her autobiographical poem, "Work of Dust": "My grandfather trudged/ 2000 *versts* through pine dark/ forests, calf deep snow to America,/ then out of his life./ He was cruel./ His carpenter tools/ collected dust/ in the room's dark corner. By fifty, grandmother's/ face was geography:/ lines of demarcation/ a dried-up river bed./ Her hands like gnarled oaks,/plucked chickens in the New/ World where dogs eat dogs/ eat..." She is a lecturer at San Diego State University where she teaches a course in Women and the Labor Movement through Poetry and Prose. She has travelled in South and Central America with novelist Harold Jaffe. Her books include *How the West Was One, Continuous Performance* and *1492: What Is It Like To Be Discovered?* with artist Deborah Small.

DAVID KHERDIAN [Spencertown, NY] is primarily a poet, but also a novelist, critic, translator and editor. His *Settling America: The Ethnic Expression of 14 Contemporary Poets* (Macmillan, 1974) is a model for multi-ethnic anthologies. His retelling of the popular Asian classic *Monkey: A Journey West* (Shambhala, 1992) is enjoying great popularity. His *Beat Voices: An Anthology of Beat Poetry* has just been published by Henry Holt. "I am currently at work on a memoir 'I Call It Home' in my Root River Cycle. Whatever else I might be, I am first and last my peasant father's son."

PHILIP LEVINE [Fresno, CA]was born and raised in Detroit and educated at Wayne State University. After a series of industrial jobs he left the city and lived in various parts of the country before settling down in Fresno where he teaches. His writing deals squarely with working class lives and includes among others: *They Feed They Lion* (1972), *1933* (1974), *One for the Rose* (1981), *A Walk with Tom Jefferson* (1988), *New Selected Poems* (1991) *What Work Is* (1991), and *The Simple Truth* (1995). He has received countless awards for his writing including two National Book Critics Circle Awards, and a Pulitzer Prize for *The Simple Truth*. In his collection of interviews (*Don't Ask*, University of Michigan Press) he writes: "I think the writing of a poem is a political act....The sources of anger are frequently social, and they have to do with the fact that people's lives are frustrated, they're lied to, they're cheated, that there is no equitable handing out of the goods of the world. A lot of the rage that one encounters in contemporary poetry has to do with the political facts of our lives. So I don't see that there is any real conflict here. I think being a poet is, in a sense, a political act—that is, if you're a real poet, not just a court singer." The editors thank Philip Levine for his contribution to this collection and to the movement of working class writing.

SUSAN LUZZARO [Chula Vista, CA] includes much of her biography in her "Working Class Education" printed here. She writes, "In my circles, to suggest you were a writer was tantamount to saying you were going to a shrink—excessive and unrealistic. On my way to my terminal degree I worked as a mother and housewife, a telephone solicitor, an electronic's factory worker, a school bus driver, a Red Cross driver. All of these jobs inform my perception as a writer." Her chapbook *Complicity* is forthcoming from Trask House Books, and a larger collection of poems will be published by West End Press.

PETER MARKUS [Interlochen, MI] grew up in the working class suburbs south of Detroit. He writes, "I was born from the rust of junkyards, from the sculpted heaps of slag you find piled along the banks of the Detroit River. My story begins there: in the river, in the rust, in the steel." He is currently writer-in-residence at the Interlochen Arts Academy in Interlochen, Michigan. His first book of poems is *Still Lives with Whiskey Bottle* (March Street Press, 1996).

LISA MARTINOVIC [Fayetteville, AR] draws most of her writing from her 25 years of being in the workforce as well as from observing others at work. She says, "I've written about everything from my thrilling experience as a temporary office worker to discovering the hidden glamour and soul-satisfaction of lap dancing. My stints as reporter and bartender have yet to be deconstructed in poetry." She is the author of five chapbooks of poetry and a performance poet, which includes poetry slams in San Francisco, New Orleans, and Austin. Her poems are included in *Coffeehouse Poetry Anthology* (Bottom Dog Press, 1996).

JOE NAPORA [Ashland, KY] is a Dayton native who has lived and worked in New York, San Francisco, Canada, Michigan, and now Kentucky where he teaches at Ashland Community College. His poetry can be found in *Portable Shelter, Tongue and Groove* (1982), *The Walum Olum* (translated from Delaware Indian classic, 1983), *Scighte* (1987), *Journal of Elizabeth Jennings Wilson* (1987) and the collection *To Recognize the Dying* (1987). He helps direct the Jesse Stuart Writing Festival and edits *Bullhead* magazine and press. He writes, "Our poetry is at home in this middle place between speech and writing, and perhaps it is through the idea of 'home' that we discover what it means to be connected not only with land and the body and the body politic but connected in specific ways to specific landscapes. Yoga, yoke, joining, is a being-at-home with the body."

EDWINA PENDARVIS [Huntington, WV] was born in eastern Kentucky and spent most of her childhood in coal towns there and in southern West Virginia. She worked at various jobs—curb hop, telephone salesperson, child-care aide—while majoring in English at the University of South Florida. "After teaching high school English for three years, I took a mandatory year's leave—schools didn't allow pregnant women to teach at that time—and got my master's degree in gifted education. I've been teaching ever since in public schools and at Marshall University." Her poetry collection *Joy Ride* will be released by Bottom Dog Press in 1997 in the *Human Landscapes* collection.

GEOFF PENROSE [Seattle, WA] writes, "I was raised in Holland, Michigan, where I unwittingly picked up the particular virulent, secular strain of the Protestant work ethic. These days, I shuttle between Seattle and coastal Alaska, working the long hours of the wild-caught salmon industry, especially with salted salmon roe products. I work the roe full-time now, after eight years of summers-only which helped pay for my college education. I hardly ever need to call upon my M.F.A. degree when hip-deep in viscera."

JIM SANDERSON [Beaumont, TX] was born in San Antonio and grew up in the Texas heartland. He was educated at Southwest Texas State University in San Marcos and at Oklahoma State University. He teaches writing and American literature at Lamar University in Beaumont, Texas. Jim studied writing with Gordon Weaver. His story collection *Semi-Private Rooms* (Pig Iron Press (1992) won the Kenneth Patchen Award.

VIVIAN SHIPLEY [New Haven, CT] teaches at Southern Connecticut State University. "I was raised in Kentucky by parents who both grew up on farms in Kentucky. They were dirt and chicken variety. I learned what it was like to do hard manual labor and never make a dent in the unending work of tending animals and crops. I also saw how people spent their entire lives working hard every day but continuing to live 'hand to mouth.' I was determined to escape that cycle of poverty and saw education as my trapdoor out. All work has dignity but it is rewarded in a very uneven manner and I think that this is the basis for social inequity that none of the politicians can resolve." She is editor of *Connecticut Review* and won the 1995 Ann Stanford Poetry Prize. Her latest books include *Poems Out of Harlan County* (Ithaca House Poetry Series of Greenfield Review Press) and *Devil's Lane* (Negative Capability Press, 1996).

DANIEL SMITH [Freeport, IL] is the third generation to own and operate his family's dairy farm in northwestern Illinois. A fulltime farmer, with his wife and three sons, he milks 120 cows and raises 500 acres of crops in a family partnership, utilizing sustainable farming practices. A graduate of the University of Wisconsin, he writes, "My poems carry a deep-rooted love of a home place. As both farmer and poet, I stress the value of a family's ties to the land and the passing of tools and knowledge from one generation to the next." His first book of poems *Home Land* is forthcoming from Bottom Dog Press in *Human Landscapes*.

ANNABEL THOMAS [Ashley, OH] lives in rural Ohio with her husband Bill, a retired veterinarian. She writes: "Generations of my people were hill farmers, and rural teachers who walked to their one-room schools over the Appalachian foothills of south-eastern Ohio. I often write stories about these kinsmen as they exist in my imagination kindled by family tales handed down through the years. When World War II came, many men left the hills and went to work in factories on the flatlands of northern Ohio. The setting of "Laying Ulajean's Ghost" comes out of memories of my son's description of the Galena, Ohio, Brick Works, where he was employed for several years stacking the new-molded bricks ready to roll into the kilns. The Brick Works are now the stuff of legend." Annabel Thomas's books include *The Phototropic Woman* (Iowa School of Letters Award winner, 1981), *A Well of Living Water* in *Human Anatomy: Three Fictions* (Bottom Dog Press, 1993), and *Knucklebones* (Helicon Nine Editions, 1995) winner of the Willa Cather Fiction Prize.

JAMES MASON VAUGHAN (Honilulu, HI) is a Navy veteral from WW II, who still suffers from Post Traumatic Stress Syndrome. He writes, "The mural of my experiences is filled with contradictory images and explosions of color, seldom pleasing, often frightening, never placid." He has lived in various states and is working now on a collection to be entitled "Desert Book."

GRANT VECERA [Richmond, IN]. Having grown up in Indianapolis, he and high school friends created College Works, doing landscaping, painting, and odd jobs. Now with a Masters of Fine Arts degree in creative writing "I continue to paint houses with one of my College Works buddies and teach part-time at Indiana University-Purdue University. It was at the University of Arkansas that I took on a part-time job as a shuttle bus driver and meal-on-wheels delivery person at a local Senior Citizens' Center. Although not affiliated with the University, folks like Lida Lewis, O.K. Mattocks, Jean Brashler and many other friends at the Senior Center were educators of the highest caliber."

MARK VINZ [Moorhead, MN] was born in a small town in North Dakota and grew up in Minneapolis and the Kansas City area. He writes, "Ten years of many different jobs as a teenager and college student convinced me, more than anything else, to stay in school and pursue a future that depended more on my head than my hands." He now teaches at the Moorhead State University where he coordinates the Master of Fine Arts in Creative Writing Program. He and his wife Betsy have two children. His books include: *Minnesota Gothic* (poems with Wayne Gudmundson photographs) and *Late Night Calls: Prose Poems and Short Fiction*. He co-edited collections: *The Party Train, Inheriting the Land: Contemporary Voices from the Midwest*, and *Imagining Home: Writing from the Midwest*.

DAVID WATTS [Mill Valley, CA] is a clinical professor of medicine at The University of California San Francisco where he has conducted a practice of medicine and gastroenterology. He also has a Masters degree in English and Creative Writing from San Francisco State University. He is the author of the poetry chapbook *The Heart's Inquiry*. He writes, "With my wife, poet Joan Baranow, I am editing an anthology entitled *Poetry in Medicine* based upon a course I created for medical students in which poetry is used to teach the human side of health and illness."

TOM WAYMAN [Winlaw, British Columbia] is co-director of the Writing Studio at the Kootenay School of the Arts in Nelson, British Columbia. He writes, "My immediate family is very much 'The Working Class Goes to College'—both my mother (a social worker) and father (a pulp mill chemist) were the first in their respective families to win the scholarships that enabled them to attend university. My grandfathers were a cabinet maker and a needle trades machine operator. 'Turn of the Tide' is partially based on my father's brother who bummed around North America in the Depression, at last settling into work as a member of the Construction Laborers' union in B.C. My own work experience is a mix of blue-collar (construction, factory) and white collar (journalism, teachers' aide) in the U.S. and Canada." He has edited a collection of working writings entitled *Paperwork* (Madeira Park: Harbour, 1991), and has also published two books of essays on the new work writing, most recent being *A Country Not Considered Canada, Culture Work* (Toronto: Anasi, 1993). His poetry collection *I'll Be Right Back* is forthcoming from Ontario Review Press.

SUKI WESSLING [Santa Cruz, CA] writes, "Driving down El Camino Real one Wednesday night in July, I passed a forlorn group of car salesmen in tuxedos. Their showroom was lit up like New Year's Eve, and they looked uncomfortable and hot in the tuxedos that, apparently, some higher-up had thought would attract business. The lot was empty, and I, along with the rest of the motorists, kept driving. My writing often starts with an image like this, many times a memory. I grew up in a smalltown where the obvious class divisions clashed with our schoolteachers' applause of 'The American Dream.' Many of the kids in my town didn't dare to dream any further than the auto manufacturing plants that were laying off their parents. In my writing I'm attracted to those who dare to dream and strive, as well as those who dared, and then gave up. 'A Strong Face' is about a small moment in a woman's life when she hesitates, and then continues on her journey."

FREDERICK WM. ZACKEL [Bowling Green, OH] now teaches creative writing at Bowling Green State University and is the author of two novels, *Cocaine and Blue Eyes* and *Cinderella After Midnight*, the first having been made into the NBC tv movie. He writes that "to stay alive and later to feed my family, I have held many jobs. I wrote advertising copywriting in Cleveland and Los Angeles, shoveled grapeskins after fermenting from vats at a California winery, collected shopping carts, was an assistant shipping manager for a fish company, and was recognized by Kelly Services as an Outstanding Kelly Girl. For years I drove taxicab at night on San Francisco's adrenaline streets."

THE PHOTOGRAPHERS

CHARLSE CASSADY, JR [Lakewood, OH] is a photographer and journalist working around Lorain, Ohio. His work has appeared in exhibits and various book publications.

LEIGH CHARLTON [Ames, IA] is a commercial photographer, photo journalist, and co-author and photographer of three books. She specializes in agricultural photography and videography. She teaches photography at Iowa State University and lives in the Midwest and on the West Coast.

REBECCA COLON [Huron, OH] is a young farmer-photographer with a Master of Fine Arts degree from Bowling Green State University. She has exhibited her photography and prints in Ohio.

ROGER PFINGSTON [Bloomington, IN] is a poet and photographer who teaches at the University of Indiana. His work has been exhibited widely and has appeared in many anthologies.